AFRICA

—————◆—————

A FOREIGN AFFAIRS READER

AFRICA

A FOREIGN AFFAIRS READER

Edited by
PHILIP W. QUIGG

Foreword by
HAMILTON FISH ARMSTRONG

Published for the
COUNCIL ON FOREIGN RELATIONS

by
FREDERICK A. PRAEGER, *Publisher*
New York   *London*

FREDERICK A. PRAEGER, Publisher
64 University Place, New York 3, N. Y., U.S.A.
77–79 Charlotte Street, London W.1, England

Published in the United States of America in 1964
by Frederick A. Praeger, Inc., Publisher

Published in the United Kingdom in 1964
by Frederick A. Praeger, Inc., Publisher

For information, address Council on Foreign Relations,
58 East 68th Street, New York 21

FIRST EDITION

Library of Congress catalog card number: 64-12589

Printed in the United States of America
by Quinn & Boden Company, Inc., Rahway, N. J.

For a list of Council publications see pages 348 and 349.

Foreword

by HAMILTON FISH ARMSTRONG

When *Foreign Affairs* was established, now over forty years ago, the chief political interest of Europeans in "the Dark Continent," as Africa was romantically called, and of the few Americans who had any such interest at all, lay in observing and comparing the different colonial systems in operation there and in speculating about the advantages which each would bring in the long run to the so-called mother country. The European nations had divided Africa up, not share and share alike, but share and share according to two principles, if they can be called that: first come first served, and the lion's share to the boldest and strongest. Following the Berlin Conference of 1884–85, the partitionment of the remaining African territories was largely, though not always, by agreement. But in general, the titles of possession were based on the same factors of power; and forty years ago these did not seem open to challenge.

The articles in the following pages, chosen from among those which have appeared in *Foreign Affairs* in the intervening forty years, reveal how the points of reference in the discussion of African affairs changed, and how remarkably quickly. Interest in the merits and demerits of the various concepts of colonial rule as such, viewed from the standpoint of the possessor and assumed to continue at his will, was replaced by concern as to where the different colonial systems (and they varied immensely) were leading the native peoples politically and socially, and how the attitudes and relations of the two parties seemed likely to be affected. Out of this evaluation of the changing scene dawned the understanding that all the colonial systems alike, whether paternalistic or purely exploitative, were in fact only phases in an African evolution which tended directly and indeed swiftly toward a much larger participation by the indigenous peoples in the conduct of their own affairs and which could be prevented from culminating in independence only by the use of repressive force.

"Colonialism" has meant so many things over the years, from benevolent to vicious, that it is futile to attempt giving it any fresh definition. At its beginnings, as William L. Langer wrote in "The Diplomacy of Imperialism," "it was taken for granted that the world was marked out by Providence for exploitation by the European white man and that the principle of every man for himself and the devil take the hindmost was natural law." Retreat from that concept has been all but complete. In some cases, the withdrawal was a rout, in others it has been more orderly than seemed likely in the circumstances and has left a residue of good will and coöperation on both sides. Whether fatal obstinacy or good sense will mark the remaining liquidations of European power in Africa remains to be seen.

Now that colonial rule has reached or is everywhere reaching its end, a retrospective view of its characteristic features becomes possible and can be valuable. The interest of such an examination is not just historical. Europeans and Africans will not agree on the motives and processes that marked colonialism's growth, sway and rapid decline; but memory of the past will make it easier for everyone to identify new manifestations of the imperialist urge that may occur.

Some say they are already occurring. The term used for them is "neo-colonialism." The new nations are right to be vigilant against fresh attempts to exploit or dominate them against their will and interest. But some of their leaders who bandy charges of neo-colonialism about are not immune to suspicion as being themselves willing to take over the white man's burden in defenseless neighboring lands. By illuminating previous experience, the articles selected by Philip Quigg for this book can help put everyone on the watch against colonialist or imperialist tendencies in whatever form they appear.

The last section of the volume sets forth the motives and aspirations of the leaders of the new Africa, and their proposals for dealing with their immense national problems in freedom yet as parts of an interdependent world. Their articles, though the product of a turmoil of spirit, are in the main argued reasonably and without animus. The authors have felt free to write just as they wished because they knew that the policy of *Foreign Affairs* is to open its pages to diverse opinions and leave the reader to form his own. Here as in the earlier sections, Mr. Quigg's prefatory notes serve to give each contribution its place in the larger scene and thus provide a pattern of developing thought and action.

Preface

If Lord Lugard and W. E. B. Du Bois could have had anything in common beyond their fascination for Africa, it would have been their disbelief, at the time they wrote for *Foreign Affairs* in the 1920s, that within 40 years they would appear together between covers in the company of six presidents or prime ministers of independent African states. Yet the arch-colonialist, who felt that Africans were children requiring generations of guidance, and the radical pamphleteer, who assumed that the white man was morally and economically incapable of letting go his empires, have both been proven wrong by the breakneck pace of political evolution in Africa. Be it added, everyone clse was wrong, too, except for a few African nationalists whose expectations were fulfilled as much by good luck as good management.

The burden of this is that events in Africa, in the span of nearly 40 years covered by this volume—and more particularly since World War II—acquired a momentum of their own. They were shaped by men only as a flooding river is contained, with here a sandbagging operation and there an evacuation, but with never a possibility of halting the force of the current. The nationalist leaders themselves no less than the colonialists were swept along in the decade of the fifties, and the tide now beats on the last strongholds of white domination— in Southern Rhodesia, the Portuguese territories and South Africa.

In the larger part of black Africa where the European did not settle, the number of independent African states has grown within a decade from three to thirty-two—a virtually bloodless transformation that surely is without precedent. If, then, a new continent has emerged, are not the articles collected here largely irrelevant and dated? Far less than one might suppose. Some are contemporary, written by African leaders after their countries achieved independence; some are of lasting historical interest; but all were selected because they have something to say that has bearing on the present and future of Africa. Here are colonialists, African nationalists, scholars, journalists, administrators and makers of policy arguing their points of view and disagreeing with one another not merely about issues but in their evaluation of the most fundamental matters having to do with the capacity of the African to govern himself. If the reader becomes confused, it is perhaps a necessary stage in groping toward an understanding of Africa. Until we have exposed ourselves to the kind of contradictory points of view expressed here—not one of which is without elements of truth—we are unlikely to apprehend the political forces that will be shaping Africa in the years ahead. It will be all too easy to adopt the neatly self-contained viewpoint either of those who judge the African uncompromisingly by the extent to which he adopts Western institutions and values or of those who embrace whatever is indigenously African as having unique virtue.

Since *Foreign Affairs* was founded 42 years ago, considerably more than 100 articles on Africa have appeared in its pages. A decision to omit articles on North Africa from this volume brought the total number to more manageable proportions. The 24 articles finally selected focus on political and social problems of black Africa (including South Africa) and touch only incidentally on the large but somewhat specialized problems of economic development. They are reprinted exactly as they originally appeared in *Foreign Affairs,* and within sections, are presented chronologically. The date of issue in which each article was first published appears at the head of its introductory note.

P. W. Q.

Contents

PART IV

AFRICAN "ISMS"

PART V

DEAD END IN SOUTH AFRICA

PART VI

THE NEW LEADERS

Part I

Zephyrs of Change

Note

THE WHITE MAN'S TASK IN TROPICAL AFRICA
BY SIR FREDERICK D. LUGARD

October 1926

Lord Lugard epitomized the colonial era in Africa—with all its virtues and not a few of its vices. Serving both the Crown and private interests, he stamped his name on Africa as few men have. It would hardly be an exaggeration to say that Uganda and Nigeria are his creations.

When Frederick D. Lugard was born in India in 1858, the interior of Africa was virtually unknown. By the time he had graduated from Sandhurst and had fought in the Afghan War, and in the Suskin and Burma campaigns, the interior of Africa, though still unoccupied by Europeans, had in a rough and ready way been carved up among the colonial powers by agreement reached in the Berlin Treaty of 1885. When Lugard sailed for East Africa in 1888, therefore, the colonial era in Africa was really only beginning, and it might well be said to have ended in the year that Lugard died, 1945. For the Second World War greatly accelerated the movement toward self-government at the same time that the major colonial powers, gravely weakened by war, lost much of that sense of mission so powerfully demonstrated in the life and writings of Lord Lugard. In the half century that intervened, the "colonialists" did virtually all of good or ill that they were to do for Africa, and Lord Lugard cut the biggest swath of all. He successfully campaigned against the slave trade in East Africa; took possession of Uganda; put the Imperial British East Africa Company, the Royal Niger Company and the British West Charterland Company in business; and carved out of West Africa the future state of Nigeria. Except for a brief tour as Governor of Hong Kong, he devoted all of his mature life to Africa, retiring from the colonial service in 1919. He was raised to the peerage as Baron Lugard of Abinger in 1928.

Lugard is best remembered by two phrases: "Indirect Rule" and

3

"The Dual Mandate," which together sum up the achievements of his career. The support and authority of local potentates had long been used in governing British possessions, but Lugard developed the concept of indirect rule to a fine administrative art, governing the most populous territory in Africa with between two and three hundred of his countrymen. The method was justified by more than necessity, as the closing pages of the following article make clear. (See also pp. 59–60.) "The Dual Mandate" provided the rationale for all that Lugard and other responsible colonialists sought to achieve in Africa. Both terms are understandably in disrepute among Africans today.

In what follows Lugard gives particular attention to the problem of African labor and the injustices that have attended its recruitment. Almost everything that he says remains relevant to the Portuguese territories—where forced labor is still practiced—and, to a lesser extent, to South Africa. What he does not say—perhaps because it was more widely known to an earlier generation—is that inducing Africans to work for cash proved to be one of the most difficult problems faced by administrators and commercial interests. Where more direct methods were not resorted to, it was generally solved by imposing a head tax on Africans that could be paid only in cash.

The White Man's Task in Tropical Africa

by SIR FREDERICK D. LUGARD

In the march of material progress in the nineteenth century probably the most outstanding event was the discovery of the use of steam as a motive power, and it is of interest to note how and why it led inevitably to the development of the tropics and their control by the white races. On the one hand the oceans ceased to be barriers passable only at the cost of long delays and great discomfort. The gateways through which trade gained access to the western half of the continent of Africa were no longer the Mediterranean ports and the camel caravan routes across the Sahara, but the ports on the West Coast, while the construction of the Suez Canal opened new and shorter sea routes to its eastern shores. On the other hand the rapid expansion of every branch of industry under the stimulus of power-driven machinery gave rise to a great demand for raw materials and for markets for the products manufactured from them. These demands were moreover increased by the phenomenal growth of population and the improvement in the standard of living of every class, which was the proximate result of the industrial revolution of the nineteenth century.

The supplies of many of these raw materials—vegetable oils, fibres, cotton, hides and skins, rubber, various minerals, etc.—were wholly insufficient, unless supplemented by the wealth of the tropics, while others were obtainable only from them. Nor was the demand for human food and the minor luxuries which now for the first time were available to the working classes less insistent—among others, sugar, rice, maize, tea, coffee, cocoa, and edible oils.

Of the great white races of the earth, the United States of America alone was for a time self-supporting, but as her population increased she too became a large importer of tropical products, both vegetable and mineral, from Africa and other tropical countries; their volume and diversity, compiled from statistical tables, would probably be a revelation to the average reader. Twenty years ago the trade of the United States with the tropics was shown by Benjamin Kidd to amount to $346,000,000 (about half that of the United Kingdom) and he sums up with the conclusion that "the development of the tropics will beyond doubt be the permanent underlying fact of the twentieth century."

His forecast has proved true, and its truth will be more abundantly proved as the century grows older. "The Control of the Tropics" (as he named his remarkable essay) was probably one of the not remote causes of the Great War, and the future is pregnant with hardly less dangers from the same cause. If this be so—if the essential needs of the white man and the jealousies and misunderstandings to which they give rise, and if the so-called "awakening of the colored races," are indeed matters of such world importance—it goes without the saying that public opinion should be well informed as to the nature of the problem. Its solution rests primarily on the shoulders of those who have assumed the immense responsibility of governing the backward races which people the tropics, nor can it be evaded by those who use the products of the tropics and who exercise influence in the councils of the civilized nations. The nations in control are, as Kidd expressed it, "trustees for civilization"—a phrase which, repeated in the Covenant of the League of Nations, has become a household word throughout the world. In carrying out this trust they exercise a "dual mandate" [1]—as trustees on the one hand for the development of the resources of these lands, on behalf of the congested populations whose lives and industries depend on a share of the bounties with which nature has so abundantly endowed the tropics. On the other hand they exercise a "sacred trust" on behalf of the peoples who inhabit the tropics and who are so pathetically dependent on their guidance.

The fulfilment of the former mandate is for the most part undertaken with avidity by private enterprise, and the function of the Power in control is limited to providing the main essentials, such as railways and harbors, to seeing that the natives have their fair share, and that material development does not injuriously affect the fulfilment of the second mandate—an even more important obligation.

Railways in Africa are generally constructed by the state. Without

[1] "The Dual Mandate in Tropical Africa." By the present writer. Blackwood & Sons, Edinburgh.

arterial railways the cost of administration in the interior would be prohibitive and the slave trade and tribal wars could not have been suppressed. Railways increase the mobility of the forces necessary to stamp out these evils and maintain law and order. They render possible the advent of trade and commerce, from which a considerable revenue is raised for administrative purposes, and they encourage native production by providing a market for native produce in return for imported goods, such as textiles and hardware, and so add to the well being and prosperity of the people. Along the lines they traverse they have superseded human porterage, and so set free vast numbers of men for productive work. Their construction, if carried out on right principles, is an educative agency of great importance, teaching tribes hitherto at war the value of coöperation, and the principle of a fair day's wage for a day's labor. Feeder roads, telegraphs and harbors are ancillaries. For such works native labor is required, for the white man cannot, or at any rate will not (except in Queensland) do manual work in the tropics. Private enterprise also requires native labor, and hence the first problem is to decide to what extent and under what conditions it can be employed without injury to the people. On the one hand the withdrawal of too large a percentage of adult males from the village community tends to destroy the social organization—slender at best—and the tribal authority and tribal sanctions. Some of these no doubt are based on superstition and barbarous traditions. In course of time they must disappear and be succeeded by a higher type of social organization, but if they are broken down too rapidly, if whatever is good in them is treated with contempt, and disappears with the bad before something better has been evolved, the result is chaos.

It is perhaps difficult for us to realise how great is the contrast between the communal life of the primitive tribe, hedged round with observances and customary rites, and the life of individualism and license of the labor camp. Much can be done, and is done, to ameliorate these conditions. Units of a tribe may be kept together under their own tribal authority, wives may be induced to accompany their husbands, and if the absence is not too prolonged little harm may be done. Something of good, as has already been said, may also result. The primitive savage in contact with civilization learns the discipline of work, and the result of coöperation. He learns on a plantation new methods of cultivation which he can apply to his own fields. If well fed and housed his physique improves with the regular day's work.

New ideas and better standards of life are opened to his mind—in housing, clothing, sanitation, and the utensils for field work.

The old order must change—as it has changed with us—and the inexorable mandate of civilization forbids to stereotype the conditions of savage life. Whether the primitive African dancing in the moonlight through the livelong night, careless and improvident for the morrow, will be the happier for it, who shall say? Is the villager of England with his wireless set and his trade unions, with motor cycles and cars dashing through the village street and rattling the bones of the elders of the past in the village cemetery, happier than they were?

To return to our subject. Men recruited from distant tribes often suffer from the change of climate, diet and mode of life before they become acclimatized. New diseases against which they have acquired no measure of immunity cause a heavy death rate. In spite of medical care, disease is sometimes carried back to the village. Not only is the mortality high among the laborers, but the birth rate decreases. In many parts of Africa it is estimated that the population since the advent of the white man has been stationary or has decreased, and this in spite of all that has been achieved in the stopping of slave raids and of tribal war, and the conquest of such diseases as smallpox which formerly ravaged Africa unchecked. The security of life which the reign of law and order has introduced is no doubt itself paradoxically in some degree responsible, for the freedom of movement has facilitated the spread of infectious diseases.

From a merely utilitarian point of view, it becomes a matter of the first importance that the demand for labor shall not lay too heavy a burden on the present generation. For essential public works and services even compulsion may in the last resort be justified and is authorized in such cases by the terms of the Mandates in tropical Africa, but "only if adequately remunerated"—important words, which were omitted from the proposed Slavery and Forced Labor Convention which is now under discussion in Geneva.

In regard to forced labor for private profit the "traditional policy of Great Britain" has been very clearly formulated in a state paper, as being "absolutely opposed to compulsory labor for private employment. . . . It is a point of fundamental importance that there is no question of force or compulsion, but only of encouragement and advice through the native chiefs."

"In no British Dominion and in no British Colony," said the Under-Secretary lately, "will it ever be tolerated that there should be compulsory labor for private profit." Indirect pressure, on chiefs by advice which they dare not disregard, by unduly heavy taxation, or by inadequate land allotment, is also reprobated. But voluntary labor is already insufficient to meet the demands of settlers in the sparsely populated highlands, which offer a congenial home for the white man, where by introducing new cultures and improved methods he has increased the material prosperity. What then is to be done? There are three possible courses; first, to reduce the demand by limiting government works to those of essential importance, and restricting European immigration and private enterprise; second, to make the existing supply go further by increasing the efficiency of the laborer and by the use of labor-saving devices; or finally, to import labor from overseas.

Each of these courses deserves brief consideration. The construction of railways may be limited to arterial lines and to such as traverse densely populated regions and therefore afford an outlet for produce, new markets, and a rapid means of transport for labor recruits. It is of no use "opening up" for white plantations sparsely peopled regions, however fertile, if there is no labor for their development. In the second place, wage labor can be made more efficient by good feeding and care of health, by training, by piece-work—which means more European supervision—and by the use of machinery, either to supplement or replace human labor. One illustration will suffice. The use of the ox in agriculture and (on European-owned estates) of mechanical plows, etc., and the abolition of human porterage by the employment of draught transport and of "road-less" mechanical vehicles, would set free hundreds of thousands of men for productive work, and add an enormous acreage to that which the natives at present cultivate by primitive methods.

Finally there is the question of supplementing African labor by importing workers from overseas. The two sources of supply in the past have been India and China. The importation of Indian labor has raised in Natal and Kenya difficulties greater than those of the problem it was hoped that it would solve. Moreover the Indian Emigration Act of 1922 has prohibited the indenture of Indian coolie labor. There remains China. It is necessary to distinguish between immigrants, whose indenture provides for compulsory repatriation, and those who on the expiration of their contracts are allowed to remain as colonists, bringing their families with them and using their period of indenture as a kind of apprenticeship, during which they can save a little money and get to know the country. For reasons which cannot be discussed here, the Chinese would no doubt belong to the former category. The cost of recruiting, transporting and repatriating Chinese, and the high wages they demand, would make the experiment a very costly one. The Chinese refuse to bring their wives with them—or the wives refuse, as in Samoa, to come unless paid the same wages as the men; they take back their earnings with them and spend little or nothing in the country; and there is the serious question of racial miscegenation. On the other hand, if the strict supervision exercised by a special official, which is adopted in Malaya, is enforced, there are no grounds for humanitarian objections so far as the Chinese themselves are concerned.

What, it may naturally be asked, in view of the difficulties with which this labor question bristles, is the nature of the demand by private enterprise, and what is the solution which it proposes itself? The demand is mainly either for mining or for European-owned plantations and estates; the requirements of traders and others are comparatively negligible.

The mining companies which export gold, diamonds, tin, copper, manganese, etc., generally make large profits, and are able to offer every attraction possible to wage labor. The extraction of coal, on the other hand, economizes expenditure on railways and steamers, and is therefore of direct benefit to the people of the country. In Nigeria, primarily on account of the labor question, it has so far been retained as a government monopoly. Foreign agricultural enterprise may either consist of plantations of rubber trees or oil-palms, etc., which grow in the lowlands and are supervised by Europeans who relieve each other periodically, or of estates owned by settlers in the highlands, whose altitude renders continued residence possible. If the crops consist of exotic species which require skilled cultivation or technical preparation for the market, such as Arabian coffee, tobacco, sisal, tea and flax, these foreign-owned plantations are a notable contribution to the economic resources of the country, and they also should be able to offer attractive conditions to wage labor, provided that the demand is not too heavy. It is, however, a disadvantage that the heaviest demand is at the season when the natives are most engaged in tending their own food crops.

But if the foreign estate owner does not limit his enterprise to these cultures, and includes products which are successfully grown by the natives, such as cotton, maize, cocoa, groundnuts, etc., it is inevitable that—unless artificially protected—he cannot compete with the native grower who has no "overhead charges" to meet and can work in his own time, in his own way, for his own profit, and with the assistance of his family. Their interests become antagonistic, and if the planter has a powerful share in the legislation and policy of the government, strict impartiality, despite the best of intentions, becomes difficult.

The planter and the settler point to the capital and the efforts expended in converting lands left derelict or used only as grazing areas for nomadic cattle-owners, into estates of great value whose produce forms the bulk of the exports. They hold that the natives can only become good citizens by contact with the Europeans. They would solve the labor problem by inducing the natives to live on their estates as "squatters" or tenants pledged to render service for specified periods. The planters of Virginia solved their labor problems three centuries ago in much the same way, by importing slaves, but what was possible in the early seventeenth century is not possible in the twentieth. The imported slaves resided on their estates, and it was equally to the owners' interest that they should be well-cared for; but in order to maintain the system they wisely made it an offense to teach the slaves to read and write, for education must doom such a system to failure. British settlers in Kenya and Nyasaland, on the contrary, show much enthusiasm for native education. And here I touch a new subject.

The policy and methods hitherto adopted in educational matters in Africa have not produced good results, and the fact has recently received official recognition in England by the appointment by the Secretary of State of a Standing Committee at the Colonial Office consisting of educational experts, representatives of the churches and missions, and others of practical administrative experience, under the presidency of the Under-Secretary. A synopsis of the policy they advocated was published with the approval of Government as a state paper. In this movement the Trustees of the Phelps-Stokes Fund, with their intimate knowledge of the methods by which such great results have been achieved in the United States at Hampton and Tuskegee, lent assistance and coöperated by sending two Missions to Africa and publishing the results of their investigations. It is, however, only just to add that the principles they so ably advocated had already been demonstrated and an attempt to give them practical effect by legislation had already been made and would have been carried out in detail had not progress been arrested by the war.

The new policy regards the education in the class-room of a comparatively small minority of the youth in the principal centers as only one phase—and that not the most important—of education. The system of set examinations based on curricula more appropriate to pupils in England, and conveyed in text books ill adapted to African experience and mentality, must in future give place to a system which shall reach the heart of the people and influence the village community. Its object will be to retain what is best in African tradition, to make the village agriculturist or craftsman more efficient, to replace superstitious fear by the ethics of a higher religion, to fill in the great hiatus between the illiterate masses and the so-called "educated" minority. Education, it is hoped, will mean the raising of the standard of the people, not the denationalization of the few, making of the African a better and more efficient African and not an imitation white man.

So regarded, the Education Department is but one of many agencies engaged in the work. And not least of the potent agencies which operate outside the class-room is that of the Administrative Officer, whose task it is to train each tribal unit or separate community to conduct its own domestic affairs under the guidance of its own appointed head.

Among the more advanced sections the task is comparatively easy. Habits of obedience to authority on the one hand, and of responsibility and initiative on the other hand, have already been acquired in a greater or lesser degree. But among the more primitive, where as yet no higher authority than the head of the family exists, where impulse to action is dictated by some prompting of superstition, or some motive hard to fathom, the District Officer's task is much harder. He will set up a petty tribunal for the settlement of minor disputes and offenses, but it will arrive at most astonishing decisions or be wholly unable to assert its authority. The very standards of right and wrong will often need to be created. It would be simpler and much more effective to assume all powers himself. The interminable delays, the inability to grasp simple fundamentals, the constant failure of one chief after another in whom he had built hopes of success, are heartbreaking to the competent energetic officer, and it becomes a chronic temptation to do the thing himself and do it well. It is thus that the proverbial efficiency of the rural administration in British India and elsewhere has been achieved.

But is the white influence as effective as it seems on the surface? No tropical administration has revenues adequate to support the army of officials required thoroughly to administer these vast areas peopled by a mosaic of tribes speaking scores of different languages. Exigencies of climate, necessitating absence on leave, together with the transfers due to departmental promotion, cause frequent changes in personnel. At best the District Officer, who thinks he is "running the show" himself, and with success, is really in the hands of his interpreters, his court messengers and his police. Every now and then a scandal comes to light which reveals the tyranny, bribery and peculation carried on in the white man's name.

Apart from such considerations, what is the ultimate result? Half a century of direct assumption of control by the Administrative Officer finds the community just where it was. The more capable and energetic he has proved himself, the less competent will it be to stand alone. Meanwhile, contact with civilization, and the spread of education, beget as their natural offspring the agitator for "self-determination" and a share in the control of domestic affairs. The tribes are without leaders of influence, for leadership has been at a discount. The only lesson they have been taught is obedience to the will of another. The agitator presses for elected representatives on the Legislative Council, and a widening of the unofficial vote. But the native lawyers, who for the most part constitute the native members of the Council, are not representative of the masses, and know less about them, their language and their needs than the District Officer. Philanthropists at home applaud the extension of "a new measure of self-government."

Better in my judgment all the early mistakes and absurdities of the primitive native tribunals, the incompetence of the petty chiefs, and the slow growth of efficiency, while the chief and his village council acquire with the support of government a steadily increasing authority. If their actions on occasion give cause for protest, they cannot at any rate be laid at the white man's door.

Democracy in the East (perhaps more logically than in the West) begins at the bottom with the village *panchayat* in India and its counterpart, the *tipao* in China—generally perhaps with autocracy enthroned as a figure-head at the top, ostensibly omnipotent but in reality with well understood limitations.

From all of these considerations there emerges, as I think, one great lesson for all of those powerful states which have accepted the grave responsibility of controlling and educating—that is to say, "bringing forth" to a higher plane—the backward races who are, in the words of the Covenant of the League of Nations "unable to stand alone in the strenuous conditions of the modern world." The lesson is this: we should abandon the idea that methods and policies found suitable to ourselves are necessarily the best suited to the ancient civilizations of the East or to the evolution of African tribes. The predominant characteristics of the English-speaking races are individual initiative, willingness to accept responsibility, and belief in the value of compromise in the settlement of affairs without strict adherence to logic. From these characteristics have sprung our system of representative government through parliaments. We are prone to assume that our methods of government, our religious formulae, our systems of education, the lessons of our history, our appraisement of the degrees of criminality and our code of punishments, because we have proved them best for ourselves, must be best for all the world. It may be so in the far future, but the attempt to bridge the centuries without adequate study of other mentalities, traditions and beliefs, is more likely to lead to failure than to success.

With the realization of the difficulty and of the importance of the work, there has come an increasing recognition of the fact that, as Sir Valentine Chirol puts it, the task demands not the average man but the very best men we have got. When I first went to Africa—and the assertion is obviously not flattering to myself—there was undoubtedly a feeling that anyone was good enough for Africa. Selection of officers was haphazard in the extreme. The Indian Service enjoyed great prestige, and next to it came the Eastern Colonial Cadet Service. To-day neither the one nor the other can boast of better men than those who serve in tropical Africa. And the credit is due to the Service itself—though many, alas! of those who pioneered the way have not lived to see the results.

Conditions in the early days, of housing, food, medical aid, and overwork for the British staff were very bad, especially in West Africa, and the mortality was dreadful, but as a result of the abounding material prosperity of these dependencies these conditions have now improved beyond comparison. Wives accompany their husbands, and the tone of European society has changed greatly for the better, a change which includes all classes,—missionaries, traders, miners and officials. Its effect is not lost on the black man. I do not refer to British colonies only.

And what are the results on the credit side of the dual task, to compensate for the death toll. In material prosperity they are amazing. Thousands of miles of railways, harbors both on the East and West

Coasts constructed at a cost of several millions each, and a trade which now aggregates many scores of millions of pounds sterling. The little colony of the Gold Coast has built a hospital at a cost of a quarter of a million pounds sterling, and is now engaged on school buildings at Achimota estimated to cost double that sum. In non-material matters the progress made cannot be so easily tabulated. I have spoken of education, of methods of rule, and of principles of employing wage labor; in these and in many other spheres there can be no doubt that the white man's standard has been raised. The endeavors of the Mandates Commission to uphold the true principles of Trusteeship on the one hand, and the loyalty of Africa and its white rulers during the war on the other are tangible tokens of progress.

A word in conclusion as to the Mandates. Has the system set up by the Covenant of the League proved useful and effective? The general verdict seems to be in the affirmative. The essential features which distinguish territories held under Mandate from Colonies and Protectorates are, first, that the Mandatory is pledged to administer the country in accordance with certain strict rules laid down in the Mandate—whether those rules are in accordance with the practice in its own colonies or not; second, that it must render an annual account of its stewardship to the Mandates Commission, a body advisory to the League, and that these reports, together with the full minutes of the discussion upon them with the accredited representative of the Mandatory, are made public; and third, that inhabitants have the right to petition the League through the Mandatory, and the world at large has the right to submit any memorial if it is considered that the conditions of the Mandate are not being carried out. Publicity and the expression of public opinion are the only forces which can be brought to bear on a Mandatory, but they are very powerful forces. Whether the right of petition is sufficiently effective or whether it may be liable to misuse are matters now engaging the consideration of the Commission.

The Commission consists of ten members of different nationalities nominated by the Council of the League for personal competence. They may not hold any appointment under their governments. The examination of the reports, laws, petitions, and the large volume of press articles, parliamentary debates and other papers circulated by the Secretariat concerning the administration of fourteen separate countries, in addition to two or three sessions each year of some three weeks' duration each at Geneva, is a task so heavy that it is perhaps doubtful whether the system can long be efficiently carried out on its present basis.

Germany, in accordance with the Treaty of Locarno, will before long become a Member of the League. Influential parties in that country have long been engaged in propaganda having for their object the restitution of one or more of her colonies. They claim that until she is adjudged worthy to control a colony she does not sit at the table of the League on a footing of equality with Portugal or Spain, and that her industrial millions need free and assured access to tropical resources. This she enjoys already in all British territories whether under a Mandate or not, and will have as of right in all other mandated areas in Africa when she enters the League. Italy proclaims that if Germany were to obtain a Mandate she would advance a similar claim. On the other hand it is repugnant to right feeling that populations, to whom solemn pledges of protection and of the permanence of the existing arrangements have been made, should be bartered about as mere chattels to suit the convenience or political exigencies of European nations, and that the pledges should be treated as "scraps of paper." Nor can a Mandate be revoked (except in theory for gross maladministration) without the consent of the Mandatory.

I have touched on but two or three of the many problems which tropical Africa presents to the twentieth century for solution, but enough I think has been said to indicate their great interest and the claim they have on the careful attention alike of those who benefit by the products of Africa, and those who acknowledge the obligations which wealth, leisure, civilization, and the ethics of a higher creed impose upon the more favored nations.

Note

THE BLACK CLOUD IN AFRICA
BY EVANS LEWIN

July 1926

How did an informed and humane Englishman view the African scene four decades ago? If we may judge from this possibly typical appraisal, he was already profoundly disturbed by events in South Africa and wherever else the settled European was uprooting and distorting the life of the black man without admitting him into the society of the white man. But in black Africa he is satisfied that things are going well. He is proud of the way his countrymen are exercising their "trusteeship" for the African, by fulfilling their civilizing mission without interfering fundamentally with the Africans' way of life. He is not smug about it, and he shows awareness that World War I has wrought changes. But he believes deeply in the white man's mission and he thinks that there is plenty of time. One of the principal needs, he says, is for more relevant education, especially to make the African a better agriculturalist.

In short, the following article is an amalgam of views that seem alternately as valid as ever and utterly antique. But this is not the only interest of the article. It reminds us that the process by which Africa has today been brought into the main stream of world affairs was in great measure natural and inevitable and that whatever shortcomings we now see in the colonial system or in particular methods used, some form of domination was inescapable as soon as so vibrant a culture as that of Europe came into contact with the more static cultures of Africa. For the greater part of the colonial history of Africa, that domination was not enforced but accepted and it was after many years of looking up to the white man (which was a principal reason why the white man looked down) that the African discovered his master had feet of clay. Thereafter, the course of events was as inevitable as the previous subjection had been.

Evans Lewin can best be described as the bibliographer of the British Empire in the twentieth century. He was librarian of the Royal Empire Society and the Royal Colonial Institute, wrote histories and geographies and prepared massive catalogues. He lived in South Africa for four years after the Boer War and for a shorter period in Australia. He published two histories of Canada, but was a particular student of Africa, not only of the British possessions there, but also of the administration of the German territories. He died in 1955 at the age of 79.

It is fashionable today to smile patronizingly at the white-man's-burden philosophy which pervades this article, but the acceptance of responsibility which it reflects was in fact the saving grace of colonialism—the element that preserved it from being purely exploitative. And though we may avoid the term today, who would deny that it motivates our programs of foreign aid and technical assistance?

The Black Cloud in Africa

by EVANS LEWIN

Dean Inge in a more than usually gloomy and brilliant article in the *Quarterly Review* in which he shows, more particularly with reference to Asiatic civilization, the menacing dangers that threaten the survival of European control in the East, and even Europe itself, has pointed out that "the suicidal war which devastated the world of the white man for four years will probably be found to have produced its chief results, not in altering the balance of power in Europe, but in precipitating certain changes which were coming about slowly during the peace." In no part of the world is this more true than in Africa.

The basis of racial supremacy throughout the whole of Africa, tropical and sub-tropical, as in India, rests upon the consent of the governed, and only to a limited extent upon the application of those superior material means of enforcing his will that civilization has placed in the hands of the white man. Without the willing coöperation of native races all attempts to compel obedience must fail inevitably in their ultimate and highest object, which is the uplifting of the great and hitherto inert masses of the African peoples to a higher plane of civilization.

White supremacy in Africa, if it be attacked at all, will not be threatened in those vast intermediate areas, sweltering under the tropical sun, which lie between the two fringes of white colonization in the north and south of the continent, but in those more favored regions where white settlement is possible and where Europeans have erected a substantial civilization—in the north upon the ruins of the ancient Roman and Arab cultures, and in the south in regions where the black man was in a state of semi-savagery when Europeans first set foot in his territories.

Two distinct problems are created through the impact of the white man upon the black. In the tropical portions of the continent, where the black man is in an overwhelming majority and where the white man merely acts as the director and pioneer of civilization, it is possible for the native to retain in a large measure his own cultural environment without being cut off from the ties of the past which bind him to his own people and serve to develop his own methods of thought, and without being swallowed by a new and alien civilization imposed upon him from abroad. He can adopt, and generally does adopt, just so much of European methods and civilization as are suited to his advance upon the paths of his own culture. He still remains among his own people, able to influence them for good or ill and to be influenced by them in return. Above all, he can rise in the scale of civilization without let or hindrance from the white man. At no point does he come into active conflict with economic or social factors that he is unable to understand; and, although acting frequently under European guidance, he is still master in his own house and suffers under no intolerable racial disadvantages.

In the more temperate portions of the continent, on the other hand, where the white man has established industries and built large cities, the native has come into direct contact with economic and social forces which, while they may help his material development, generally tend to retard his spiritual and cultural advancement. He is a social outcast. If he attain some degree of the higher culture of those who have opened new avenues of educational advance, he is unable to make effective use, in the service of the whole community, of the knowledge he has assimilated by slow and painful processes and in spite of the almost overwhelming prejudices, well founded or otherwise, that are arraigned against him. In a country of white settlement he is faced by the inertia of racial antipathy and is met everywhere by a stubborn and ineradicable opposition, should he attempt to climb into the preserves of the white man. Politically he does not count; socially he cannot mix on terms of anything approaching equality with the white man. He is not permitted to enter a church attended by Europeans, and he is doomed to remain a "hewer of wood and drawer of water" because all avenues of economic advance are closed upon him.

The problems, therefore, in tropical and sub-tropical Africa are entirely different. In the former the black man is free to work out his own destinies. In the latter he is at the beck and call of the European and, under present conditions, cannot, even if he would, evolve his own type of civilization; he is racially but not yet economically segre-

gated. It is this profound difference between the treatment accorded
to the black man in tropical Africa and in South Africa that is bringing about the pressing problem of the present age in Africa known
generally as the "color question."

Prior to the war there was an uneasy stirring of the black masses
of humanity who were being slowly influenced by the penetrating
genius of the European races. Vast and important changes were being
brought about by the gradual, but not too rapid, economic development of African countries. Missionaries, traders, and administrators
were performing their allotted tasks well or indifferently well, or even
badly in some cases, in the midst of primitive peoples who were only
slowly awaking to the nature of the new methods being introduced
among them.

The war, however, set in operation new and perplexing influences in
Africa. Not only did the African races see thousands of white men,
professing the Christian religion, engaged in a deadly struggle upon
African soil, especially in such regions as the Cameroons, German
East Africa, and German South-West Africa—a struggle with its
inevitable reactions in other parts of the continent—but they wit-
nessed great numbers of their own race entering upon this fight on
one side or the other and also leaving Africa itself to assist their masters in the main theatre of the war. The French native troops who
were withdrawn from West Africa and the northern protectorates,
and the natives who left South Africa for employment on the lines
of communication in Europe itself, must have returned with enlarged ideas of the prowess of the white man but with a changed
view of his cultural and spiritual superiority; and the repercussions
throughout Africa of the ideas thus engendered have had far-reaching
and important results.

It may be stated as a general axiom that Christianity as preached
by the missionaries has received a setback wherever native Africans
have come into direct contact with Europeans. The black man has
come more and more to realize that precept and practice are not the
inevitable accompaniments of European civilization. But of one fact
he is still generally convinced, more particularly in the tropical portions of the continent. He believes that Europeans, as a whole, are
desirous of helping him to rise in the scale of civilization, and that in
spite of certain ugly economic factors an outstanding feature of European control is the idea of trusteeship, held by most administering

nations, on behalf of the native races that have fallen under their charge.

This conception of "trusteeship" as presented to the African peoples is not a new one. It goes back at least as far as the great movement which ended in the abolition of slavery, though until recently it has been but a still small voice crying in the wilderness of the somewhat ineffective, and certainly self-interested, administration that was introduced into numerous African territories when the race for African land first assumed considerable proportions in the 'eighties of the last century. It is, however, one of the most satisfactory features of the new administrative policy that has come to the front since the war that this underlying principle has been recognized officially as the guiding force of European effort in tropical Africa. While, on the one hand, economic penetration and development is undoubtedly the factor that causes European governments to shoulder the vast responsibilities of administrative work in Africa, on the other, the recognition of these responsibilities has become an essential feature of government; and African natives in the tropics have not been slow to appreciate all that is involved in this new orientation of European policy.

In all British colonies and protectorates in Africa the doctrine of trusteeship has been firmly laid down as a guiding principle of government. The Kenya White Paper of 1923 stated that the basis of our position in East Africa is the duty of trusteeship for the native population under our charge, and this duty has been emphasized more recently by Mr. Ormsby Gore, Under-Secretary of State for the Colonies, in the remarkable report of the East African Commission. He states that "it is difficult to realize without seeing Africa what a tremendous impact is involved in the juxtaposition of white civilization, with its command over material force, and its comparatively high and diversified social system, on the primitive people of eastern Africa. The African native is confronted with a whole range of facts entirely beyond his present comprehension and he finds himself caught in a maelstrom of economic and cultural progress which in the majority of cases baffles him completely." He then goes on to say that "the status of trusteeship involves an ethical conception; that is to say, it imposes upon the trustee a moral duty and a moral attitude. This derives in part from the influence of Christianity upon western civilization, and in part from what is claimed to be a specifically British conception, namely that of 'fair play for the weaker.' "

A great African administrator, Sir Frederick Lugard, has pointed
that this trusteeship involves a double duty. "We are not only trust
for the development and advance in civilization of the African, bu
we are also trustees for the world of very rich territories. This means
that we have a duty to humanity to develop the vast economic resources of a great continent." It is precisely how far these two conceptions can be embodied in a harmonious policy, fair alike to the
natives, to white settlers where they exist, and to the outside world,
that constitutes to-day the problem of tropical Africa.

British policy in Africa may perhaps be best exemplified by a study
of the work being done in the two West African colonies of the
Gold Coast and Nigeria and in Uganda and the Kenya Colony.
In no part of tropical Africa are the natives generally so far advanced
on the paths of civilization as they are in the Gold Coast, Nigeria,
and Uganda, and the main reason for this advance is that not only
was there a foundation of native civilization upon which to erect the
present edifice but the native has been left under suggestive guidance
to work out his own salvation. His lands have not been alienated, his
tribal system has not been broken up, and no attempt has been made
to force upon him alien methods of government or to turn him into
a mock Englishman. Compared with German administration in the
Cameroons, where a strictly plantation system was followed and where
the tribal lands frequently fell into the hands of speculating companies and private individuals, the system has proved a distinct success.

At the basis of all prosperity and contentment in Africa is the land
question. Where the native has obtained security of tenure, either on
a community basis or as a private owner, there is unlikely to be any
serious attempt to question the right of the European to control. It
is only where, as is frequently the case in South Africa, the native
has been de-tribalized and is a "landless" man, that serious unrest is
likely to occur—assuming, of course, that the natives have passed out
of the purely savage state. In the Gold Coast, the natives, almost by
their unaided efforts, have built up a great cocoa industry, which now
supplies half the world with its cocoa, worked entirely by native
cultivators and owned by native peasant proprietors. Similarly in
Nigeria, the natives own their own land and are encouraged to work
out their own salvation. In Uganda also a great cotton-growing industry has been established by the natives, worked and owned entirely
by them. It is not in every part of Africa, however, that native peasant

proprietorship is possible or, perhaps, desirable; and it is precisely where the natives are too backward in civilization to adopt readily the methods that have been so successful elsewhere that other means, such as European plantations, must be tried. Here the largest amount of unrest in the near future is to be expected.

British policy in Africa generally is to establish control by means of what is generally termed "indirect rule," that is to say, so far as possible the prestige of the native chiefs is maintained and extended and the people are ruled mainly through their hereditary or chosen leaders. Though some individuals do, perhaps not unsuccessfully, break away from their tribal surroundings and influences and ape the Englishman, especially in the coastal towns, the vast majority still retain all that is best in their native cultures and gradually take from European civilization the things best suited to their own mental and cultural development. In comparison of French and British methods in this respect it need only be said here that while the French are eminently successful as administrators in Africa, their policy is intensely nationalistic and makes for unity of administration rather than for diversity. The Frenchman looks upon his colonies as forming part of France and the native is trained to look upon himself as a Frenchman. In the British colonies, on the other hand, the natives remain to all intents and purposes sons of the soil that gave them birth.

At the back of all progress in tropical Africa is the question of education. Recently an American Commission under Dr. Thomas Jesse Jones, sent out by the Phelps-Stokes Fund, has reported on this subject, and though the conclusions of the Commission are not to be accepted in all cases without demur, it has undoubtedly performed a most useful work in a hitherto almost unexplored field. It is remarkable that both so much and so little has been done in the educational sphere in Africa. In some cases, apart from missionary endeavor, very little has been achieved and that, not infrequently, upon wrong lines. It seems to be admitted universally, however, that the bad old system of a purely literary education only survives in regions where the authorities, and the missionaries themselves, have not been awakened to what should be the true purpose of native education. The Phelps-Stokes Commission has plainly indicated that in its opinion, while a literary education may well form the apex of the system, the main purpose of African training should be to instruct the natives how to use their lands, their hands, and their intelligence. In other words training in agriculture, in craftsmanship, in hygiene, is quite as essential as a knowledge of reading, writing, and arithmetic.

Up to the present, agricultural and craft education have been much neglected, although definite steps have been taken in many cases to show the native how essential these subjects are to his well-being. It is almost incredible that in the whole of Africa there is, apparently, but one school that is exclusively engaged in teaching agriculture to natives and it is, perhaps, the more remarkable that this institution, the Tsolo Agricultural School, is situated in South Africa and is supported by funds supplied by the native Bhunga, a council of the native Transkeian Territory of the Cape Province. Such establishments should be everywhere in Africa to supplement the work of the ordinary schools, and the funds used to spread education, and especially to educate native teachers, should be increased at least tenfold in every colony in Africa. Efficient education—not mere book learning— and native tenure of land, will do everything to stabilize the position of the European as the controller of the destinies of tropical Africa.

The status and prospects of the native present a different picture in that portion of the continent where he comes into direct contact with European civilization in, to him, some of its ugliest and most detrimental forms. It is not easy for those who have not lived in the Union of South Africa to visualize the position of the natives in those provinces. The problems are so complex, the danger is so pressing, the outlook is so uncertain, that one may be pardoned for taking a gloomy view both of the future of the white race in the sub-continent and the future of the natives themselves. To state the position frankly and concisely, it must be admitted that the impact of European civilization upon the natives in South Africa in certain respects, though fortunately not in all, has been disastrous, because there the native can only be assimilated into the social system as a helot rather than as a sharer in the full benefits of white civilization.

The problem may be approached from two points of view: the result upon the white population of a preponderating black element in a country otherwise eminently suitable for European settlement, and the effect upon the natives of the conditions by which they have been gradually surrounded and into which they are continuously being drawn. The black man in South Africa is a man entrapped. The white man is tending to become an aristocrat in the center of a civilization that may be compared with the slave-holding states of antiquity and where in the future he may only remain as a master existing on the sufferance of his servants. Sooner or later his position, unless he take effective steps to alter his present policy, will be comparable with that of Europeans settled in the West Indies, and he will be swamped by an ever-swelling tide of black humanity.

In the Union of South Africa there are at present some 5,404,000 non-Europeans, of whom 4,698,000 are pure Bantus, compared with a white population of 1,522,000.* In addition there are 497,000 natives in Basutoland, 150,000 in the Bechuanaland Protectorate, and 112,-000 in Swaziland, three native territories under the direct rule of the Colonial Office, the control of which is urgently desired by the Union Government. There is thus a total native and colored population of 6,163,000 who are increasing at a much more rapid ratio than the Europeans. The former Director of the Census, Mr. Cousins, has pointed out that the European race can only hold its own numerically in South Africa by seeking accessions from abroad and that failing a constant immigration it must abandon the prospect of maintaining a white civilization, except as a diminishing minority in face of an overwhelming majority. It may then, he thinks, be forced to give up its domination or even to leave the country.

There seems, however, little possibility of any considerable immigration, owing to the fact that South Africa cannot easily absorb newcomers unprovided with a considerable capital and also owing to the general hostility both of the Nationalist and Labor parties to any active policy of immigration. The immense reservoir of unskilled labor, at cheap rates of pay, which the natives supply, makes it useless to import unskilled white laborers, without capital, expecting to find employment; and, moreover, the threat of widespread unemployment for white unskilled workers already in the Union is very serious. So far little has been done to meet this pressing internal problem of the "poor white" or "bywoner."

The effect in South Africa of the juxtaposition of the white and black races has been that Europeans will not do what is regarded as kaffir's work and reserve to themselves every employment requiring any degree of technical skill and resolutely refuse to perform what are regarded as the inferior kinds of manual labor. Unfortunately in a country circumstanced as South Africa is to-day the result of this selective policy of aristocratic exclusion has been that there has grown up the large class of almost unemployable whites who have no place

* For more up-to-date figures, see p. 200.—ED.

in the economic system because they are not trained to take "white men's jobs" and are unable to live on the wages that would be paid to kaffir labor. This class is continuously increasing and Dr. Edgar Brookes, a leading Transvaal educationalist, quoting from the Director of the Census, has pointed out that "only 50 percent of our boys and girls annually leaving school can now be placed in employment," with the ultimate effect that to her other difficulties South Africa is adding year by year a problem that strikes at the root of the economic relations of white and black.

But the most far-reaching effect of the European colonization of South Africa has been the change it has wrought upon the native modes of life. Originally a pastoralist, owning cattle, sheep, goats, and, in some cases, horses, the kaffir has been taken in too many cases from his natural surroundings and thrown into the vortex of a new economic life foreign to all his experiences. To-day more than 12 percent of the natives are town dwellers, living in locations on the outskirts of the cities or in compounds in the mining areas, frequently amidst squalid surroundings and under hygienic conditions unworthy of a great and progressive community. The housing of the native workers in South Africa is a problem that affects the well-being of the black-and-white structure of South African society and is a serious cause of much of the native unrest.

The growth of the mining industry in the Transvaal and elsewhere has been detrimental to the true welfare of the natives in many ways. Moreover, those natives who have not been caught in the industrial machine, or who have returned to their tribal areas, only too frequently with the vices and few of the virtues of white civilization, find that the lands placed at their disposal are in many cases entirely inadequate for their needs, while, speaking generally, they have not been trained to make the best use either of the poorer lands at their disposal or of some of the undoubtedly fertile territories that still remain to them. There is something pathetic in the inexorable way in which the natives have been forced back into the remoter and less fertile parts of the country, although in contradistinction to many native races in like circumstances the kaffirs have not gone to the wall in the fight between the energy and business acumen of the European and the simplicity and lack of forethought of the native. They are, instead, intensely alive and are loudly clamoring for land in a country where the average per head on the native reserves available for their occupation is in some cases as low as 4.8 acres (Transvaal and

Orange Free State) and nowhere more than 12.8 acres (Cape) as compared with the enormous farms held by Europeans. It is estimated that in South Africa only 13 percent of the land is set aside for 4,500,000 natives while 87 percent is reserved for 1,500,000 whites. The question of native reserves, coupled with the policy of racial and industrial segregation, is the immediate problem that faces the Union Government to-day.

The policy of General Hertzog, the Premier, outlined at Smithfield, Orange Free State, on November 13th, is one of segregation for the natives; but the whole question is so complicated by numerous factors that it is difficult to conceive how such a policy can be put into practice, even approximately. In no case is it possible to return the natives to the lands from which they originally came, to withdraw from the economic life of the community the vast numbers that have broken away from their tribal allegiance, to take from the white community the lands it already possesses, or to deprive the black man of his present means of education or to prevent its ultimate extension and improvement. By segregation General Hertzog probably means the extension, if that be possible, of the areas allotted to natives, in accordance with definite promises made in 1913, and the creation of some political means whereby the black man may be enabled to express his opinion and to press his views upon the white community. The political aspect of General Hertzog's plan for the establishment of a Native Council to meet annually is already attracting great attention in the Union, where that part of the native population that has received some measure of education is clamoring for an effective constitutional means of expressing its desires.

His policy also involves what may be termed industrial segregation, or rather industrial reservation, a policy that strikes directly at the economic aspirations of the natives and is intended to prevent them from acquiring positions of trust, as skilled mechanics and workmen, to the detriment of the white workers. This policy is not new in South African politics for a color bar has long existed in the mines of the Witwatersrand by virtue of departmental regulations whereby special occupations, skilled and half skilled, were reserved for Europeans and half-castes. The regulation which provided that "the operation of, or attendance on, machinery shall be in charge of a competent shiftsman, and in the Transvaal and Orange Free State such shiftsman shall be a white man," was unanimously declared to be *ultra vires* by the Transvaal Supreme Court in 1924, in a judgment which created great satisfaction among the black workers and produced a corresponding opposition among the white. This year, however, a Color Bar Bill was introduced, as the beginning of the government's native segregation policy, which extended the industrial disability to the Cape Province and ran counter to Cecil Rhodes's well-known policy of "equal rights to all civilized men south of the Zambesi." This bill was thrown out by the Senate upon its first presentation, after the natives had been refused a hearing before the Select Committee dealing with it; it was reintroduced and again rejected by the Senate on March 17, 1926, and now will be submitted to a joint session of the two Houses of Parliament, under the terms of the South Africa Act of 1909.

Only the extension and radical reform of the present inadequate and, generally, inappropriate educational system is likely to lead to a solution of the racial trouble. The kaffir in South Africa must be trained for agricultural work, not exclusively on the farms of the white community, but in his own settlements. Industrial training must go hand in hand with agricultural education, but in this case it must be made certain that the black man be placed in a position where he can employ his training amongst his own people. Otherwise the economic pressure exerted by thousands of trained workers, competent to perform many jobs now exclusively confined to Europeans, will prove overwhelming in a country where the black flood, unless offered adequate safety-gates, will inevitably sweep away the economic barriers of an aristocratic civilization. At the root of the whole native question in Africa is vocational training for the land and one cannot do better than echo the words of Dr. Thomas Jesse Jones that "it has been a surprise that so few Europeans or Africans have realized that the most fundamental demand vocationally is for training to develop the soil possibilities of the great African continent"—a demand equally applicable to the Union of South Africa and the great tropical territories in the north. Given this fundamental change and a gradual removal of the barriers that shut out the educated black man from employment for which he has fitted himself, the problem of South Africa may be settled eventually by mutual consent.

Note

WORLDS OF COLOR
BY W. E. B. DU BOIS

April 1925

At the time this article was written, William Edward Burghardt Du Bois was the recognized leader and most eloquent spokesman of the Negro in America. Teacher, author and publicist, he found his most effective platform in *Crisis*, the journal of the National Association for the Advancement of Colored People, which he edited for 22 years. In his fight for racial equality he was strident, autocratic, militant, arrogant and (for a time) enormously effective. He was also unequivocally racialist, and it was his advocacy of Negro separatism that finally caused a sharp break in 1934 with the N.A.A.C.P., of which he had been a founder. Thereafter he was a leader largely without followers.

Always a socialist, he greatly admired the Soviet Union, although he effectively fought the American Communist Party during the twenties and thirties. But after World War II he devoted his attention increasingly to "peace and socialism," and his support of Communist causes became less qualified. In 1951 he was indicted by a Federal Grand Jury for failing to register his Peace Information Center as the American agent of a foreign power. He was acquitted, but his fellow-travelling continued unabated; in 1958 he was awarded the Lenin Peace Prize and in 1961 he finally joined the Communist Party. He then became a citizen of Ghana, where he lived his last years, working on an African encyclopedia. Born in a New England town two years after the abolition of slavery, he died 95 years later and 5,000 miles away during the night before the Great March on Washington of August 28, 1963. Not one of the speakers there mentioned his name.

Du Bois was one of the first American Negro leaders to demonstrate an informed and effective interest in Africa and the Africans. Although he opposed Marcus Garvey's Back-to-Africa movement, he believed that American Negroes should speak for Africa, which was then largely inarticulate. He himself took a leading part in a succession of Pan-African Congresses in the twenties and it was he who organized the important Fifth Congress of 1945 in London. Although he was not the most reliable or objective observer of Africa—for example, he was blind to the evils practiced by the Liberian Government of that time—his knowledge of Africa was considerable and his comments were invariably interesting.

This is the first of five articles he wrote for *Foreign Affairs* over a period of two decades. Like Lord Lugard (see page 5), than whom he could hardly be more different, he starts with the problem of labor, probably the major concern of the twenties in Africa, as elsewhere. He then moves to a comparative examination of the style and performance of the various colonial powers in Africa. Understandably, his criteria for judging the colonial powers depend heavily on the degree of race consciousness shown by the administering authorities. Hence Britain gets very low marks, and ironically his kindest words are reserved for Portugal. Today, an objective evaluation of the performance of the colonial powers in Africa would have to give far more credit to Britain, which was the first to prepare its territories systematically for self-government and independence. Nevertheless, even today there is much truth in Du Bois's analysis, and he reminds us again that for the African there is no substitute for acceptance and respect.

Du Bois was the first Negro to be elected to the National Institute of Arts and Letters. A Phi Beta Kappa graduate of Harvard, from which he also obtained a Ph.D., he spent his early years teaching—Greek, Latin, economics, history, sociology. Among a score of books that he wrote were "Suppression of the Slave Trade" and "The World and Africa." His last book, written in 1961, bore the same title as this article, written 38 years ago.

Worlds of Color

by W. E. B. DU BOIS

Once upon a time in my younger years and in the dawn of this century I wrote: "The problem of the Twentieth Century is the problem of the color line." It was a pert phrase which I then liked and which since I have often rehearsed to myself, asking how far was it prophecy and how far speculation? Today, in the last year of the century's first quarter, I propose to examine this matter again, and more especially in the memory of the great event of these great years, the World War. How deep were the roots of this catastrophe entwined about the color line? And of the legacy left, what of the darker race problems will the world inherit?

THE LABOR PROBLEM

Most men would agree that our present Problem of Problems is what we call Labor: the problem of allocating work and income in the tremendous and increasingly intricate world-embracing industrial machine which we have built. But, despite our study and good-will, is it not possible that our research is not directed to the right geographical spots and our good-will too often confined to that labor which we see and feel and exercise right around us rather than to the periphery of the vast circle and to the unseen and inarticulate workers within the World Shadow? And may not the continual baffling of our effort and failure of our formula be due to just such mistakes? At least it will be of interest to step within these shadows and, looking backward, view the European and white American labor problem from this external vantage ground—or, better, ground of disadvantage.

With nearly every great European empire today walks its dark colonial shadow, while over all Europe there stretches the yellow shadow of Asia that lies across the world. One might indeed rede the riddle of Europe by making its present plight a matter of colonial shadows and speculate wisely on what might not happen if Europe became suddenly shadowless—if Asia and Africa and the islands were cut permanently away. At any rate here is a field of inquiry, of likening and contrasting each land and its far off shadow.

THE SHADOW OF PORTUGAL

I was attending the Third Pan-African Congress and I walked to the Palacio dos Cortes with Magellan. It was in December, 1923, and in Lisbon. I was rather proud. You see Magalhaes (to give him the Portuguese spelling) is a mulatto—small, light-brown and his hands quick with gestures. Dr. José de Magalhaes is a busy man: a practising specialist; professor in the School of Tropical Medicine whose new buildings are rising; and above all, deputy in the Portuguese Parliament from São Thomé, Africa. Thus this Angolese African, educated in Lisbon and Paris, is one of the nine colored members of European Parliaments. Portugal has had colored ministers and now has three colored deputies and a senator. I saw two Portuguese in succession kissing one colored member on the floor of the house. Or was he but a dark native? There is so much ancient black blood in this peninsula.

Between the Portuguese and the African and near African there is naturally no "racial" antipathy—no accumulated historical hatreds, dislikes, despisings. Not that you would likely find a black man married to a Portuguese of family and wealth, but on the other hand it seemed quite natural for Portugal to make all the blacks of her African empire citizens of Portugal with the rights of the European born.

Magalhaes and another represent São Thomé. They are elected by black folk independent of party. Again and again I meet black folk from São Thomé—young students, well-dressed, well-bred, evidently sons of well-to-do if not wealthy parents, studying in Portugal, which harbors annually a hundred such black students.

São Thomé illustrates some phases of European imperialism in Africa. This industrial rule involves cheap land and labor in Africa and large manufacturing capital in Europe, with a resultant opportunity for the exercise of pressure from home investors and the press. Once in a while—not often—a feud between the capitalists and the manufacturers at home throws sudden light on Africa. For instance, in the Boer War the "cocoa press" backed by the anti-war Liberals attacked the Unionists and exposed labor conditions in South Africa.

In retaliation, after the war and when the Liberals were in power, the Unionists attacked labor conditions in the Portuguese cocoa colonies.

For a long time the cocoa industry flourished on the islands of São Thomé and Principe, on large plantations run by Portuguese and backed by English capital. Here under a system of labor recruiting and indentures which amounted to slavery these little islands led the world in cocoa production and here was the basis of the great English and American cocoa industry. When this system was attacked there immediately arose the situation which is characteristic of modern industrial imperialism and differentiates it from past imperialism. Modern expansion has to use democracy at home as its central authority. This democracy is strangely curbed by industrial organization but it does help select officials, and public opinion, once aroused, rules. Thus with a democratic face at home modern imperialism turns a visage of stern and unyielding autocracy toward its darker colonies. This double-faced attitude is difficult to maintain and puts hard strain on the national soul that tries it.

In England the attack of the Unionists on the Liberals and the "cocoa press," proving slavery on the São Thomé plantations, led to a demand for drastic labor reform in Portuguese Africa. Now the profits of the great Portuguese plantation owners could not afford this nor could they understand this sudden virtue on the part of capitalists who had known all along how labor was "recruited." They charged "hypocrisy," not understanding that English capitalists had an inconvenient democracy at home that often cracked its whip over them. The cocoa industry was forced by public opinion to boycott Portuguese cocoa; the great Portuguese proprietors were forced to give place to smaller Negro and mulatto cultivators who could afford smaller profits. At the same time the center of cocoa raising crossed the straits and seated itself in the English colonies of the Gold Coast and Nigeria, formerly the ancient kingdoms of Ashanti, Yoruba, Haussaland and others. Thus in this part of Portuguese Africa the worst aspects of slavery melted away and colonial proprietors with smaller holdings could afford to compete with the great planters; wherefore democracy, both industrially and politically, took new life in black Portugal. Intelligent black deputies appeared in the Portuguese parliaments, a hundred black students studied in the Portuguese universities and a new colonial code made black men citizens of Portugal with full rights.

But in Portugal, alas! no adequate democratic control has been established, nor can it be established with an illiteracy of 75 percent; so that while the colonial code is liberally worded and economic power has brought some freedom in São Thomé, unrestrained Portuguese and English capital rules in parts of Angola and in Portuguese East Africa, where no resisting public opinion in England has yet been aroused.

The African shadows of Spain and Italy are but drafts on some imperial future not yet realized, and touch home industry and democracy only through the war budget. As Spain is pouring treasure into a future Spanish Morocco, so Italy has already poured out fabulous sums in the attempt to annex north and northeast Africa, especially Abyssinia. The prince who yesterday visited Europe is the first adult successor of that black Menelik who humbled Italy to the dust at Adowa in 1896.

Insurgent Morocco and dependent Egypt, independent Abyssinia and Liberia are, as it were, shadows of Europe on Africa, unattached, and as such they curiously threaten the whole imperial program. On the one hand they arouse democratic sympathy in home lands which makes it difficult to submerge them; and again they are temptations to agitation for freedom and autonomy on the part of other black and subject populations.

THE SHADOW OF BELGIUM

There is a little black man in Belgium whose name is Mfumu Paul Panda. He is filled with a certain resentment against me and American Negroes. He writes me now and then but fairly spits his letters at me and they are always filled with some defense of Belgium in Africa or rather with some accusation against England, France and Portugal there. I do not blame Panda although I do not agree with his reasoning. Unwittingly, the summer before last, I tore his soul in two. His reason knows that I am right but his heart denies his reason. He was nephew and therefore by African custom heir of a great chief who for thirty years, back to the time of Stanley, has coöperated with white Belgium. As a child of five young Panda was brought home from the Belgian Congo by a Belgian official and given to that official's maiden sister. This sister reared the little black boy as her own, nursed him, dressed him, schooled him, and defended against the criticism of her friends his right to university training. She was his mother, his friend. He loved her and revered her. She guided and loved him.

When the second Pan-African Congress came to Brussels it found Panda leader of the small black colony there and spokesman for black Belgium. He had revisited the Congo and was full of plans for reform. And he thought of the uplift of his black compatriots in terms of reform. All this the Pan-African Congress changed. First it brought on his head a storm of unmerited abuse from the industrial press: we were enemies of Belgium; we were pensioners of the Bolshevists; we were partisans of England. Panda hotly defended us until he heard our speeches and read our resolutions.

The Pan-African Congress revealed itself to him with a new and inexplicable program. It talked of Africans as intelligent, thinking, self-directing and voting men. It envisaged an Africa for the Africans and governed by and for Africans and it arraigned white Europe, including Belgium, for nameless and deliberate wrong in Africa. Panda was perplexed and astonished; and then his white friends and white mother rushed to the defense of Belgium and blamed him for consorting with persons with ideas so dangerous and unfair to Belgium. He turned upon us black folk in complaining wrath. He felt in a sense deceived and betrayed. He considered us foolishly radical. Belgium was not perfect but was far less blood-guilty than other European powers. Panda continues to send me clippings and facts to prove this.

In this last matter he is in a sense right. England and France and Germany deliberately laid their shadow across Africa. Belgium had Africa thrust upon her. Bismarck intended the Congo Free State for Germany and he cynically made vain and foolish Leopold temporary custodian; and even after Bismarck's fall Germany dreamed of an Africa which should include the Congo, half the Portuguese territory and all the French, making Germany the great and dominant African power. For this she fought the Great War.

Meantime, and slowly, Belgium became dazzled by the dream of empire. Africa is but a small part of Britain; Africa is but a half of larger France. But the Congo is eighty-two times the size of little Belgium, and at Tervurien wily Leopold laid a magic mirror—an intriguing flash of light, set like a museum in rare beauty and approached by magnificent vistas—a flash of revealing knowledge such as no other modern land possesses of its colonial possessions. The rank and file of the Belgians were impressed. They dreamed of wealth and glory. They received the Congo from Leopold as a royal gift—shyly, but with secret pride. What nation of the world had so wonderful a colony! And Belgium started to plan its development.

Meantime the same power that exploited the Congo and made red rubber under Leopold—these same great merchants and bankers—still ruled and guided the vast territory. Moreover Belgium, impoverished by war and conquest, needed revenue as never before. The only difference, then, between the new Congo and the old was that a Belgian liberal public opinion had a right to ask questions and must be informed. Propaganda intimating that this criticism of Belgium was mainly international jealousy and that the exploitation of black Belgium would eventually lower taxes for the whites was nearly enough to leave the old taskmasters and methods in control in spite of wide plans for eventual education and reform.

I remember my interview with the socialist Minister for Colonies. He hesitated to talk with me. He knew what socialism had promised the worker and what it was unable to do for the African worker, but he told me his plans for education and uplift. They were fine plans, but they remain plans even today and the Belgian Congo is still a land of silence and ignorance, with few schools, with forced industry, with all the land and natural resources taken from the people and handed over to the State, and the State, so far as the Congo is concerned, ruled well-nigh absolutely by profitable industry. Thus the African shadow of Belgium gravely and dangerously overshadows that little land.

THE SHADOW OF FRANCE

I know two black men in France. One is Candace, black West Indian deputy, an out-and-out defender of the nation and more French than the French. The other is René Maran, black Goncourt prize-man and author of "Batouala." Maran's attack on France and on the black French deputy from Senegal has gone into the courts and marks an era. Never before have Negroes criticized the work of the French in Africa.

France's attitude toward black and colored folk is peculiar. England knows Negroes chiefly as colonial "natives" or as occasional curiosities on London streets. America knows Negroes mainly as freedmen and servants. But for nearly two centuries France has known educated and well-bred persons of Negro descent; they filtered in from the French West Indies, sons and relatives of French families and recognized as such under the Code Napoleon, while under English law similar folk were but nameless bastards. All the great French schools have had black students here and there; the professions have known many and the fine arts a few scattered over decades; but all this was enough to make it impossible to say in France as elsewhere that Negroes cannot be educated. That is an absurd statement to a Frenchman. It was not that the French loved or hated Negroes as such; they simply grew to regard them as men with the possibilities and shortcomings of men, added to an unusual natural personal appearance.

Then came the war and France needed black men. She recruited them by every method, by appeal, by deceit, by half-concealed force. She threw them ruthlessly into horrible slaughter. She made them "shock" troops. They walked from the tall palms of Guinea and looked into the mouths of Krupp guns without hesitation, with scarcely a tremor. France watched them offer the blood sacrifice for their adopted motherland with splendid *sang-froid*, often with utter abandon.

But for Black Africa Germany would have overwhelmed France before American help was in sight. A tremendous wave of sentiment toward black folk welled up in the French heart. And back of this sentiment came fear for the future, not simply fear of Germany reborn but fear of changing English interests, fear of unstable America. What Africa did for France in military protection she could easily repeat on a vaster scale; wherefore France proposes to protect herself in future from military aggression by using half a million or more of trained troops from yellow, brown and black Africa. France has 40,000,000 Frenchmen and 60,000,000 Colonials. Of these Colonials, 845,000 served in France during the war, of whom 535,000 were soldiers and 310,000 in labor contingents. Of the soldiers, 440,000 came from north and west Africa. The peace footing of the French army is now 660,000, to whom must be added 189,000 Colonial troops. With three years service and seven years reserve, France hopes in ten years time to have 400,000 trained Colonial troops and 450,000 more ready to be trained. These Colonial troops will serve part of their time in France.

This program brings France face to face with the problem of democratic rule in her colonies. French industry has had wide experience in the manipulation of democracy at home but her colonial experience is negligible. Legally, of course, the colonies are part of France.

Theoretically Colonials are French citizens and already the blacks of the French West Indies and the yellows and browns of North Africa are so recognized and represented in Parliament. Four towns of Senegal have similar representation; but beyond this matters hesitate.

All this, however, brings both political and economic difficulties. Diagne, black deputy from Senegal, was expelled from the Socialist Party because he had made no attempt to organize a branch of the party in his district. And the whole colonial bloc stand outside the interests of home political parties, while these parties know little of the particular demands of local colonies. As this situation develops there will come the question of the practicability of ruling a world nation with one law-making body. And if devolution of power takes place, what will be the relation of self-governing colonies to the mother country?

But beyond this more or less nebulous theory looms the immediately practical problem of French industry. The French nation and French private industry have invested huge sums in African colonies, considering black Africa alone. Dakar is a modern city superimposed on a native market-place. Its public buildings, its vast harbor, its traffic are imposing. Conakry has miles of warehouses beneath its beautiful palms. No European country is so rapidly extending its African railways—one may ride from St. Louis over half way to Timbuktu and from Dakar 1,500 miles to the Gulf of Guinea.

The question is, then, is France able to make her colonies paying industrial investments and at the same time centers for such a new birth of Negro civilization and freedom as will attach to France the mass of black folk in unswerving loyalty and will to sacrifice. Such a double possibility is today by no means clear. French industry is fighting today a terrific battle in Europe for the hegemony of reborn Central Europe. The present probabilities are that the future spread of the industrial imperialism of the West will be largely under French leadership. French and Latin imperialism in industry will depend on alliance with western Asia and northern and central Africa, with the Congo rather than the Mediterranean as the southern boundary. Suppose that this new Latin imperialism emerging from the Great War developed a new antithesis to English imperialism where blacks and browns and yellows, subdued, cajoled and governed by white men, form a laboring proletariat subject to a European white democracy which industry controls; suppose that, contrary to this, Latin Europe should evolve political control with black men and the Asiatics hav-

ing a real voice in Colonial government, while both at home and in
the colonies democracy in industry continued to progress; what would
this cost? It would mean, of course, nothing less than the giving up
of the idea of an exclusive White Man's World. It would be a revolt
and a tremendous revolt against the solidarity of the West in opposition to the South and East. France moving along this line would
perforce carry Italy, Portugal and Spain with it, and it is the fear of
such a possible idea that explains the deep-seated resentment against
France on the part of England and America. It is not so much the
attitude of France toward Germany that frightens white Europe, as
her apparent flaunting of the white fetish. The plans of those who
would build a world of white men have always assumed the ultimate
acquiescence of the colored world in the face of their military power
and industrial efficiency, because of the darker world's lack of unity
and babel of tongues and wide cleft of religious difference. If now
one part of the white world bids for dark support by gifts of at least
partial manhood rights, the remainder of the white world scents treason and remains grim and unyielding in its heart. But is it certain that
France is going to follow this program?

I walked through the native market at St. Louis in French Senegal
—a busy, colorful scene. There was wonderful work in gold filigree
and in leather, all kinds of beads and bracelets and fish and foods.
Mohammedans salammed at sunset, black-veiled Moorish women
glided like sombre ghosts with living eyes; mighty black men in pale
burnooses strode by—it was all curious, exotic, alluring. And yet I
could not see quite the new thing that I was looking for. There was
no color line particularly visible and yet there was all the raw material
for it. Most of the white people were in command holding government office and getting large incomes. Most of the colored and black
folk were laborers with small incomes. In the fashionable cafés you
seldom saw colored folk, but you did see them now and then and no
one seemed to object. There were schools, good schools, but they
fell short of anything like universal education for the natives. White
and colored school children ran and played together, but the great
mass of children were not in school.

As I look more narrowly, what seemed to be happening was this:
the white Frenchmen were exploiting black Africans in practically
the same way as white Englishmen, but they had not yet erected or
tried to erect caste lines. Consequently, into the ranks of the exploiters
there arose continually black men and mulattoes, but these dark men

were also exploiters. They had the psychology of the exploiters. They looked upon the mass of people as means of wealth. The mass therefore had no leadership. There was no one in the colony except the unrisen and undeveloped blacks who thought of the colony as developing and being developed for its own sake and for the sake of the mass of the people there. Everyone of intelligence thought that Senegal was being developed for the sake of France and inevitably they tended to measure its development by the amount of profit.

If this sort of thing goes on will not France find herself in the same profit-taking colonial industry as England? Indeed, unless she follows English methods in African colonies can she compete with England in the amount of profit made and if she does not make profit out of her colonies how long will her industrial masters submit without tremendous industrial returns? Or if these industrial returns come, what will be the plight of black French Africa? "Batouala" voices it. In the depths of the French Congo one finds the same exploitation of black folk as in the Belgian Congo or British West Africa. The only mitigation is that here and there in the Civil Service are black Frenchmen like René Maran who can speak out; but they seldom do.

For the most part, as I have said, in French Africa educated Africans are Europeans. But if education goes far and develops in Africa a change in this respect must come. For this France has a complete theoretical system of education beginning with the African village and going up to the colleges and technical schools at Goree. But at present it is, of course, only a plan and the merest skeleton of accomplishment. On the picturesque island of Goree whose ancient ramparts face modern and commercial Dakar I saw two or three hundred fine black boys of high school rank gathered in from all Senegal by competitive tests and taught thoroughly by excellent French teachers in accordance with a curriculum which, as far as it went, was equal to that of any European school; and graduates could enter the higher schools of France. A few hundred students out of a black population of nineteen millions is certainly but a start. This development will call for money and trained guidance and will interfere with industry. It is not likely that the path will be followed and followed fast unless black French leaders encourage and push France, unless they see the pitfalls of American and English race leadership and bring the black apostle to devote himself to race uplift not by the compulsion of outer hate but by the lure of inner vision.

As yet I see few signs of this. I have walked in Paris with Diagne who represents Senegal—all Senegal, white and black—in the French parliament. But Diagne is a Frenchman who is accidentally black. I suspect Diagne rather despises his own black Wolofs. I have talked with Candace, black deputy of Guadaloupe. Candace is virulently French. He has no conception of Negro uplift, as apart from French development. One black deputy alone, Boisneuf of Martinique, has the vision. His voice rings in parliament. He made the American soldiers keep their hands off the Senegalese. He made the governor of Congo apologize and explain; he made Poincaré issue that extraordinary warning against American prejudice. Is Boisneuf an exception or a prophecy?

One looks on present France and her African shadow, then, as standing at the parting of tremendous ways; one way leads toward democracy for black as well as white—a thorny way made more difficult by the organized greed of the imperial profit-takers within and without the nation; the other road is the way of the white world, and of its contradictions and dangers English colonies may tell.

THE SHADOW OF ENGLAND

I landed in Sierra Leone last January. The great Mountain of the Lion crouched above us, its green sides trimmed with the pretty white villas of the whites, while black town sweltered below. Despite my diplomatic status I was haled before the police and in the same room where criminals were examined I was put through the sharpest grilling I ever met in a presumably civilized land. Why? I was a black American and the English fear black folk who have even tasted freedom. Everything that America has done crudely and shamelessly to suppress the Negro, England in Sierra Leone has done legally and suavely so that the Negroes themselves sometimes doubt the evidence of their own senses: segregation, disfranchisement, trial without jury, over-taxation, "Jim Crow" cars, neglect of education, economic serfdom. Yet all this can be and is technically denied. Segregation? "Oh no," says the colonial official, "anyone can live where he will—only that beautiful and cool side of the mountain with fine roads, golf and tennis and bungalows is assigned to government officials." Are there black officials? "Oh yes, and they can be assigned residences there, too." But they never have been. The Negroes vote and hold office in Freetown—I met the comely black and cultured mayor—but Freetown has almost no revenues and its powers have been gradually absorbed by the autocratic white colonial government which has five million dollars a year to spend. Any government prosecutor can abolish trial by jury in any case with the consent of the judge and all judges are white. White officials ride in special railway carriages and I am morally certain—I cannot prove it—that more is spent by the government on tennis and golf in the colony than on popular education.

These things, and powerful efforts of English industry to reap every penny of profit for England in colonial trade, leaving the black inhabitants in helpless serfdom, has aroused West Africa, and aroused it at this time because of two things—the war, and cocoa in Nigeria. The burden of war fell hard on black and British West Africa. Their troops conquered German Africa for England and France at bitter cost and helped hold back the Turk. Yet there was not a single black officer in the British army or a single real reward save citations and new and drastic taxation even on exports.

But British West Africa had certain advantages. After the decline of the slave trade and before the discovery that slavery and serfdom in Africa could be made to pay more than the removal of the laboring forces to other parts of the world, there was a disposition to give over to the natives the black colonies on the fever coast, and the British Government announced the intention of gradually preparing West Africans for self-government. Missionary education and the sending of black students to England raised a small Negro intelligentsia which long struggled to place itself at the head of affairs. It had some success but lacked an economic foundation. When the new industrial imperialism swept Africa, with England in the lead, the presence of these educated black leaders was a thorn in the flesh of the new English industrialists. Their method was to crowd these leaders aside into narrower and narrower confines as we have seen in Sierra Leone. But the Negroes in the older colonies retained possession of their land and, suddenly, when the cocoa industry was transferred from Portuguese Africa, they gained in one or two colonies a new and undreamed of economic foundation. Instead of following the large plantation industry, cocoa became the product of the small individual native farm. In 1891 a native sold eighty pounds of the first cocoa raised on the Gold Coast. By 1911 this had increased to 45,000 tons and in 1916 to 72,000 tons. In Nigeria there has also been a large increase, making these colonies today the greatest cocoa producing countries in the world.

Moreover this progress showed again the new democratic problems of colonization, since it began and was fostered by a certain type of white colonial official who was interested in the black man and wanted him to develop. But this official was interested in the primitive black and not in the educated black. He feared and despised the educated West African and did not believe him capable of leading his primitive brother. He sowed seeds of dissension between the two. On the other hand, the educated West African hated the white colonial leader as a supplanter and deceiver whose ultimate aims must be selfish and wrong; and as ever, between these two, the English exploiting company worked gradually its perfect will.

Determined effort was thus made by the English, both merchants and philanthropists, to cut the natives off from any union of forces or of interests with the educated West Africans. "Protectorates" under autocratic white rule were attached to the colonies and the natives in the protectorates were threatened with loss of land, given almost no education and left to the mercy of a white colonial staff whose chief duty gradually came to be the encouragement of profitable industry for the great companies. These companies were represented in the governing councils, they influenced appointments at home and especially they spread in England a carefully prepared propaganda which represented the educated "nigger" as a bumptious, unreasoning fool in a silk hat, while the untutored and unspoiled native under white control was nature's original nobleman. Also they suggested that this "white" control must not admit too many visionaries and idealists.

This policy has not been altogether successful, for the educated Negro is appealing to English democracy and the native is beginning to seek educated black leadership. After many vicissitudes, in 1920 a Congress of West Africa was assembled on the Gold Coast, and from this a delegation was sent to London "to lay before His Majesty the King in Council through the colonial ministry certain grievances." This was an epoch-making effort and, as was natural, the Colonial Office, where imperial industry is entrenched, refused to recognize the delegation, claiming that they did not really represent black West Africa. Nevertheless, through the League of Nations Union and the public press this delegation succeeded in putting its case before the world. They described themselves as "of that particular class of peaceful citizens who, apprehensive of the culminating danger resulting from the present political unrest in West Africa—an unrest which is silently moving throughout the length and breadth of that continent— and also appreciating the fact that the present system of administration will inevitably lead to a serious deadlock between the 'Government and the Governed,' decided to set themselves to the task of ameliorating this pending disaster by putting forward constitutionally a programme, the carrying of which into operation will alleviate all pains and misgivings."

The final resolutions of the Congress said, "that in the opinion of this Conference the time has arrived for a change in the Constitution of several British West African colonies, so as to give the people an effective voice in their affairs both in the Legislative and Municipal Governments, and that the Conference pledges itself to submit proposals for such reforms."

The reasons for this demand are thus described:

"In the demand for the franchise by the people of British West Africa, it is not to be supposed that they are asking to be allowed to copy a foreign institution. On the contrary, it is important to notice that the principle of electing representatives to local councils and bodies is inherent in all the systems of British West Africa. . . . From the foregoing it is obvious that a system by which the Governor of a Crown Colony nominates whom he thinks proper to represent the people is considered by them as a great anomaly and constitutes a grievance and a disability which they now request should be remedied."

Since the war not only has West Africa thus spoken but the colored West Indies have complained. They want Home Rule and they are demanding it. They asked after the war: Why was it that no black man sat in the Imperial Conference? Why is it that one of the oldest parts of the empire lingers in political serfdom to England and industrial bondage to America? Why is there not a great British West Indian Federation, stretching from Bermuda to Honduras and Guiana, and ranking with the free dominions? The answer was clear and concise—Color.

In 1916 a new agitation for representative government began in Grenada. The fire spread to all the West Indies and in 1921 a delegation was received by the Colonial Office in London at the same time that the Second Pan-African Congress was in session.

Here were unusual appeals to English democracy—appeals that not even commercial propaganda could wholly hush. But there was a force that curiously counteracted them. Liberal England, wanting world peace and fearing French militarism, backed by the English thrift that is interested in the restored economic equilibrium, found as one of its most prominent spokesmen Jan Smuts of South Africa, and Jan Smuts stands for the suppression of the blacks.

Jan Smuts is today, in his world aspects, the greatest protagonist of the white race. He is fighting to take control of Laurenço Marques from a nation that recognizes, even though it does not realize, the equality of black folk; he is fighting to keep India from political and social equality in the empire; he is fighting to insure the continued and eternal subordination of black to white in Africa; and he is fighting for peace and good will in a white Europe which can by union present a united front to the yellow, brown and black worlds. In all this he expresses bluntly, and yet not without finesse, what a powerful host of white folk believe but do not plainly say in Melbourne, New Orleans, San Francisco, Hongkong, Berlin, and London.

The words of Smuts in the recent Imperial Conference were transcribed as follows: "The tendencies in South Africa, just as elsewhere, were all democratic. If there was to be equal manhood suffrage over the Union, the whites would be swamped by the blacks. A distinction could not be made between Indians and Africans. They would be impelled by the inevitable force of logic to go the whole hog, and the result would be that not only would the whites be swamped in Natal by the Indians but the whites would be swamped all over South Africa by the blacks and the whole position for which the whites had striven for two hundred years or more now would be given up. So far as South Africa was concerned, therefore, it was a question of impossibility. For white South Africa it was not a question of dignity but a question of existence."

This almost naïve setting of the darker races beyond the pale of democracy and of modern humanity was listened to with sympathetic attention in England. It is without doubt today the dominant policy of the British Empire. Can this policy be carried out? It involves two things—acquiescence of the darker peoples and agreement between capital and labor in white democracies.

This agreement between capital and labor in regard to colored folk cannot be depended on. First of all, no sooner is colored labor duly subordinate, voiceless in government, efficient for the purpose and cheap, than the division of the resultant profit is a matter of dispute. This is the case in South Africa and it came as a singular answer to Smuts. In South Africa white labor is highly paid, can vote, and by a system of black helpers occupies an easy and powerful position. It can only retain this position by vigorously excluding blacks from certain occupations and by beating their wages down to the lowest point even when as helpers they are really doing the prohibited work. It is to the manifest interest of capitalists and investors to breach if not overthrow this caste wall and thus secure higher profits by cheaper and more pliable labor. Already South African courts are slowly moving toward mitigating the law of labor caste and in retaliation the white labor unions have joined Smuts' political enemies, the English-hating Boer party of independence, and have overthrown the great premier.

But how curious are these bedfellows—English capital and African black labor against Dutch home-rulers and the trades unions. The combinations are as illogical as they are thought-producing, for after all if South Africa is really bent on independence she must make economic and political peace with the blacks; and if she hates Negroes more than she hates low wages she must submit even more than now to English rule.

Now what is English rule over colored folk destined to be? Here comes the second puzzling result of the Smuts philosophy. I was in London on the night of the Guild Hall banquet when the Prime Minister spoke on "Empire Policy and World Peace" and gave a sort of summing up of the work of the Imperial Conference. It was significant that in the forefront of his words, cheek by jowl with Imperial "foreign policy," stood the "intensity of feeling in India on the question of the status of British Indians in the Empire." What indeed could be more fundamental than this in the building of world peace? Are the brown Indians to share equally in the ruling of the British Empire or are they an inferior race? And curiously enough, the battle on this point is impending not simply in the unchecked movement toward "swaraj" in India but in Africa—in the Union of South Africa and in Kenya.

In South Africa, despite all Imperial explanations and attempts to smooth things out, Smuts and the Boers have taken firm ground: Indians are to be classed with Negroes in their social and political exclusion. South Africa is to be ruled by its minority of whites. But if this is blunt and unswerving, how much more startling is Kenya. Kenya is the British East Africa of pre-war days and extends from the Indian Ocean to the Victoria Nyanza and from German East Africa to Ethiopia. It is that great roof of the African world where, beneath the silver heads of the Mountains of the Moon, came down in ancient days those waters and races which founded Egypt. The descend-

ant races still live there with fine physique and noble heads—the
Masai warriors whom Schweinfurth heralded, the Dinka, the Galla,
and Nile Negroes—the herdsmen and primitive artisans of the beautiful highlands. Here was a land largely untainted by the fevers of the
tropics and here England proposed to send her sick and impoverished
soldiers of the war. Following the lead of South Africa, she took over
five million acres of the best lands from the 3,000,000 natives, herded
them gradually toward the swamps and gave them, even there, no
sure title; then by taxation she forced sixty percent of the black adults
into working for the ten thousand white owners for the lowest wage.
Here was opportunity not simply for the great landholder and slave-
driver but also for the small trader, and twenty-four thousand Indians
came. These Indians claimed the rights of free subjects of the empire—a right to buy land, a right to exploit labor, a right to a voice in
the government now confined to the handful of whites.

Suddenly a great race conflict swept East Africa—orient and occi-
dent, white, brown and black, landlord, trader and landless serf. When
the Indians asked rights the whites replied that this would injure the
rights of the natives. Immediately the natives began to awake. Few
of them were educated but they began to form societies and formulate
grievances. A black political consciousness arose for the first time in
Kenya. Immediately the Indians made a bid for the support of this
new force and asked rights and privileges for all British subjects—
white, brown and black. As the Indian pressed his case, white South
Africa rose in alarm. If the Indian became a recognized man, landholder and voter in Kenya, what of Natal?

The British Government speculated and procrastinated and then
announced its decision: East Africa was primarily a "trusteeship" for
the Africans and not for the Indians. The Indians, then, must be
satisfied with limited industrial and political rights, while for the
black native—the white Englishman spoke! A conservative Indian
leader speaking in England after this decision said that if the Indian
problem in South Africa were allowed to fester much longer it would
pass beyond the bounds of domestic issue and would become a question of foreign policy upon which the unity of the Empire might
founder irretrievably. The Empire could never keep its colored races
within it by force, he said, but only by preserving and safeguarding
their sentiments.

Perhaps this shrewd Kenya decision was too shrewd. It preserved
white control of Kenya but it said in effect: "Africa for the Africans!"

What then about Uganda and the Sudan, where a black leadership exists under ancient forms; and above all, what about the educated black leadership in the West Indies and West Africa? Why should black West Africa with its industrial triumphs like Nigeria be content forever with a Crown Government, if Africa is for the Africans?

The result has been a yielding by England to the darker world— not a yielding of much, but yielding. India is to have a revision of the impossible "diarchy;" all West Africa is to have a small elective element in its governing councils; and even the far West Indies have been visited by a colonial undersecretary and parliamentary committee, the first of its kind in the long history of the islands. Their report is worth quoting in part: "Several reasons combine to make it likely that the common demand for a measure of representative government will in the long run prove irresistible. The wave of democratic sentiment has been powerfully stimulated by the war. Education is rapidly spreading and tending to produce a colored and black intelligentsia of which the members are quick to absorb elements of knowledge requisite for entry into learned professions and return from travel abroad with minds emancipated and enlarged, ready to devote time and energy to propaganda among their own people."

Egypt is Africa and the Bilad-es-Sudan, Land of the Blacks, has in its eastern reaches belonged to Egypt ever since Egypt belonged to the Sudan—ever since the Pharaohs bowed to the Lords of Meroe. Fifty times England has promised freedom and independence to Egypt and today she keeps her word by seizing the Sudan with a million square miles, six million black folk and twenty million dollars of annual revenue. But Egypt without the Sudan can never be free and independent and this England well knows, but she will hold the Sudan against Egypt as "trustee" for the blacks. That was a fateful step that the new Conservatives took after the Sirdar was murdered by hot revolutionists. Its echo will long haunt the world.

If now England is literally forced to yield some measure of self-government to her darker colonies; if France remains steadfast in the way in which her feet seem to be tending; if Asia arises from the dead and can no longer be rendered impotent by the opium of international finance, what will happen to imperialistic world industry as exemplified in the great expansion of the nineteenth and early twentieth centuries?

LABOR IN THE SHADOWS

This is the question that faces the new labor parties of the wurld—
the new political organizations which are determined to force a larger
measure of democracy in industry than now obtains. The trade union
labor movement dominant in Australia, South Africa and the United
States has been hitherto autocratic and at heart capitalistic, believing
in profit-making industry and wishing only to secure a larger share of
profits for particular guilds. But the larger labor movement following
the war envisages through democratic political action real democratic
power of the mass of workers in industry and commerce. Two questions here arise: Will the new labor parties welcome the darker race
to this industrial democracy? And, if they do, how will this affect industry?

The attitude of the white laborer toward colored folk is largely a
matter of long continued propaganda and gossip. The white laborers
can read and write, but beyond this their education and experience
are limited and they live in a world of color prejudice. The curious,
most childish propaganda dominates us, by which good, earnest, even
intelligent men have come by millions to believe almost religiously
that white folk are a peculiar and chosen people whose one great accomplishment is civilization and that civilization must be protected
from the rest of the world by cheating, stealing, lying, and murder.
The propaganda, the terrible, ceaseless propaganda that buttresses
this belief day by day—the propaganda of poet and novelist, the un-
canny welter of romance, the half knowledge of scientists, the pseudo-
science of statesmen—all these, united in the myth of mass inferiority
of most men, have built a wall which many centuries will not break
down. Born into such a spiritual world, the average white worker is
absolutely at the mercy of its beliefs and prejudices. Color hate easily
assumes the form of a religion and the laborer becomes the blind
executive of the decrees of the masters of the white world; he votes
armies and navies for "punitive" expeditions; he sends his sons as
soldiers and sailors; he composes the Negro-hating mob, demands
Japanese exclusion and lynches untried prisoners. What hope is there
that such a mass of dimly thinking and misled men will ever demand
universal democracy for all men?

The chief hope lies in the gradual but inevitable spread of the
knowledge that the denial of democracy in Asia and Africa hinders

its complete realization in Europe. It is this that makes the Color Problem and the Labor Problem to so great an extent two sides of the same human tangle. How far does white labor see this? Not far, as yet. Its attitude toward colored labor varies from the Russian extreme to the extreme in South Africa and Australia. Russia has been seeking a *rapprochement* with colored labor. She is making her peace with China and Japan. Her leaders have come in close touch with the leaders of India. Claude McKay, an American Negro poet traveling in Russia, declares: "Lenin himself grappled with the question of the American Negroes and spoke on the subject before the Second Congress of the Third International. He consulted with John Reed, the American journalist, and dwelt on the urgent necessity of propaganda and organization work among the Negroes of the South."

Between these extremes waver the white workers of the rest of the world. On the whole they still lean rather toward the attitude of South Africa than that of Russia. They exclude colored labor from empty Australia. They sit in armed truce against them in America where the Negroes are forcing their way into ranks of union labor by breaking strikes and underbidding them in wage.

It is precisely by these tactics, however, and by hindering the natural flow of labor toward the highest wage and the best conditions in the world that white labor is segregating colored labor in just those parts of the world where it can be most easily exploited by white capital and thus giving white capital the power to rule all labor, white and black, in the rest of the world. White labor is beginning dimly to see this. Colored labor knows it, and as colored labor becomes more organized and more intelligent it is going to spread this grievance through the white world.

THE SHADOW OF SHADOWS

How much intelligent organization is there for this purpose on the part of the colored world? So far there is very little. For while the colored people of today are common victims of white culture, there is a vast gulf between the red-black South and the yellow-brown East. In the East long since, centuries ago, there were mastered a technique and philosophy which still stand among the greatest the world has known; and the black and African South, beginning in the dim dawn of time when beginnings were everything, have evolved a physique and an art, a will to be and to enjoy, which the world has never done without and never can. But these cultures have little in common, either today or yesterday, and are being pounded together artificially and not attracting each other naturally. And yet quickened India, the South and West African Congresses, the Pan-African movement, the National Association for the Advancement of Colored People in America, together with rising China and risen Japan—all these at no distant day may come to common consciousness of aim and be able to give to the labor parties of the world a message that they will understand.

THE COLOR LINE

My ship seeks Africa. Ten days we crept across the Atlantic; five days we sailed to the Canaries. And then, turning, we sought the curve of that mighty and fateful shoulder of gigantic Africa. Slowly, slowly we creep down the coast in a little German cargo boat. Yonder behind the horizon is Cape Bojador, whence in 1441 came the brown Moors and black Moors who, through the slave trade, built America and modern commerce and let loose the furies on the world. Another day afar we glide past Dakar, city and center of French Senegal. Thereupon we fall down, down to the burning equator, past Guinea and Gambia, to where the Lion Mountain glares, toward the vast gulf whose sides are lined with silver and gold and ivory. And now we stand before Liberia—Liberia that is a little thing set upon a hill— thirty or forty thousand square miles and two million folk. But it represents to me the world. Here political power has tried to resist the concentration in the power of modern capital. It has not yet succeeded, but its partial failure is not because the republic is black but because the world has failed in this same battle; because the oligarchy that owns organized industry owns and rules England, France, Germany, America, and Heaven. And it fastens this ownership by the Color Line. Can Liberia escape the power that rules the world? I do not know. But I do know that unless the world escapes, world democracy as well as Liberia will die: and if Liberia lives it will be because the world is reborn as in that vision splendid that came in the higher dreams of the World War.

And thus again in 1925, as in 1899, I seem to see the problem of the Twentieth Century as the Problem of the Color Line.

Part II

The Differing Faces
of Colonialism

Note

BRITISH AND FRENCH COLONIAL TECHNIQUE IN WEST AFRICA

BY DERWENT WHITTLESEY

January 1937

The two most important colonial powers in Africa have been Britain and France. As Du Bois suggested in the previous article, the manner in which they governed their subject peoples could hardly have been more different. Both reflected their own national characteristics, their differing values and purposes. And increasingly what they have done or failed to do has affected all of Africa. The Portuguese believe that everything would be fine in their territories if it had not been for the madness and irresponsibility of the British in encouraging the hope of self-government and independence. And it was events across the Congo River in French Equatorial Africa that as much as anything persuaded the Belgians to abandon their long-range hopes for creating a rich and stable state in the heart of Africa.

The following article was written in an earlier era, however, when Britain and France too believed that they had almost unlimited time in Africa. The author, Derwent Whittlesey, who died in 1956, was a political geographer—indeed, one of the creators of that discipline in the United States. He had a particular interest in Africa, traveled there often and at the time of his death was planning the completion of a major work on Africa.

The special quality of his work can be attributed partly to his training as a historian before he was attracted to geography, first at the University of Chicago, and after 1928 at Harvard. For 12 years he was editor of the *Annals* of the Association of American Geographers, and was president of the Association in 1924. He was a fellow of the American Academy of Arts and Sciences, and consultant to innumerable Government departments and agencies. His most important work is generally considered to be "The Earth and the State," which was completed two years after this article was written.

Whittlesey's analysis will bear recall when readers turn to the last section of this volume, where the men who grew up under these contrasting colonial systems and who now head independent African states reflect in their purposes and attitudes some of the differences noted here.

British and French Colonial Technique in West Africa

British and French Colonial Technique in West Africa

by DERWENT WHITTLESEY

The annexation of Ethiopia has presented the Italian Government with a tremendous problem in colonial administration. No other area in Africa of equal size offers such variety of topography, climate, language, and religion. The task of ruling so conglomerate an empire will certainly not be easy. The British and the French have already acquired a fund of experience as a result of their administration of vast and populous domains; the Italians, if they are wise, will study carefully what these predecessors in colonial government can teach them.

In tropical Africa, it is true, European rule is a thing of scarcely more than a generation. Though various nations had gained toeholds on the coast during the four hundred years following the Portuguese explorations of the late fifteenth century, only by the middle of the nineteenth century was the continent effectively penetrated. The sketchy information brought back from the interior by explorers and traders was used by the colonizing powers as the basis for extravagant territorial claims. The Berlin Conference on the Congo in 1884–85 gave impetus to this scramble in which each nation sought to stake out for itself the largest possible holdings. By 1900 the political map of tropical Africa had by and large assumed its present appearance; the only important changes since then have been the ousting of Germany during the World War and the recent Italian conquest of Ethiopia.

Once in possession of these tracts of largely unexplored land, the colonial powers proceeded to create systems for administering them. The two nations which had acquired the largest prizes—Great Britain and France—embarked upon quite divergent programs. In fact, we might go so far as to say that at only one point do their policies agree: both recognize the fact that Europeans cannot make permanent homes in tropical lowland Africa but must regularly return to the middle latitudes for periods of recuperation. On every other fundamental issue of both theory and practice the British and the French colonial techniques differ widely.

One of the most significant differences concerns the degree to which the natives are permitted to govern themselves. In the admin-

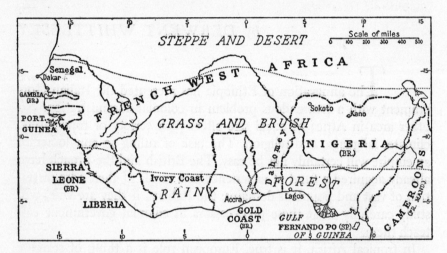

istration of the French colonies Frenchmen occupy all the important positions, though properly trained Africans are allowed to fill subordinate posts, and in special circumstances even to become French citizens. Great Britain, on the other hand, has generally adopted the plan of governing Africans whenever possible through their native rulers. This is accomplished by setting up a hierarchy of European officials alongside the native administration. The two methods have come to be known as "direct" and "indirect" rule. Direct rule is the current practice nearly everywhere throughout the world. Indirect rule is being attempted in only a few places. One of those few places is British West Africa—the composite designation for Nigeria, Gold Coast, Sierra Leone, the Gambia and the British mandated areas in Cameroons and Togoland.

Conditions are propitious in West Africa for a comparative study of direct and indirect rule. British and French colonies alternate with one another along the coast, yet the environment differs very little. As can be seen from the accompanying map, the political frontiers, which run north and south, cut at right angles, generally speaking, the lines separating the climatic belts. The student of colonial government thus finds in these colonies an excellent laboratory for observing and comparing the results of unlike systems of administration.

The first British experiment in indirect rule in West Africa took place in Northern Nigeria, and it came about not through any premeditated design but as the necessary result of circumstances. Geographically, Northern Nigeria belongs to the Sudan. For some centuries prior to European penetration it had been under the rule of a number of independent Arab emirs who had imposed their culture and their religion on the Negro aborigines.

During the years following the Berlin Conference the British and French governments sought to convert their grandiose territorial claims into valid title by effective occupation. In order to chastise some of the emirs who had repudiated certain trading concessions, the British in 1900 sent against them a small force under Colonel (now Lord) Lugard, who almost bloodlessly entered one walled capital after another. In thus forestalling French penetration from Dahomey, he unexpectedly found himself after a few months in control of nine million people and a quarter million square miles. Lacking the trained men necessary to govern this great area, Lugard was obliged to leave each emir in control on condition that he governed temperately. The only drastic changes insisted upon were the suppression of slave-raiding, the substitution of an equitable tax system for the arbitrary impositions commonly practised, and the abolition of cruel punishments. To insure that British requirements were fulfilled, a Resident was appointed to the court of each native ruler of the first rank. Thus, indirect rule was set up in Northern Nigeria as a means of "muddling through" a particular emergency.

The arrangement worked from the very beginning. A few emirs, unable or unwilling to relinquish practices disapproved by the Residents, have had to be deposed in favor of more adaptable rulers, but care is always taken to make the selection from the group of heirs eligible according to local usage. As a rule, the emir is amenable to the rebuke which he is sure to receive from the Resident if his administration becomes notoriously lax or venal. The first small group of Residents has expanded into a modest hierarchy of eleven provincial residencies divided into forty districts, each under a subordinate political officer. A district may range in area from 1,000 to 33,000 square miles and in population from 30,000 to 2,000,000. The officer and two or three assistants cover at recurrent intervals all the outlying territory within the district, spending two-thirds to three-fourths of their time in the bush. They hear complaints, sit in judgment on those appealed cases which can properly come before them, ferret out injustice, suggest improvements to be made by the local authorities, and generally maintain the standards of British colonial government. This haphazard device not only functions well, it operates at low cost— a fact very welcome to the Colonial Office in London, ever called upon to justify expenditure in the colonies.

As soon as the efficacy of indirect rule was proved in Northern Nigeria, steps were taken to extend it to Southern Nigeria, where the geographic and cultural pattern is quite different. Northern Nigeria has a long dry season. But here there is rainfall nearly the year round. Here, then, instead of grassy plains are dense forests, wide river deltas, and teeming vegetation. As an inevitable consequence of these conditions the natives were found segregated into numerous small tribes, each with its own language and gods, separated alike from each other and from the outside world. Along the coast, too, there were settlements of Europeans which tended to de-tribalize the natives without substituting any new bond of interest or loyalty. The introduction of sectarian missions only accentuated this disintegrating process, for the natives naturally sought to improve upon Christianity by inventing sects of their own, such as the Anglican polygamous church. There were a few large tribes which were well adapted to indirect rule. Other groups, though small in size and occupying only a few square miles of territory, were arbitrarily lumped into provinces staffed by British administrative offices. Though the conditions were not propitious, indirect rule proved flexible enough to function.

In time the scheme was adopted in other British West African colonies. In the Gold Coast, the Ashanti, a tribe on the northern margin of the dense forest, had (like some of those similarly placed in Nigeria) a powerful political organization prior to the coming of the British. A bitter contest (the Ashanti War of 1899–1900) led to the suppression of the native government and the exile of the ruler. Now, after the lapse of a generation, the son of the exiled chief occupies the "stool" of his father, and the native government, which appears to have been operating all the time *sub rosa*, has been drawn from hiding. Small tribes are being accorded similar rights, all the way from the Gambia to British Cameroons.

As has just been intimated, the imposition of indirect rule on pagan tribes often drives the real government under cover, leaving a usurper to represent his people before the British officer. The underground government sometimes goes undiscovered for years—generally until some administrator learns the local language and obtains the confidence of the real leaders of the tribe. He then usually finds that the aboriginal government has been functioning all along and that the usurper has no authority over the people beyond the backing he has been able to obtain from the British. The persistence of traditional tribal government, even when it is deprived of tax money and the sanction of the powerful European, raises a question as to the ultimate success of any sort of government imposed by whites. The Italians might do well to keep this doubt in mind as they proceed with the creation of their administrative system in Ethiopia.

The excuse for the imposition of British rule in West Africa is that Englishmen desired to increase their trade in goods while putting a stop to trade in human beings. The consequences of this double aspiration are the trading firm and the mission. Traders, missionaries, and administrators make up European society in British West Africa. Their total number is small: about 1,300 in Lagos (the metropolis of all British West Africa; a few score in each chief center of the interior; three or four individuals in the many small outlying stations. Until recently there were few women there except missionaries, and even now wives often stay in Africa for short terms only. Practically no children are brought out. Everybody lives in houses owned either by the government, the trading firm or the missionary society. The white man comes out for a definite tour of duty, usually eighteen months, at the end of which he "goes home" on long leave, generally eighteen weeks. When he comes back he is likely to find himself posted to a new station, and frequently he is shifted about during his tour. Nobody contemplates a time when it will be possible for Europeans to put down roots in British West Africa.

Government is administered to benefit British trade only to the extent that it does not prejudice native interests. Concessions to work mineral resources are thus favored, because the Africans have neither the capital nor the skill to initiate mining; but farmland cannot be alienated to Europeans, since agriculture is the basis of African existence. The only exception of importance is a group of plantations, started by Germans in Cameroons and inherited by Britain, which are still owned and operated by Europeans. This guarantee to the Africans of their farmland in perpetuity grows out of the recognition by the British that the West African environment forbids settlement by Europeans. It is the logical foundation for indirect rule. To the African tribe and individual it is more valuable than the form of government which happens to be imposed.

The French mode of administration is in theory the flat antithesis of the British. France is in Africa to make Frenchmen out of the Africans. To this end African life is given no official recognition. Administrative officers from France rule directly, native leaders being allowed to handle their own people only by sanction of custom, never of law. All land is French, except that which an individual African registers with the French authorities. This amounts to very little in total acreage, because the African tribes hold their land collectively and individual ownership is a novel idea. Large concessions to exploit forests and mines, as well as allotments for agricultural plantations, may be and are made to Europeans. Since no land is set aside for native reserves, the concessionaires in effect obtain the local labor with the land.

The Europeans in French Africa comprise the same three groups as in British colonies—administrators, traders, and missionaries—although the proportion of administrators is higher. They come for longer tours, generally two years (sometimes three the first time out), and they go home for shorter leaves, usually three months. As many as can arrange it bring their wives and children, and the larger capitals have quite the aspect of European provincial centers. Yet this semblance of European life on alien soil is only a semblance. "Home" is always France, even for the few planters who have taken up more or less permanent abode on the land. The number of Frenchmen living in the colonial centers is considerable: nearly 7,000 in Dakar, the capital, and about a thousand in each of four or five other towns, besides smaller numbers in lesser places.

All France's West African colonies combined—in local parlance known as "A.O.F." (Afrique Occidentale Française)—have an area three times that of Britain's West African possessions. Yet the population of A.O.F. is only five-eighths that of British West Africa. Nevertheless, to administer A.O.F. the French employ a larger personnel. The total white population of the British colonies is about 11,000, that of the French about 31,000. The proportion of traders is notably higher in the British territory because the British employ approximately twice as large a personnel to manage a store as do the French. The ratio of missionaries is probably about the same. The proportion of functionaries is therefore much higher in the French possessions. Obviously more political officers are needed for direct than for indirect government. Even though qualified Africans may fill lesser positions in the French colonies, they have not yet taken over so large a percentage of the offices as is the case in the Native Administrations of the British colonies.

The discrepancy in numbers between British and French administrators appears in the technical as well as in the political staffs. The engineering needed to bring Africa into the machine age had to be performed by trained men sent from Europe. Africans could neither build railroads nor drive their engines; they had no doctors who could vaccinate for smallpox, to say nothing of discovering the secrets of yellow fever. With time, many Africans have acquired the skill necessary to run a motor-car, a railroad locomotive, or a gasoline launch. Others have become licensed doctors. In British territory such men have been worked as fast as possible into the expanding technological services of the native administrations. In Gold Coast, for example, all trains are operated by Africans, except for the European inspectors who check up on the honesty of the ticket takers. Hospitals for natives in all the British colonies are manned largely by Africans, although the heads of both the medical and nursing staffs are still European. Road building is generally let out to African contractors whose work is not supervised beyond the final inspection prior to acceptance and payment, an inspection which every such contract job receives the world over. In some of the more advanced emirates of Northern Nigeria the administration of public works is in native hands, assisted by a few Europeans lent from the British service. In Kano the highly technical topographic office, although started by Europeans, is now entirely manned by Africans, who are continuing the detailed mapping of the emirate. Finally, all routine clerical work in store and office is performed by Africans. When the British undertook the administration of the interior at the beginning of the century, they tapped a small local reservoir of Africans who could read and write English, most of them trained in mission schools in Sierra Leone. The increased number of schools in all the colonies, especially in the coast towns, has more than kept pace with the demand for graduates, and nearly every colony is now turning out clerks faster than jobs open up for them.

In the French colonies there is no division between the European and native technical services. Africans who have adequate training may hold practically any post, although few of them do occupy positions of much responsibility. True, there was no group already trained in the French language and in French methods of business when France undertook serious administration of the country. Nevertheless, a full generation after the inauguration of French schools, jobs requiring only moderate technical proficiency are still performed by Europeans. White men staff many railroad trains, and white men and women sell stamps at the post office windows. Occasionally an African is found occupying a good position. For instance, one may run across a native as secretary of an important Chamber of Commerce or as a uniformed official in full charge of a principal custom house. But these exceptions only stress the gap between theory and practice. The French continue to draw upon Europeans for their technical and clerical staffs far more than do the British.

The educational system in the French colonies is extensive, unified, and admirably organized. The school is perhaps the most vital cog in France's colonial administration. Her control of West Africa is postulated on the conversion of the Africans into Frenchmen. The French colonial officials recognize that adults are fixed in their African mold, but they expect to model the plastic natures of the young. With this goal in view, the African children are taught French, which they learn easily, and they are steeped in French traditions. Although there is no compulsion to adopt Christianity, missions are everywhere, and an imposing church stands conspicuously in every town, even in Moslem areas. If built to serve solely the religious needs of the European population, smaller edifices would be quite adequate.

All this is markedly opposed to British procedure. Churches there are, but in the Moslem area no missionaries are allowed unless invited by the native ruler. In the pagan country, where proselyting is permitted, church buildings generally bear the cross of sectarianism; scarcely one of them is attractive in architecture or imposing in scale. British schools are likewise left mainly to chance, though a well-planned institution of higher education is sustained by the government of each larger colony. The emirates maintain intermediate schools, conducted in the language of the country, with whatever advice and coöperation they may seek from British authority. Except in the case of mission enterprises, all schools are staffed by Africans.

The contrast between British and French personnel is nowhere so striking as in the realm of law enforcement—the police and the army. Wherever native administrations in territory annexed by the British already had native police forces, they were retained and even increased. Elsewhere the police are officered by two or more European commissioners in each headquarters, but manned and sub-officered entirely by Africans. The small consolidated army of the four colonies —Nigeria, Gold Coast, Sierra Leone and Gambia—is similarly organized. European officers are seconded from their home regiments for not more than six years, and non-commissioned personnel is selected from the African troops. This is a volunteer force for duty in Africa only. Except for aiding in the occupation of the country at the outset, and helping conquer Germany's African colonies during the World War, its job has been mainly drilling.

The French colonial police may not be more numerous than the British, but a large army cantonment is a feature of every important town in A.O.F. To officer this army requires a commissioned staff of nearly 500, besides the non-commissioned personnel which is also European. Universal conscription is the law in the colonies, no less than in France itself. By no means every male African who reaches military age is ushered into the army; yet no traveller in French North Africa or Southern France can have escaped the frequent sight of Negro troops, sent north for two of their five years' service.

Since 1926 conscripts have been divided into two classes: the superior group is trained as troops, the rest are organized into labor units, serving in Africa in peacetime, but available, like the fighting forces, for service anywhere in case of need. Here we come upon the major objective of the French in developing these colonies. They represent an extension of France not merely economically, but in every phase of life, and most of all in providing for a larger army than can be recruited in the homeland. That is not to say, as has often been said, that France is training a Negro army primarily for use in Europe. Nevertheless, black troops have in the past seen active service on European fronts. The best of the conscripts are at present being regularly sent to France, supposedly to absorb civilization, and perhaps to become hardened to the rigors of the European climate. It must not be supposed that the natives strenuously object to military service. On the contrary, most of them love it. The African likes a uniform, and police and soldiers in both British and French colonies are proud of the hot and inappropriate clothing which their calling compels them to wear. A group of native police is said once to have become thoroughly disaffected because a humane officer ordered them to leave off their woolen wrap puttees.

The French colonials who show the most proficiency obtain preferment in government and business, all of which is conducted in French. In no aspect of administration is the contrast between British and French more interesting than in this matter of language. As a result of British ships having for several generations frequented the settlements of the West African coast, a debasement of English, salted with many Portuguese words, has become the local *lingua franca*. This jargon, like pidgin English on the coast of China, has penetrated inland wherever its knowledge will aid in getting a job as servant or in turning an honest penny in trade. But every British political officer is required to learn at least one of the African languages of the region where he works, and in this region he normally lives out his official life. Africans are not encouraged to learn English, and few officials of the native administrations can speak it. The French administrator, in contrast, need not learn an African language. Indeed, the prospects of his career discourage his doing so, because he is likely to be sent to quite different parts of West Africa for successive tours, and for some of his official life to other of the major French colonial regions—North Africa, Madagascar, Indo-China. Army officers even more than administrators expect to be shifted about the empire. Moreover, an effective fighting force should speak a single language.

It would be unfair to say that French interest in creating a native army is the sole reason why France practises direct administration. It is a method of political control which happens to fit the character and traditions of the French people. Their feeling for logical systems and order would not accept a scheme of government which varied from place to place in conformity with local usage. Furthermore, to govern Africa according to African models would seem to any Frenchman nonsensical, criminal almost, when Africans might be privileged to be governed as Frenchmen. In contrast, it suits the British taste to accept a problem and solve it on the spot with minimum reference to the problems of other places. Besides, the notion that British Africa is being governed for the Africans pleases that powerful liberal and non-conformist element of the British public which first became interested in Africa during the agitation for the abolition of the slave trade. If at the same time good money can be made by legitimate commerce, neither the humanitarians nor the traders are likely to object.

In some details the two opposed modes of administration are approaching each other. Theoretically at least, direct rule looks toward the extension of the franchise and the ultimate democratization of French Africa by incorporating it with France itself. Already several thousand Africans are French citizens, mainly those who live in Dakar and some of the other old French settlements. These men enjoy the right of electing a deputy to the Chamber in Paris. British rule, on the other hand, tends to perpetuate the form of government found among those groups already highly organized in 1900. The autocratic authority of the emirs has been modified only in so far as necessary to make it conform with British ideals of fair play and justice. The application of indirect rule to small forest tribes has often meant substituting autocracy for local self-government. Village government, instead of being autocratic, is generally in the hands of an oligarchy of the older men.

The British hierarchy appears to be developing into a bureaucracy, which is admittedly one of the chief evils of direct rule. Political officers are required to spend increasing amounts of their time on paper work, the curse of the bureaucratic system. And as the organization becomes set in its mold with the passage of years, elbowing for hierarchical preferment increases. Nevertheless, the British and French systems are still poles apart, and will remain so as long as England concentrates on trade with a minimum of interference in local government, while France organizes her colonies with at least half an eye to the protection of her Rhineland frontier.

Finally, in both the British and French colonies individual land tenure is beginning to supplant collective ownership. The French policy is to encourage individual ownership by emphasizing its legality. In general, the British make no effort to alter the local system of tribal land tenure, although in the coast towns private ownership has long since replaced communal holding. Furthermore, the law permits individuals to register specific parcels of land anywhere so long as the title is clear. Registration is becoming increasingly common, since individual tenure is best adapted for those who produce for the market. The salable crops—cotton, peanuts, and particularly tree products, such as cacao, coffee and oil palm—occupy the same land year after year, in sharp contrast to the aboriginal practice of shifting the farms to virgin soil every few seasons. Since local usage recognizes the planter as the owner of his crop, his long-term occupancy of specific plots tends to become identified with ownership of the land. In this way the concept of individual tenure is making headway.

That Italy will adopt indirect rule in Ethiopia is hardly to be anticipated. But the experiments in West Africa have not progressed to the stage where it can be asserted that direct rule is changing the African into a European, and there is a good deal of evidence that the aboriginal organization of life goes on beneath forms imposed by both British and French governments. The Italian acquisition of the penultimate slice of independent Africa by no means signalizes the European administrative conquest of that continent. The vitality of native African institutions has not yet been measured.

Note

BELGIAN "COLONIALISM"

BY PIERRE RYCKMANS

October 1955

Altogether different from the colonial administration of France and Britain was that of Belgium. More paternalistic and methodical, less conscious of the hot breath of nationalism breathing down their necks, the Belgians were building for a distant future. At the time this article was written in 1955 (and for some years thereafter) there was not a single Congolese with a university education outside the Church; but it was equally true that in no dependent territory of Africa was there a higher proportion of African children in primary school (save possibly Basutoland). Africans had no political representation whatever, but neither did the white settlers; the Congo was governed from Brussels by professional administrators in Leopoldville. With independence less than five years away, there were no identifiable nationalist leaders, no petitions in circulation, no demonstrations for freedom and independence. All these came later.

Belgian colonialism had no more effective or dedicated a spokesman than Pierre Ryckmans, Governor-General of the Congo from 1934 until 1947 and thereafter, until his death in 1959, Belgian representative on the U.N. Trusteeship Council. Except for a few years in mid-career, when he practiced law in Brussels and was professor of Colonial Law at the Universities of Antwerp and Louvain, he devoted his life to the colonial service of his country. The fruit of his experience and his philosophy of governing subject peoples were brought together in two major works: "Dominer Pour Servir" and "La Politique Coloniale."

No one who reads the following article can doubt the sincerity of Ryckmans' sense of mission, or that he truly believed his cause was to liberate and not to oppress or retard. That he and his countrymen whose thinking he helped to shape were hopelessly and disastrously

Belgian "Colonialism"

wrong, the whole world now knows, but their error was not so much in their objectives as in their misreading of the times. If Belgium had had the 30 additional years that Ryckmans asks for here, the Congo might well have lived up to his high expectations. As it was, Ryckmans died a year before the roof fell in on his life's work.

Belgian "Colonialism"

by PIERRE RYCKMANS

It has often been said that Belgium has no official colonial doctrine, and that is true enough in the sense that there is none which is complete and systematic. Leopold II had no firm plans when he founded the *Association Internationale Africaine* in 1876, nor yet in 1879 when he secured Stanley's services. Neither he nor anyone else could have foreseen then that in 1885 he would be recognized by all the Powers as "Sovereign of the Congo Free State." One thing is certain, namely that Leopold II, acting alone and without the military and financial support of a government behind him, could never have hoped to *conquer* the Congo by force of arms, to impose himself there against the will of the inhabitants. Therefore no attempt at conquest was made. That was a fortunate beginning.

When Leopold II's political and national ambitions became more specific, he based his right on *occupation*, not conquest; on peaceful coexistence with the natives who occupied a very small part of the African Equatorial belt. It is true that in the 1890's Central Africa was not uninhabited; but neither was it fully occupied. The King, and later Belgium, never questioned the prior rights of the natives as first occupants. There was plenty of room for everybody—wide empty spaces where one could take up land without interfering with anyone else, without disturbing the natives in their peaceful possession of widely scattered patches of land, without infringing any existing rights.

In the vast area of the Congo basin there lived a few million natives, lost in the jungle and the bush, tolerated at best by their physical environment, leading a precarious life on what one might call the fringe of nature. Surface and underground wealth were unknown and unexploited. Belgian colonization aimed at tapping these unexploited resources, at occupying unused land, at filling voids.

The concern for native rights can be traced through Congo legislation from the very beginning. Thus an Order by the Administrator General dated July 1, 1885—the very day the Congo Free State was proclaimed—specifies that "no one may dispossess natives of the land they occupy" and that "vacant land should be considered as belonging to the State." The Civil Code, Book 2, Section 12, is more general as well as more explicit: "All ownerless property belongs to the State, subject to customary rights of natives being reserved." According to a Decree of September 14, 1886, "Territory occupied by natives under the authority of their chiefs continues to be governed by local customs and practices." The Decree of May 21, 1935, states that no land may be granted to non-natives except after an investigation aimed at "establishing vacancy and assessing any rights which natives may claim regarding the land concerned"—such as hunting rights and rights of way. According to the Mining Law, natives may continue exploiting their mines under the conditions prevailing at the time the law came into force. The same applies to gathering of produce or such undertakings as salt works. For instance, where natives used to cut palm nuts in a wild grove for their domestic needs, or where by their primitive methods they gained, say, a ton of salt a year from some salt springs, the state could grant a concession for exploitation of the palm grove or the salt springs only subject to reserving the customary rights of the natives. In such cases they were supplied free of charge with all the palm oil they needed or were given their ton of salt ready packaged.

This was the rule which prevailed throughout the turbulent history of the Congo Free State. All the extensive concessions of land granted by the state to private corporations—concessions which became the subject of severe criticism—referred exclusively to vacant land, and were made subject to the reserved rights of natives.

In fact, though, criticism was amply deserved. It would be useless to deny that under the Free State natives suffered grievous wrongs; but they were abuses of existing laws. A rubber concessionnaire, for instance, was entitled to employ only gatherers who agreed to work for freely negotiated wages; in practice, however, natives only too often were put to forced labor. Again, the head tax owed to the state was (in the absence of currency) figured in working days, and working days were translated into weights of dry rubber; but in practice calculations were often forgotten and rubber deliveries became an arbitrary and exorbitant tribute exacted from the people. Endless discussion followed between philanthropists who denounced abusive prac-

tices and jurists who upheld the written law. The state was no doubt
to blame for failing to exercise proper supervision. It is a question,
however, whether the same abuses could not have been committed as
well under a free-enterprise system.

Similar principles prevailed in the political field. The existing native
political structure was allowed to stand. No native chief was deprived
of his authority. It is stated in the preamble of the Decree on Native
Areas that the Decree "does not intervene in the internal life of native
communities, where tribal custom remains sovereign." Native custom
recognized no authority higher than the tribal level. In the years between 1880 and 1885, before the Congo Free State was founded,
some thought was given by King Leopold to establishing a "Confederation of Free Natives"—that is, a Federal Authority above the tribal
chiefs. When the state came into existence, it did not supersede any
existing authority; it simply filled a political void.

This is a long way from the concepts which prevailed at the time
the New World was conquered. Then conquered territories were considered as chattels of the mother country to be exploited by it for its
own profit. The supremacy of European over native interest was never
questioned. If the aborigines resisted, war resulted; and in more than
one case the natives were wiped out. A new European society was
born upon the ruins of Indian societies. And when the American
colonies rose in rebellion against the European mother countries, it
was not the conquered Indians but the conquering whites who gained
their freedom. The exception was in Haiti, where by an ironic reversal
of things the white colonizers who had exterminated the Indians were
in turn exterminated by the slaves they had imported from Africa.

So far as American natives were concerned, the revolution staged
by the colonials against the motherland did not put an end to the
"colonial régime;" the natives simply changed masters. The process of
gradual conquest of Indian lands continued, and in the jungles of the
Upper Amazon and Upper Orinoco it has not yet been completed
even today. In the United States, the colonial problem was settled in
two successive stages. The first ended—for the colonists—with their
victory over the motherland in the American Revolution. The second
ended a century later—for the Indians—with the capture of Sitting
Bull, which put a close to the Indian Wars and marked the final tri-
umph of the immigrants over the original population.

For a citizen of a European colonial nation it is rather irritating to
find how much ignorance of fact and confusion of ideas are displayed

about the so-called "colonial system." Among those who condemn it
a priori are some who were, and still are, the main beneficiaries of
colonial rule. Thus we find that Latin America is "against" Belgian
rule in the Congo because the Spaniards of America, the very heirs of
the conquistadores, rose against Spain. Guatemala and Ecuador vote
"against" the colonial Powers in the General Assembly of the United
Nations because they believe that by casting a "pro-colonial" vote they
would be false to their own history.

Of course, the fact that the original inhabitants of America were
subject to abuses by the white man in the past would not justify the
Belgians if they inflicted similar abuses on the people of the Congo
today. But then we do not look for excuses. Americans today are the
first to condemn the wrongs inflicted by their ancestors and make
every effort to repair them in so far as it is still possible. Times have
changed since the days of slavery and the Indian Wars. But do
Americans really believe that in Europe times have not changed as
well? Do they think that we still hold to doctrines and practices of
two centuries ago? An Australian representative in the United Nations once very pointedly remarked that at the time abuses were
prevalent in the colonies, the people at home were treated hardly any
better by the governing classes. Today the people make the laws.
The people of Asia and America do not have a monopoly of human
feelings. Parliaments and public opinion in London, Paris or Brussels
are not less concerned about native rights than parliaments and public
opinion in Washington or New Delhi or in Monrovia or Addis Ababa.

The attitude of most members of the United Nations toward the
colonial problem could hardly be summed up better than in a phrase
used by Secretary of State John Foster Dulles in addressing the General Assembly: "The colonial system is obsolete and should be done
away with as soon as possible." This saying was warmly applauded and
is often quoted. Applied to my country, it might be translated: "Belgium's authority over the Congo is outdated and should be put an end
to as soon as possible."

I like to believe that this is not what Secretary Dulles intended, and
indeed his statement is open to a less injurious interpretation since
it holds at least two ambiguities. If by "the colonial system" he means
"exploitation of the colony for the profit of the mother country,"
everybody agrees that this is definitely to be condemned. But since
that sort of régime is ended, it no longer needs to be put an end to.
Present colonial systems have nothing in common with those of the

eighteenth or even the nineteenth century. I use the plural, for there are nearly as many colonial systems as there are colonies. The colonial system of Papua applied to Malta would certainly be outdated, just as the colonial system of Malta applied to Papua would certainly be premature and would carry that colony back very rapidly into total barbarism.

In the same way the colonial Powers could subscribe to the Dulles formula if "as soon as possible" means "as soon as the colonial peoples are able to govern themselves along the lines of civilized democracy." But that is not the way the phrase is understood by a large number of U.N. members, mainly Asian nations who themselves have become independent only recently. They take the words "as soon as possible" as meaning "the soonest moment will be the best." Perhaps in their ignorance about the specific conditions in each colony, and with their tendency to identify those conditions with the conditions in their own country, they believe that all colonies have the ability to provide themselves with excellent governments. Alternatively, they may consider independence so much the highest achievement that any national government, however bad, is preferable to any foreign government however good it may be. Mr. Krishna Menon, for one, seems to hold the opinion that the special virtue which resides in independence can of itself make everything right. He said recently that if natives who are still in a primitive state reject necessary measures, it is because these measures are enacted by a foreign authority. "People," he said, "are such that they do not appreciate good things when they are imposed upon them; but they will adopt them spontaneously if left free to choose."

However that may be, it is the fact of colonialism *as such* which the majority of the General Assembly condemns: the mere fact of control by a foreign authority. Or should the word "foreign" perhaps be replaced by "European?" For if the foreign authority happens to be a colored people, nobody dreams of condemning this form of colonialism. The domination of the Javanese over the Dayaks of Borneo, or of the Burmans over the Karens and the Shans, or of the Ethiopians over Bantu tribes, or of the American Negroes over the autochthonous tribes of Liberia, does not seem to find disfavor in the eyes of many anti-colonialists.

The anti-colonialism of the Asians, of the Moslem Powers and of the Soviet bloc we find understandable enough. Less explicable, however, is the anti-colonialism of Anglo-Saxon Americans and of Latin Americans.

We believe in the civilizing mission of the West. We think our Western Christian culture is superior to the native culture of Africa and that to have planted it there was good in itself and for it to disappear would be bad in itself. We believe that, if emancipation jeopardized the existence of Western civilization in Africa, that would not represent progress but the reverse. If we were not so convinced we should have no justification for being in Africa.

But an Indian does not believe in the superiority of Western civilization. On the contrary, he is convinced of the superiority of his own civilization. He feels, moreover, that Western influence in his country has been an evil in itself, and from his point of view he may be right. He therefore doubts the superiority of Western culture over Bantu culture. He does not believe that the West has a civilizing mission. He understandably rejects for Africa the civilization which he also rejects for himself. If therefore emancipation would bring the natives back to the culture of their ancestors that does not strike him as something terrible; quite the opposite. The misunderstanding between him and us is irreconcilable.

The American anti-colonial attitude, on the other hand, would seem to be justified only if the flowering of European culture in Africa were not going to wither away as a result of our departure. Everyone who knows the Congo—all the Congo, not just the large towns—is convinced that Belgian rule there is indispensable, and that the end of it would be the end of all that we have built up during three-quarters of a century.

These explanations are necessary for an understanding of the Belgian attitude toward political progress. We do not believe that the extension of the right to vote is an end in itself; we consider political progress to be a means to an end, the end being social, cultural and economic progress. If it is correct to say, "Good government is no substitute for self-government," it is equally correct to say, "Self-government is no substitute for good government."

If we were to grant political rights in the Congo today, we would have the choice between a competent but restricted electorate and a general but incompetent electorate. Restricting the suffrage to the enlightened would mean handing over power to the European minority, with the risk that it might be used against the interests of the native masses. On the other hand, primitive tribesmen are obviously incapable of recognizing the common good. Extending the suffrage to them could only mean establishing a caricature of democracy and might endanger the future of civilization in Africa.

Such being the situation, nobody in the Congo has been given the right to vote, neither white nor black. Councils are advisory and their members are appointed. The metropolitan authority holds the balance between the divergent interests of the Europeans, the "evolved" natives and the tribal masses. This solution avoids political friction. The natives prefer it to the domination of the local European minority, because it grants no privilege to the white minority, implies no discrimination and does not set a precedent for the future. The Europeans submit to it, though with more and more reluctance; many of them have settled in the country for good and demand that they be allowed to have a part in governing it. They nevertheless realize the threat which they would face if the right to vote were extended to more and more strata of natives. The system is far from ideal, but it works. In order to make it acceptable, the Administration strives to make the Councils steadily more representative. And since the Councils are merely advisory, they for their part tend to be moderate, knowing that proposals of an extreme nature would inevitably be rejected; and in practice the Administration almost always does follow their advice.

The French and British systems are different. The French have tried to find a solution by establishing dual electoral colleges, one French, the other native; the English, by multi-racial councils in which each race is represented by a given number of members or by qualified suffrage. Both systems are unsatisfactory in that they emphasize the inequality of status and create racial rivalries.

It is noteworthy that native representatives in Congo councils have insisted on continuing government officials in ex officio capacities. It seems to prove their confidence that the Administration acts as a fair arbiter. Indeed, it may well be that equality in the lack of political privileges has been a contributing factor to the Congo's peaceful development.

We are convinced, besides, that political advancement will best be promoted by working for economic and social progress, without which political rights would remain a delusion. By promoting such progress we are forging the weapons with which the natives will conquer their political freedom, if we do not have the wisdom to grant it gracefully when the time is ripe.

The absence of a color bar works powerfully in favor of economic progress for the natives. They are not excluded from any profession. On the other hand, we are being taken to task for inequality of wages, for violating the principle of "same work, same pay" which we allegedly qualify by adding "taking into account the different standards of living of Negroes and whites." It is true that on the whole native wages are too low. It is also true that for nearly the same work the natives receive wages far below the wages of the whites. In order to discuss this problem dispassionately and without bias some historical facts must be borne in mind.

First of all, it has to be remembered that we literally started from scratch in the Congo. Economic equipment was nonexistent; previous generations had left no capital; current resources were nil; technique was totally absent. In all the vast country there was not one mile of road, not a single wheel, not one stone building, not one literate native. There were neither draft nor pack animals. The only known means of transportation were the dugout canoe on the rivers, and everywhere else the human beast of burden. The country simply could not afford to pay for building roads, harbors and a minimum of basic equipment at wage rates even remotely comparable to those of civilized countries. There was not, as in the early days of the Soviet Union, a choice between consumer goods and industrial equipment; the choice was between rudimentary industrial equipment at low wages or no industrial equipment and no wages at all.

The first workers who went into the service of the whites had an extremely low standard of living. Moreover, the European peace had relieved them from their most absorbing traditional occupation: armed protection of their working women. They had time on their hands. A job which secured them their daily meat, white protection for themselves and their families, and better lodgings than their huts seemed an acceptable exchange for some of their leisure. If, in addition, they were offered textiles and glassware, which they valued highly and were unable to produce themselves, their very modest wages became an appreciable net gain to them. Recruits by the chiefs for military service were slaves who thus escaped from bondage. Similarly, the majority of those who volunteered for labor did not take jobs so much to earn money as to free themselves from the heavier forced labor which was demanded of them in the village, to escape from the persecution of the tribal chief, from the accusations of the magician, from the menace of powerful enemies. A little work was not too high a price to pay for security—even had no salary been attached. Thus labor's demands were cheap.

On the other hand, employers could hardly afford to offer generous wages. All enterprises were "marginal," and one had better admit that many of them still are today. On account of the light traffic, railway rates would be considered prohibitive in an industrialized country; and distances from world markets are long. Katanga copper is carried 1,200 miles to the nearest port, and copper has no local market. Transport rates thus increase considerably the cost of imports and reduce the worth of exports. Dams for hydroelectric plants are built with concrete which sells at a higher price than flour. Skilled European labor costs at least three times as much as it does in Europe and the output of semi-skilled native labor is very low.

These circumstances explain, even though they do not entirely justify, the low native wages. Even today employers tend to link any increase in wages to an increase in output. This would be justified if the initial wage had been freely and normally negotiated, but such was not the case. The initial wage guaranteed the worker a higher standard of living than he had known in his native village; but it would not have allowed him to live and raise a family according to the standards of a civilized society. It is therefore imperative that wages rise faster than the output of labor, and that is what is happening today. Many employers no doubt could raise wages still further without risking bankruptcy, but many businesses were built (doubtless unwisely) on the level of wages in force at the time they started and would collapse if they suddenly had to face substantial wage increases. In the interest of the workers themselves it therefore is necessary to envisage a period of gradual adjustment.

As to the equalization of black and white wages in accordance with the principle of "same work, same pay," that presents one of the most difficult problems facing Africa. Careful study shows that there is no perfect solution. Wages can be levelled up or they can be levelled down: those of the Negroes can be raised or those of the whites can be reduced. Levelling down by reducing the wages of the whites would have just one effect: whites would no longer come to Africa. They are urgently needed and the conditions of life there are such that they can be attracted only by the offer of a higher standard of living or higher pay than they would enjoy in their own country. Africa cannot offer them all the facilities that life offers in Europe; one must make up for what is lacking with higher pay and the possibility of saving for an easier future. On the other hand, raising the average wages of the Negroes to the level of European wages would be charging a country with an average income of $50 with the same burdens carried by a country with an average income of $500—quite obviously an impossibility.

The only justification for the higher wages paid to white people lies in the fact that they are indispensable specialists. One could preserve this qualification for them artificially by establishing a color bar, that is, by excluding the natives from qualified jobs. The Belgian Government has always refused to do this. All professions are open to the natives. A number of jobs which were formerly filled by whites—though without being reserved for them—are filled by natives today. They do not receive the wages which were enjoyed by the whites, and that is normal. Progressive Africanization is the only solution. By reducing the ratio of high-wage whites to low-wage natives, savings on the white payroll may be applied to raising the average native pay without increasing the total payroll to an uneconomic level.

This explains the Belgian attitude toward European immigration into the Congo. We aim at attracting only selected immigrants who can fulfill functions which the natives still cannot. Immigrants who would not be able to resist native competition are discouraged from coming. But under these conditions, functions which the natives can perform just as well as the whites ought no longer to enjoy preferential treatment.

What is to become of the whites ousted in this process? In general, they will be entrusted with higher functions. A skilled worker, for instance, will be promoted to foreman or instructor. If he is unfit for promotion, he will go on drawing his current wage, but there will be no further recruiting of labor from Europe for any jobs for which there are African candidates. This is not a wholly satisfactory solution since it perpetuates inequality. However, the situation is eased somewhat by the fact that even today most Europeans do not settle for good in Africa and that immigration remains controlled. If Africanization were carried through in one big operation, in large sections, all the whites in such and such a category being simultaneously replaced by Negroes, the inequality in pay would be less noticeable, for Negroes and whites would not be performing the same work at the same time. But that is not how things work. It is a gradual shift, and Negroes and whites find themselves working at the same time on the same jobs.

How is one to make the first black doctor agree to receive a lower salary than that which his European colleague gets in a neighboring hospital, when both have the same qualifications? And yet it is precisely because the country is too poor to be able to afford white doctors in large quantities that it is necessary to supply it with a native medical corps. Adoption of the solution which seems fair and right, the invariable application of the "same work, same pay" principle, would lead Africa into a dead-end road. The formula of "expatriation pay" for white immigrants has been tried. It is easier to apply in a country under a native government, like the Gold Coast, where officials are not suspected of delaying the process of Africanization, than in a colony where the administration may be suspected of holding on to useless whites out of a sense of racial solidarity. The French have gone very far—probably too far—with full assimilation of local and French officials. This makes it impossible to increase the staff to desirable levels without imposing a load which with its present poverty Africa is unable to carry. It is only by increasing national income that the difference between white and black wages can gradually be reduced. The immigrants will be less exacting once colonial life has fewer hazards and inconveniences than it has today; and the increase in average income will be accompanied automatically by an improvement in average wages.

But then, one may ask, why does not the Administration set out resolutely on the road to Africanization by preparing a selected native "élite" to undertake public duties? Why has it not sent natives to the universities of Europe long ago? Is it because it deliberately wishes to keep the natives in subordinate positions that it excludes them from higher education? Unfortunately, statements by certain Europeans from time to time tend to confirm this interpretation. They want their cook to make a good soup and not to write letters. They praise the Administration for its "policy" of limiting its efforts to primary instruction and to teaching handicrafts.

That is *not* in fact the policy of the Administration. It aims at endowing the country with a complete educational system, in all grades, as perfect as the limited resources available will permit. Opinions as to how this can best be done differ. Some believe that the best approach will be to divide all available resources among all the branches of education—primary, middle and advanced. Others believe that it would be better to begin at the bottom and to start by organizing as broad a system of primary education as possible. The choice was before us, but it was impossible for us to do everything at once. In order for a few to be given a university training they had to be sent to Europe at a very young age indeed. It is difficult to foresee if a child of seven will be able to go successfully through a complete cycle of training up to the point of obtaining a university degree. If the chosen child does not succeed, all the money the colony has spent for his education will be lost and what is to become of the unsuccessful? If he succeeds, is there any assurance that he will let his compatriots benefit from the knowledge he has received? And will he not have lost all contact with native society after having spent 10 or 15 years in Europe? Will he not have been made into a black-skinned European, as much a stranger in Africa as the white man himself?

But that is not all: How many children must be deprived of the primary education which they might be given in order to achieve the hazardous result described? This is the issue. Sending one single child to Europe for a full training means having a thousand fewer children in primary schools in the Congo. During an interim period we can supply the colony with all the university élite which it needs—an élite selected at the end and not at the beginning of studies, whose education has not cost the colony anything and who can be sent back home if they prove unsatisfactory. But the mother country cannot make up for the primary training taken away from a thousand native children. We have preferred to give primary training to the mass of children right on the spot; to organize secondary education later, as soon as available resources allow; and to give the natives at home, in the Congo, the university to which they are entitled as soon as sufficient recruitment for it can be guaranteed.

The value of this program is open to discussion, but it has to be admitted, I think, that it is at least a defensible one, that it is not inspired by selfish motives. The Belgian Congo and Ruanda-Urundi together have almost the same population as French West Africa. French West Africa has a thousand children and young people studying in France, while we have just a handful studying in Belgium. Very likely French West Africa spends as much for public education as we do. But we have ten times more children than they have in primary schools, where they learn reading, hygiene and some notions of less primitive agriculture. I sincerely believe that in 30 years' time we shall have in the Congo at least as many university graduates, at least as many high school graduates, and infinitely fewer illiterates than do our French neighbors in West Africa, even though the first university in the Congo opened its doors only last year.

Will 30 years of peaceful progress be given to us?

France and the Netherlands are blamed for not having prepared the élites of Indo-China and Indonesia for independence in good time. The chaos in which these countries are struggling today is charged to former colonialism. The French and the Dutch reply that they are not responsible for the Japanese invasion and that if at the end of the war they were not allowed to reëstablish their authority and finish the job they had undertaken, the Allies were partly responsible. We, in the Congo, cannot afford any mistakes. We know that we cannot maintain our position there by sheer force of arms. This demands that we establish in the Congo "government *for* the people" until the time is ripe for "government *by* the people." We must deserve the consent of the governed. Failing that, the association between Belgium and the Congo sooner or later will be broken.

But Africa is a ferment. The Gold Coast has an African Prime Minister; Nigeria is on the eve of self-government. Shocking violence troubles Kenya. The United Nations countenances all forms of nationalism, whether premature or not. Will not these various outside influences upset the Congo? There is danger of it, no doubt. We are no longer quite free to set the pace of progress according to reason only. Yet I am full of hope. When a visitor asked some Congo chiefs if they did not fear an extension of the Mau Mau movement, they replied, "No, because the reasons for Mau Mau do not exist here." Congolese who have travelled elsewhere in Africa find that, all in all, life at home is best.

Note

PORTUGAL IN AFRICA
BY JAMES DUFFY

April 1961

A generation ago, it was not unusual to see Portugal cited as the most admirable of the colonial powers (see page 33). One factor alone was responsible for this: the apparent absence of racial feeling. The Portuguese appeared to accept Africans as their equals, frequently intermarried with them and gave them equality of status if they were able to attain an education and were willing to adopt Western ways.

Today the reality of even this much is under serious question, and Portugal is almost universally condemned for her policies and practices in Africa. An ugly, running war in Angola poisons relations between black and white men throughout the continent and burdens the West with a serious liability in the Cold War; its impact may be measured by the fact that 300,000 Angolan refugees have fled to the Congo, where their presence complicates the already staggering problems of that country. While Portugal resists every effort to pry her out of Africa, the Western world—and the Africans of Angola and Mozambique—pay a fearful price for her intransigence.

What follows, however, is no wholesale condemnation of Portugal, but an effort to provide a balanced appraisal, including an account of Portugal's professed objectives and measures to speed the development of her "overseas provinces." Though giving Portugal every benefit of the doubt for sincerity and determination, the account makes clear—even before active revolution had broken out in Angola—that its effort is at best too little and too late.

Since this article was written the situation has further deteriorated from the Portuguese point of view. The war continues, the Angolan nationalists are more united, and they are better trained and armed. The war has spread to Portuguese Guinea and a new Mozambique nationalist organization can be expected to start trouble at any time. The 32 independent states of Africa are united in their determination

84

to rid the continent of colonialism, and by a combination of pressure in the United Nations and direct action in Africa, they are destined to make the Portuguese presence in Africa increasingly costly, difficult and dangerous. And for the United States, which is allied with Portugal in NATO but condemns her conduct in Africa, the situation represents one of those dilemmas in which—by standing in the middle—we get gouged by both horns.

Informed and objective students of Portuguese Africa are a rare breed, of which James Duffy, Professor at Brandeis University, is one. He is the author of "Shipwreck and Empire," "Portuguese Africa" and "Portugal in Africa." He has also done a study for the Carnegie Endowment for International Peace on "Portugal's African Territories" and is editor (with Robert Manners) of "Africa Speaks."

Portugal in Africa

by JAMES DUFFY

Today small Portugal is still mistress of three African territories which are the oldest European colonies (or, as the Portuguese insist, "overseas provinces") in the world, and with a little luck she may soon regain an earlier distinction of being the only colonial power in Africa. In the course of her long history in Africa, Portugal has survived at one time or another every manner of crisis, and from Prime Minister Oliveira Salazar ("This is the mission of our life") down to chiefs of post in the remote Angolan bush, the Portuguese seem serenely confident that they will once more ride out the storm.

The stakes are high. No other European nation has been so long accustomed to possessing an African empire, and for the majority of the Portuguese people the thought that their small country owns African territories equivalent in size to the area of Western Europe has always been reassuring. Nor is the attraction only sentimental. In recent years the two largest of the colonies, Angola and Mozambique, have come to occupy an important position in the nation's total economy. The Portuguese colonies are not as materially prosperous as some neighboring areas, particularly the Congo, the Rhodesias and South Africa, but they are not as naturally poor as many of the new independent states. Angola and Mozambique are paying their own way, in spite of the reluctance of Portuguese capital to invest in Africa and the relative lack of investment capital from abroad. A large part of Portuguese exports, notably wine and cotton goods, is destined for Africa, and increasing percentages of Portuguese African products—coffee, tea, sisal, copra, diamonds—go into the world market. The economic picture is not entirely favorable, but it has never been better, and without the African provinces continental Portugal's economy would suffer seriously.

But, as the Portuguese themselves acknowledge, the problems which must be solved have never been greater and the room for manoeuvre has never been less. The relative tranquility of Angola, Mozambique and Portuguese Guinea is not necessarily an accurate indication of political reality. But it is certain that outside the colonies, Portuguese African opposition groups, particularly those in Leopoldville and Conakry, grow daily in size and influence. Elsewhere in the continent African national sentiment is united against the continuing presence of Portugal in Africa. Abroad, Asian and Communist nations, with the support of anti-colonial groups elsewhere, have taken up the attack against alleged Portuguese repressions, and each United Nations session rings with denunciations of Portuguese policy. This concerted opposition lost Portugal a seat on the Security Council last December. There is a question how much longer Portugal may count on even qualified support by Britain and the United States. Finally, in Portugal itself, where there are unrest and dissent and the Salazar era may be coming to an end, the turn of political events could have unpredictable repercussions in Africa. To devise an African policy which can meet even several of these challenges will test the capacities of any Portuguese Government.

The first, and easiest, task which the Salazar Government has recently undertaken has been to strengthen Portugal's sense of solidarity with the African territories. Not since the 1930s, when the régime in a moment of imperialist zeal concocted the concept of the Third Empire and created an overseas mystique which is still the basis for its African policy, has the Government labored so conscientiously to develop and sell the spirit of Lusitanian identity at home and overseas. The purposes of the program are three: to assure popular support for the Government's position in Africa; to distract attention from unrest at home; to convince the growing number of Portuguese citizens in Africa that the mother country has not forgotten them and stands ready to meet the emerging crisis.

Twice before, in the years following the Conference of Berlin in 1885 and again in the 1930s, Portuguese governments were successful in creating and exploiting a consciousness of Africa in order to solidify the Portuguese position in Angola and Mozambique. The technique is by now a familiar one. Speeches, colonial congresses, exhibits and postage stamps keep Africa constantly in the public eye. High officials make publicized visits to the territories. Journalists, teachers and students are sent on government-sponsored tours of Guinea, Angola and Mozambique, and groups of old colonists are brought back from Africa to visit—and be seen—in Portugal. A steady diet of colonial news is fed the controlled press and radio. Street rallies are organized to demonstrate popular support for Portuguese colonial solidarity.

In 1960 the campaign reached an extended climax in the cere-monies attending the five-hundredth anniversary of the death of Prince Henry the Navigator, the man most responsible for Portugal's overseas expansion. In Portugal and Brazil, in Africa and the remain-ing fragments of the vast sixteenth-century empire, the particularly Portuguese contribution of Prince Henry was extolled in thousands of speeches and articles. The words had a certain sameness, for one of the calculated purposes of the celebrations was to abstract from Henry's life and works the traditional ideals of Portugal's overseas conduct: Christianity, racial tolerance and human idealism. Dr. Pedro Theotónio Pereira, Minister of the Presidency (Dr. Salazar's administrative assistant), spoke at the formal opening of the com-memorative sessions in these familiar phrases: "We live in an age of renascence which links us with the past and which we will try to project into the future. . . . Our national values are more vigorous and rejuvenated than ever. The unity and solidarity which hold to-gether the pieces of Portuguese territory have never been stronger, and the sentiment of all the peoples has never been more unani-mous."

To give greater substance to the claim that the Portuguese world shares a unique cultural tradition, the Salazar Government has begun to talk of a Lusitanian community made up of continental and over-seas Portugal and Brazil. Although a treaty of friendship and consulta-tion has been signed by the two nations, the new Brazilian Govern-ment of President Janio Quadros may not be altogether sympathetic to Portugal's aspirations. Certainly, the *Santa Maria* affair has demon-strated that Quadros will not dance to Salazar's tune. However this may be, it is apparent that for the Portuguese the creation of a Portuguese-Brazilian commonwealth would be a resounding demon-stration of their claims for the spiritual unity of the Lusitanian world. Brazil, whose population is in large part Negro or Mulatto, has long been heralded as the success story of Portugal's overseas policies, and her presence in a commonwealth would, Portuguese planners hope, offer a convincing argument against anti-colonial attacks. While for the moment the creation of a Lusitanian community would be ex-ploited by the Portuguese primarily for diplomatic and propaganda purposes, ultimately the commonwealth could be Portugal's last trump in Africa; it could provide a framework in which Portuguese Africa could be granted independence.

To achieve the maximum benefits from what will at best be an amorphous commonwealth, and to heighten the implied analogy between Brazil and the African territories, Portugal must make Angola, Mozambique and Guinea overseas provinces in fact as well as in name. Historically, the three areas have always been colonies, no matter whether they were called "overseas provinces," as in the nineteenth century, or "colonies," as in the early days of the Salazar régime, or, as in the 1950s when the régime began to build up its case for remaining in Africa, "overseas provinces" again. The fact is that more than 95 percent of the population of Portuguese Africa are not enfranchised citizens of Portugal; they have no civil rights and are legally regarded as wards of the state governed under a *regime do indigenato* administered by officials of the Overseas Ministry, formerly the Colonial Ministry. At the United Nations, Portugal has been increasingly harassed by African and Asian delegates who argue that the African territories are colonies, no matter what they are called, and that Portugal has a responsibility to report on conditions there to the General Assembly's Trusteeship Committee. Although the Portuguese delegate responds that "Portugal is a unitary state with the overseas provinces and the homeland considered as a single entity," Portugal's vulnerability to this attack grows each year, and present indications are that the *regime do indigenato* will soon be modified, or even abolished, and a substantial portion of the African population granted token rights of citizenship or possibly even the same civil rights as the white and assimilated Portuguese citizens possess.

The formation of a Lusitanian community and the granting of meaningless citizenship to Portuguese Africans are gestures intended to bolster the persuasions of Portuguese diplomacy. Portugal has survived in Africa during the last 100 years chiefly through the skill of her diplomats, and recently she has effectively used the political leverage derived from her membership in NATO. For the last eight years the United States, and usually England, has sided with Portugal on almost every issue touching the Portuguese colonies. But this close association is coming to an end. One of the more important repercussions of Captain Galvão's seizure of the *Santa Maria* may be that it precipitated a change in Portugal's relations with her three major allies, Brazil, Britain and the United States. Portugal deeply resented the hasty about-face of the British and American Navies and began

to speak, *sotto voce,* of "reëxamining the NATO Alliance." Early
in its life the Kennedy Administration took a public stand which em-
barrassed Portugal, and she must sense that this was the beginning of
the United States' reëxamination of an alliance which has already cost
us a great deal in Africa.

Within the continent of Africa, Portuguese diplomacy, to be successful, must face in two directions—toward the free African nations
and toward the white governments of the Central African Federation
and the Union of South Africa. The former must be conciliated while
the bonds with the latter must be strengthened. The second task is
the easier, for it seems clear that Southern Rhodesia, South Africa and
Portuguese Africa will be the last white pockets in a black continent,
and the simple question of survival has in recent years led the three
governments to exchange numerous ceremonial visits and to emphasize the firm bases of their economic and political associations. With
the African countries, the problem is quite different, and Portuguese
diplomacy has followed a course of discretion and, where possible,
coöperation. Criticism of the leaders or policies of the independent
nations seldom appears in the Portuguese press; Emperor Haile Selassie has been welcomed to Lisbon. Portugal diligently takes part in all
African conferences on health, education and economic matters to
show that she is a reasonable and good neighbor. So far, Portugal
has been rebuked by African governments mostly in the United Nations. But as the frontiers of independent black Africa are extended,
it seems certain there will be a burgeoning traffic of men and ideas
into Angola and Mozambique, a traffic which diplomacy alone will
be hard put to contain.

II

The intent of all Portuguese policy in Africa itself is to preserve
the status quo. Tradition rests heavy in the Portuguese African world.
Over the centuries, colonial attitudes have formed which dominate
Portuguese life in Africa and the making of overseas policy in Lisbon.
The attitudes include a kind of racial tolerance, a self-acknowledged
Christian paternalism toward the African, suspicion of outside interference in the colonies, the notion that the African must be obliged
to work, and the simple faith that the Portuguese way is the right
way, perhaps the only way. At one time or another in the last century these concepts have been written into Portuguese colonial legis-

lation, and to a large extent they explain the present state of affairs in the territories.

That the administration of the African colonies is paternalistic the Portuguese themselves admit. The chain of authority passes in unbroken succession from the Overseas Ministry in Lisbon down to the hand-picked village chiefs. Political rights for Africans do not exist. Nor has paternalism brought measurable material benefits to the African population. The imbalance between the cost of living in Angola and Mozambique and the average wage (about $6 a month) is extreme. Education for the Africans, less than 3 percent of whom are literate, is totally inadequate; the possibilities for the African child to obtain more than three years of so-called rudimentary education are remote. Beyond the cities, large towns and several mission stations, health services scarcely exist. Partly by necessity, but also partly by intent, the African has been maintained in a world of medieval ignorance and isolation.

The Portuguese admit that such conditions do exist, but they argue that the spiritual advantages of their traditional policies more than compensate for material shortcomings. They refer repeatedly to the good will and understanding between the races. They boast that there are no real political or racial problems in Portuguese Africa. They insist that independence has led to Communism in Ghana and Guinea, to bloody chaos in the Congo, and to African racism in the rest of the continent. They speak of the Mau Mau terror in Kenya, uprisings in the Union of South Africa and Southern Rhodesia, armed strife in several of the new African republics, and of the "American-controlled dictatorship" in Liberia. We Portuguese have been here a long time, they say; we know Africa and we know the African. Whether or not the recent bloody rioting in Angola has shaken Portuguese faith in the rightness of their policies, it is certain that it will be increasingly difficult from now on to advertise the colonies as peaceful multi-racial paradises.

The Portuguese have indeed been in Africa a long time, and their policies have consistently been distinguishable from those of other colonial powers. Since the fifteenth century the Portuguese have followed an informal policy of individual assimilation—that is, the social and political acceptance without strong prejudice of Africans who were able to obtain an education and who chose to accept Portuguese cultural values. Although this easy relationship never affected more than a small percentage of the native population—hardly more than the number of settlers or traders who were assimilated by the African —it did provide a safety valve for potential resentments and it has given the Portuguese a basis for justifying their presence in Africa. On the other hand, a massive slave trade (which in its day took from four to six million people from the lands of Guinea, Angola and Mozambique), various forms of forced labor within the colonies and the destruction of tribal institutions have contributed to the subjugation of the African will.

Now, as Portuguese Africa enters the most critical decade of its history, Lisbon's goal is to reconcile the two opposing characteristics of Portuguese practice in Africa—the simultaneous acceptance and exploitation of the Africans. The reconciliation is to be accomplished by the assimilation of the Africans into a Portuguese world. What in essence the Government proposes to do is to convince the Africans that it is better to be Portuguese than to be independent.

This new policy is intended to go far beyond the rigorously selective assimilation of the past 30 years. In numerical terms selective assimilation has been an admitted failure (there are about 35,000 *assimilados* in Angola, out of an African population of some 4,500,000, and about 5,000 of Mozambique's 5,500,000 Africans are *assimilados*). The African who chooses to become assimilated, that is, to be governed by Portuguese common law instead of the *regime do indigenato*, is obliged to demonstrate, among other things, that he has severed all tribal contacts, is self-supporting, and can read and speak Portuguese with facility. The requirements have been stringently applied. Several *assimilados* have recently reached the upper echelons of the colonial and military services, still more have distinguished themselves in the professions, while others, to Portugal's dismay, have become leaders of opposition groups in exile. The Portuguese African intellectual is naturally viewed with suspicion in these troubled days, but at the same time the Salazar Government needs to encourage, if only for propaganda purposes, the emergence of a responsible élite committed to the Portuguese cause in Africa. In consequence, it is willing to permit the training and education each year of a handful of Africans.

But total assimilation means something else. What colonial theorists have in mind might be called psychological integration, and what the Government hopes to achieve in a few years is to transform African society into a semblance of Portuguese peasant society: devout, diligent, semi-literate and politically conservative. To an outsider, the proposal to make more than 11,000,000 Africans into loyal

Portuguese citizens before the winds of change sweep across the colonies seems visionary, but the Portuguese are apparently undisturbed by the scope of the task. They regard it as the next logical step in their overseas history.

The elaboration of the Salazarian mystique of faith, toil and family into a practical program of change in Africa is not yet accomplished. The policy was vaguely formulated, however, in a speech made in July 1960 by Adriano Moreira, Under Secretary of State for Overseas Administration, whose appointment to the key administrative position of the Overseas Ministry has generally been interpreted as a positive step toward a more liberal course in Africa. Sr. Moreira points out that while the number of *assimilados* is insignificant, the number of African Catholics in Angola and Mozambique is nearly 2,000,000. He emphasizes that although "political loyalty does not depend upon Christian qualifications . . . Catholic missionary activity is inseparably linked to patriotism" and that the formation of Christian qualities leads to the formation of Portuguese qualities. According to Sr. Moreira, the Catholic Church can play a vital role for Portugal, as historically it always has, in developing and consolidating national institutions and in helping to confront materialistic influences with spiritual values.

Christianity and the family are, in the Portuguese view, interdependent, and the Under Secretary goes on to stress the need for social action among African women as a second important aspect of the policy of assimilation. Instead of being a reactionary force within the society that passively resists the process of acculturation, the African woman must be made a dynamic force whose interests center in the home and the family. "The effort for integration must be directed . . . toward attracting native women to our culture, for they are simultaneously a stabilizing factor . . . and precious agents for accelerating the integration of [African] men into the social forms which correspond to the objectives of our action." Sr. Moreira envisages various programs of assistance and education for African women.

The more spiritual side of the new African program is to be accompanied by changes in the contract labor system, although there does not for the time being seem to be any real change in the deeply rooted belief that the African must be obliged, one way or another, to work. The moral justification for the obligation has been, and still is, that through work the African's traditional mode of existence is altered and he is made a productive member of his society, responsible to his family and his country. But a minimum wage law has recently been introduced into Portuguese Africa, penal sanctions for breach of labor contracts have been abolished, and sentences of forced labor for political crimes forbidden. It remains to be seen whether these changes are implemented—for it is axiomatic in Portuguese Africa that only the repressive clauses of the labor code are carried out— and whether they will lead to a more enlightened labor legislation. Finally, Sr. Moreira speaks of large-scale advances in health and social programs to assist the work of assimilation. These are, of course, desperately needed in Portuguese Africa, as in fact they are in most of the continent. But progress can only be slow.

III

Will the Portuguese succeed? Can they convert Angola, Guinea and Mozambique into overseas provinces which are patriotically, as well as legally, extensions of the mother country? Can they convince 11,000,000 Africans to resist the tide of nationalism which has swept the continent? Can they lead them to believe that they are Portuguese, not Africans? Leaving to one side such imponderables as a change in government in Portugal (and there is no reason to believe that another government, even a democratic one, would immediately cast off the African provinces), and the possibility of an invasion of the colonies from neighboring nations, it is difficult to see how Portugal can prevail in Africa on her own terms.

There are several crucial factors working against Portugal. The first is time. One senses that history is at last catching up with Portuguese Africa. Portuguese policy for the future is, with some modifications, only an intensification of policies which various governments, liberal and conservative, have tried to effect for the last one hundred years; and the Africans are not appreciably closer to assimilation than they were in the 1850s. Does Portugal have another hundred years in which to inoculate the African people against the fever of independence? In the last several years, sporadic open resistance has flared up in all three colonies. The resistance has now reached dangerous proportions.

A second reason is economic. Portugal, even if she wanted to, cannot afford to carry out any large-scale program of social and educational reform. Portugal is a poor country. She has the lowest per capita income in Western Europe—slightly over $230 a year—as well as the highest illiteracy rate, about 45 percent. A considerable portion of her people live on a subsistence level. The infant mortality rate is very high, as is the incidence of tuberculosis. These conditions in part explain why colonial spokesmen in Africa refer constantly to spiritual values and deprecate the materialism they see dominating life and thought in the rest of the continent. Social reform in Africa, of course, carries implicit dangers, as the Portuguese well realize, but human poverty and ignorance are no less dangerous fuel for the fires of resentment. So far, there has been no African leadership to fan them, but the isolation of the colonies from outside influence and the containment from within of dissident elements cannot for long continue.

A part of the economic picture of Portuguese Africa is the perennial problem of contract labor. Angola and Mozambique, and, to a lesser extent, Guinea, are committed to a policy of economic growth. Large sums are being spent on development projects. Most of the funds go for dams, port facilities, expansion of transportation systems and colonization projects, from all of which the white population obtains the greater benefit. To carry out the program of development, and to work the plantations, fisheries and mines, a steady supply of cheap African labor must be assured. Forced or contract labor has been the answer. Every African male must prove that he is productively employed six months out of the year. Those who cannot—and many of those who can—are rounded up and taken to work for the Government or for private employers. The system leads to abuse and corruption. The Portuguese speak of the African's obligation to learn the dignity of labor, but as countless critics have declaimed, the disruptive influences of the contract labor system more than counteract the theoretical advantages. The effect of the system on African life can scarcely be measured. Each year hundreds of thousands of African workers cross the frontiers into the Congo, the Rhodesias and even into the Union of South Africa to escape the labor draft. Contract labor is the most obvious form of human injustice in the colonies; it provides the focus abroad for the condemnation of Portuguese rule, and in Africa itself it is becoming the source of growing African unrest.

Another factor working against the Portuguese is racialism. The white population of Mozambique and particularly of Angola has shown an extraordinary increase in the last 20 years, from about 45,000 to approximately 160,000 in Angola, and from about 27,000 to 70,000 in Mozambique. White immigration is to a large extent the success story of contemporary Portuguese Africa. It explains the growth of the colonies' economic life, the emergence of cities and large towns along the coast and in the interior, and the urgency of development programs. Poverty and overpopulation in Portugal are driving more and more peasants and laborers to try their luck in Africa. Although in Mozambique the local administration has attempted to be selective, in Angola the door is open to all. The Government has expanded its program of colonization projects for Portuguese peasants in both provinces. The pressures of the white influx are already being felt. The economic mobility of the African worker, never high, is now being contained at a low level by Portuguese skilled or semi-skilled workers.

But the ultimate effect of the white immigration is not merely economic. It is also racial. The Salazar Government apparently has assumed that the Portuguese lack of racial prejudice, so evident in Portugal, would keep tensions to a minimum between the new white population and the Africans. What has happened is that the Portuguese are creating exclusively white communities in the colonies and that racist tendencies are now intruding into what was once a situation of relative tolerance. The Portuguese peasant or worker often has little with which to justify his presence in a strange land, and his fears and uncertainties lead him to assert a racial superiority. Life in Angola and Mozambique has begun to follow sharply segregated patterns. The Portuguese speak of cultural and economic distinctions, but these are not very meaningful arguments, and the Portuguese will discover, if they have not already, that white racialism creates its opposite image in the African.

The Salazar Government is perfectly aware that the direction of Angola and Mozambique is toward a Rhodesian, if not a South African, way of life. Such a possibility does not seem to upset Portuguese colonialists. Since the Conference of Berlin, the Portuguese have smarted under a sense of inferiority; they have seen their neighbors in Africa prosper while their own lands and resources remained undeveloped. Now it is Portugal's turn, and it appears that nothing will be allowed to stand in the way. The Portuguese are sincere when they talk about assimilation, but it is doubtful that they intend the assimilated African population to have any more voice in national affairs than does the Portuguese peasant. And what meaning can assimilation have when the Government permits and encourages the establishment of two worlds in the provinces, one white and one black, with an ever-deepening frontier between them?

The policy of total assimilation cannot work. At its best it is paternalism, at its worst it is obscurantism. Portuguese policy is implicitly founded on the time-worn concept that the African is a child with no culture or civilization worthy of recognition. His language is forbidden in schools, his traditional chiefs have been subverted or eliminated. The majority of the Africans are landless; African agricultural production is sharply controlled, and even exploited, as in Mozambique where African-grown cotton is sold at a fixed price, processed in Portugal and sold in the colony at a price few Africans can pay. Corporal punishment for Africans is common procedure; suspected troublemakers are jailed or exiled. Portuguese Africa, like Portugal, is increasingly dominated by police action. These repressions are hardly the way to persuade Africans of the advantages of assimilation.

For centuries the Portuguese have been able to contain discontent in the African territories and to ignore sporadic humanitarian protests from outside. Now the protests are constant, they are louder and they reach a larger, more sympathetic audience. Two important African organizations have been formed to work for the independence of Angola, Mozambique and Guinea. The first, the "União das Populações de Angola," has its headquarters in Leopoldville where it publishes a newspaper and is attempting to organize the Angolans living in the Republic of the Congo. The second group, the "Frente Revolucionaria para a Independencia Nacional das Colónias Portuguesas" (FRAIN) is a combination of four opposition groups. It has its headquarters in Conakry. Both are growing in size and importance. They have the support of a number of African nations, and they maintain representatives at the United Nations and in several world capitals. They have begun to talk of underground activities in Portuguese Africa, of sabotage and reprisals against collaborators.

The Portuguese Government is preparing for whatever may come. Beneath the optimistic phrases about assimilation and brotherhood there is determination to resist. "We are not," said President Américo Thomaz last November, "in Africa . . . like so many others. We will continue as always our policy of integration. . . . To this end it is necessary for us to be what we have always been, and we will not change." The present Government is not bluffing. Military garrisons have been augmented; naval patrols are posted along the Angola coast; paratroop and bombing manoeuvres have taken place; military plans have been made for emergencies; pistol-shooting clubs have sprung up among the Portuguese population. There is nothing conciliatory in the Government's attitude or in that of the white residents. In a recent speech in Mozambique, Dr. Castro Fernandez, head of the National Union, Portugal's ruling party, said bluntly, "Portugal is in Africa and Portugal will remain in Africa."

On November 30, 1960, at the peak of anti-Portuguese sentiment at the United Nations, Dr. Salazar chose to address the National Assembly on the subject of "Portugal and the Anti-Colonialist Campaign." His stern remarks were the most extensive statement he had made in recent years on Portugal's overseas policy, and they reveal that his government has no intention of abandoning its position.

Surely they [the Portuguese people] are not going to suppose that the fate of millions of men, the order and peace of their way of life, the fruit of their work, the principles of the civilization they have adopted, can be handed over to the emptiness of speeches at meetings and the anarchy of the so-called movements of liberation. . . .

A multi-racial society is therefore possible, whether of Luso-American stock, as in Brazil . . . or Luso-African stock, as we see in Angola and Mozambique. . . . It would be most unwise for us now to innovate with practices, feelings and concepts different from those which have been the secret of the work we have achieved and which are still the best safeguard for the future. . . .

I do not see that we can rest in our labors nor can we have any other care than to hold with one hand our plough and with the other our sword. . . . Great sacrifices will be called for, as well as the most absolute devotion and, if necessary, also the blood from our veins.

In the face of such unyielding attitudes it is difficult to foresee any area of compromise. Certainly the Portuguese are not following the example of the English, and they looked upon Belgium's action in the Congo with a mixture of scorn and disbelief. Their words and deeds find a closer parallel with Afrikaner policy in South Africa. Perhaps a concert of international pressures would persuade Portugal to change her course in Africa. Perhaps popular uprisings would have the same effect. But such possibilities are speculative. In Portuguese Africa there will be no easy answer.

Part III

Self-Government, Ready or Not

Note

NATIVE SELF-GOVERNMENT
BY MELVILLE J. HERSKOVITS

April 1944

In the two decades since the following article was written, we have become more aware of the contribution that the cultural anthropologist can make to an understanding of political problems. As our contacts with "underdeveloped" societies have increased, he has insistently demanded that we ask, " 'Underdeveloped' in what way?" He has impressed upon us how narrow our vision is, how dubious our assumptions, in measuring other societies by the particular standards of our own. In the compelling essay that follows we are reminded that Africa was never a cultural vacuum waiting to be filled by whatever we happened to cherish, that Western values and institutions cannot be imposed, but must be induced in such a way that the indigenous culture can adapt to it. At a time when the newly independent countries of Africa appear to be drifting "backward," away from Western ways to those more purely African—or, hopefully, to some new synthesis—the article is as relevant and important as when it was written.

Melville J. Herskovits, before his death in 1963, was the dean of American Africanists and one of the most widely known social anthropologists of his generation. He was particularly admired by African intellectuals, for his cultural relativism, his sympathetic estimate of the African's capacities, gave them encouragement and confidence.

Though Herskovits' field experience was by no means limited to Africa, he devoted almost all his mature life to the study of that continent and to the training of young Africanists. As Director of African Studies at Northwestern University he established the first African area program in the United States, and when Africa burst on the world's consciousness, his former students were among the few Africanists available in this country. He took an active—not merely a scholar's—part in African affairs and in helping to shape American policy toward Africa. "United States Foreign Policy in Africa," prepared for the Senate Foreign Relations Committee, is referred to as the Herskovits Report, and just before his fatal heart attack he had led the American delegation at the first International Congress of Africanists meeting in Accra. He was the first president of the African Studies Association, and only months before his death, 40 years of research in Africa were capped with the publication of "The Human Factor in Changing Africa."

In this article, so thoroughly characteristic of the author's work, both in substance and in tone, Herskovits expresses ideas that are now generally familiar, if not universally accepted. It is good that he lived to see the great period of change to African independence and to hear shouted on every hand arguments for which he so long sought a hearing.

Native Self-Government

by MELVILLE J. HERSKOVITS

A primary obligation of Europeans and Americans toward colonial peoples is generally held to be to "educate the native" for self-government. In postwar plans this obligation is usually expressed in the form of an injunction that colonial Powers, or any agency which is set up to control colonial areas, shall preserve the interests of the native populations during some undetermined transitional period and instruct them in the art of governing themselves. It is implied or promised that autonomy shall be theirs when their "education" has been completed. On the political side, this represents an extension of the mandates idea; as it applies to native ways of life, it is a blend of the older concept of European colonial policy embodied in the phrase "the white man's burden" and the more modern statement of administrative technique known as "indirect rule."

The principle of tutelage from which the obligation just described is supposed to derive rests on the assumption that native peoples are less developed than peoples whose cultures are marked by a machine technology and the scientific approach to natural phenomena. Native peoples are rarely held to be innately inferior because of race. They are supposed, rather, to be culturally inferior; and because their "backwardness" is believed cultural, the efficacy of education is taken for granted. The length of time a certain native people must be subject to tutelage will depend upon how "advanced" it becomes—that is, how readily it accepts European and American ways of life.

This approach to the problem is regrettably over-simplified. The fact is that native peoples all over the world have in many respects a high degree of competence for self-government, and that much of the present ill-feeling between native peoples and their European rulers is due to the failure of westerners to understand this fact. A still greater degree of friction between rulers and ruled is to be expected in the future if the former do not adopt a different attitude toward the problem of integrating colonial areas into a peaceful world economic and political system.

It should be made clear at the outset that the problem is not approached here on the unrealistic assumption that the hands of the clock can be turned backward. The fact of European and American occupation and control cannot be waved out of existence, nor can the requirements of the world economy be ignored. The basic problem is to find and adopt a policy toward native peoples which will contribute to a growing confidence among all the peoples of the world.

II

Only in recent years have we come to perceive how tenaciously "backward" peoples cling to their own ways of life, how devoted they are to what in their eyes has worth and substance. For uncounted centuries in all parts of the non-European world, native folk, unmolested in their relative isolation, created and preserved patterns of living which permitted them to survive. They developed bodies of tradition adapted to the natural settings in which they found themselves, technological skills and economic systems to provide for their physical needs, social and political institutions to regulate relationships within the group, and forms of religious and artistic expression to cope with the unknown and the unknowable and to satisfy their non-material needs.

The advent of European control changed native political and economic systems radically, but many other facets of native culture were not affected to any comparable degree. In some colonies it even happened that native economic and political institutions were not considered prejudicial to the interests of the colonial Power and were permitted to continue relatively unchanged. In fact, all over the native world, many petty chiefs today still carry on much as they did before the coming of the Europeans, and native markets still are held as they always have been. Now, however, a chief acts on the advice of a colonial officer and is paid by the European administration; and the market contributes to the operation of a fiscal system quite outside the control of those whose lives are influenced by it. In many native societies there never was much democracy, as we define it; nevertheless, the change to the district officer from the native ruler and his council of elders is no mere substitution of one power for its equivalent. It is a change from a socially sanctioned system of controls which was a part of the people's cultural heritage to a system imposed and administered from outside the group. The European system is as foreign to the native psychologically as it is politically.

Characteristic of current approaches to the problem of colonial government is the fact that the native is rarely consulted, and that when the colonial administrator takes the native point of view into account he rarely does so realistically. As a result, often unwittingly, the rôle assigned the native in the postwar world is essentially that of a pawn. Although he enjoys better sanitation, a higher standard of living, security from petty depredations, new goods to fill new wants, and our type of religious truth, he still is consumed by the desire to return to "the old days" of freedom from foreign dominance and to ways of life that were satisfactory to him. Yet even when the existence of that desire is recognized, the decision as to whether it would be "best" to gratify it is held to lie in the wisdom of the foreign ruler, not in the desire of the ruled; and this not out of devotion to the autocratic principle but because the native is believed to be like the child whose parent has the advantage of superior intelligence and maturity.

This point of view is acceptable to us because it feeds a congenial belief in our own superiority, for among Europeans and Americans ethnocentrism has been raised almost to an article of faith. It is given the appearance of validity by the military power which colonizing countries always have at their command in order to overwhelm any native opposition. "He who makes the powder," says a West African proverb, "wields the power." Our control of the machine, in contrast to the rude technologies of native folk, has heightened our sense of cultural superiority by providing it with objective proof. When we compare the complexity of our economic system with the economies of primitive folk, and when we consider the advantages that come to us from our possession of the art of writing, we secure further satisfactory evidence of our own preëminence.

It is generally assumed that native ways of life must inevitably yield when they come into contact with "higher" cultures; but the hard fact is that they do not. Evidence from all over the world is at hand to show that contact with another culture can just as easily make the native determined to continue in what seems to him a more desirable way of living. If he cannot do so on the surface of daily life, he will do it sub rosa. In many parts of West Africa, for example, European authorities have tried to suppress worship of a supposed god of smallpox, and numerous officials believe they have succeeded. What is not understood is that this deity is but one manifestation of the earth-god, who must be worshipped if crops are not to fail; worship goes on as always, in a form sufficiently changed to ensure adequate disguise.

III

What is known, it may be asked, of the ability of native peoples to govern themselves? The range of political systems in primitive society is vast. It includes a great number of civilizations, each with its own set of institutions. Just as the societies of native folk vary in size from small autonomous bands to stable kingdoms with populations counted in the millions, so the political structures range from rudimentary forms almost not discernible in any institutionalized pattern to great dynasties which have held sway for generations. So varied are these forms, indeed, that in many instances they defy the definitions set up by specialists in government, which perhaps is why the latter seem to have given over any attempt at a scientific consideration of native political methods.

Yet whether simple or complex, whether appertaining to societies small or large, these political systems perform the functions of the state as we know it—that is, they control the relations of a man to his fellows, and regulate the drive for power. Functionally, the question whether such controls are exerted by family groups or by designated officials is beside the point. The man who refrains from misconduct through fear that the son of his maternal uncle will subject him to public ridicule is responding to the same type of control as the individual in our society who avoids wrongdoing through fear of the police and the courts—except that the former system perhaps works out the more efficiently of the two.

The problem of how competent native folk are to govern themselves differs in various parts of the world. The political situation on a coral atoll in the Pacific is not the same as in a populous island such as Java. The type and degree of native contact with Europeans often differ from tribe to tribe even within a relatively restricted region, and this adds another complicating factor. Yet the underlying principles are everywhere the same. Colonial peoples the world over were affected by the victories of Japan and have reacted to the implications of the Japanese slogan "Asia for the Asiatics." Similarly, a reaction has been noted to the proclamation of the Atlantic Charter and the Four Freedoms among widely different primitive tribes.

We may assume, then, that while particular situations differ the basic motivations do not, and we may proceed to examine the conditions which antedated European control in various regions in order to find clues as to how the problem might be solved aright. There seem certain advantages in choosing to study Africa particularly in this connection. Though racial disunity does not manifest itself in Africa as it does, for example, in India, the tribal tensions there are equally strong. Moreover, Africa is the largest single land area under foreign control. It lies outside the immediate range of the "Asia for the Asiatics" slogan, and it usually is not considered as politically important as the Dutch East Indies, French Indo-China or Malaya; yet the problems it presents are quite as pressing as those arising in the latter areas. Indeed, it is especially desirable that students of international affairs begin to accord African problems closer attention than they have done in the past, for this continent seems a likely center of many future irritations.

All over Africa, before the advent of the Europeans, there existed societies ruled under a system of delegated authority which assured a reign of law and order. The Fula, Hausa, Wolof, Fulbe and other empires of the western Sudan have long been famous. The story of their dynastic struggles and of their wars of conquest reads like a page of European history—not of too distant a date at that. On the Gold Coast were the Ashanti and the Fanti kingdoms. The constitutional principles governing the former, and the legal system of the latter, show that these Negro societies were capable of developing a high degree of organization in conformity with their own patterns of government. The Kingdom of Dahomey exhibited an even more closely-knit government structure, as shown, for example, by the annual census, the techniques of levying taxes and the planned agricultural regimen. In Nigeria, the Yoruban people, and those of Benin, were likewise carefully and efficiently organized. Even in such a region as the Niger Delta, where the political unit was small and restricted to an aggregate of villages, the African tradition of regulated procedures to govern all phases of life was as prominent as elsewhere. The Kingdom of Kongo at the mouth of the Congo River was well-established when the Portuguese explorers reached it in the first part of the sixteenth century, while inland lay the countries of the Bushongo and other Bantu rulers. East and South Africa similarly had well-organized political units. Among Africanists, Uganda was long a standard example of the African "genius for organization." Almost mythical was the Kingdom of Monomotapa, in the southern part of the continent. And we have the well-authenticated historical accounts of the rise of the Zulu Kingdom under Chaka, and the establishment of the Matabele domain.

Regular processes of law were the rule in the larger aggregates as well as in the smaller autonomous village units of herding bands. The indigenous court systems of the Africans have been commented on by every early traveller who saw them in operation. In the larger groupings, appeals could be taken to a higher court from an adverse decision in a lower one. Litigation—especially in East and South Africa, where issues arose over the ownership of the cattle that passed from one family to another incident on marriage—could go on for generations. That a man argued his own case instead of retaining a specialist to do this for him, that he might cite proverbs instead of legal precedents, merely meant that the outer trappings of the system differed from those known to ourselves. The result was the same: the individual knew his rights, and could expect protection in the exercise of them.

The principles underlying African political systems were of a different order from those in present-day American and European countries. African polity was based on a conception of disciplined obedience in accord with status. The best European analogy to the African monarchy is the feudal kingdom of the Middle Ages, though the analogy, as might be expected, does not hold true in any great detail. The African system was more flexible than the European, and change of status was far easier for the African commoner and even slave than for the European yeoman or serf.

Beneath the seeming differences in position, also, was a democratic reality that is to be grasped only when one understands the basic assumptions concerning the relation of man to man. This was reflected in part in the political realism which inhibited a ruler, no matter how absolute his power in theory, from exercising that power without first ascertaining the reactions of his people to specific edicts. For the rest, this democratic reality was to be seen in the bearing of a man—in the manner in which, once the formalities of greeting were over, he would meet and treat with other members of his tribe.

There were, of course, many aspects of the political systems of Africa (or of other parts of the native world) which from our point of view appear undesirable, distasteful and even repulsive. The institution of slavery was the rule in most of the continent, and the object of most wars between native states in the more densely populated portions, particularly during the period of the slave trade to the New World, was the acquisition of human booty. It is true that, except in special instances, slavery in Africa was not the institution it became in the Americas; it was customarily of the household type, and the adoption of a slave or the child of a slave could on occasion give the bondsman the position of tribesman. But the slave did suffer one peril he did not know in the New World; he might be sent to accompany his master to the realm of the dead, to serve him there as he had served him in the world of the living. When a king died an impressive retinue accompanied him to the other world. We need but read the descriptions given by Canon Roscoe of the funerary rituals of the Baganda royalty, or those by Sir Richard Burton of the Dahomean "customs," to realize how lightly on occasion life could be held.

In the larger groupings, also, not only was life held cheaply; property, too, was owned at the pleasure of the ruler. At this distance in time from the days of autonomous rule it is not easy to obtain information on native taxation systems. But we can reconstruct something of the facts from the chronicles of the early explorers, and in some parts of Africa old men can be found whose memories reach beyond the colonial régime to the autonomous past. Land, whether of a large kingdom or of a village state, belonged in principle to the ruler. When he granted it for use he gave up his rights over it while it was under cultivation; at least he abandoned the right to take the produce. In the larger groupings, however, the ruler often could appropriate a considerable proportion of a man's wealth as taxes. A man's sons could be impressed for military service; his daughter could be taken for the royal household. When there were especially favorable channels for trade, or particularly good opportunities to dispose of produce, the ruler profited first from them; and he exercised other monopolies that offered special chances for gain.

In general, autocratic tendencies predominated in societies in which political institutions were most highly developed, whereas democratic aspects of government bulked larger in groupings "lacking centralized authority, administrative machinery, and constituted judicial institutions," to quote the phrase employed by Fortes and Evans-Pritchard. Yet whether the systems were democratic or autocratic, they operated successfully for longer periods of time than the historic record covers, to say the very least. They were cast in the patterns of the culture as a whole. Their burdens, which might seem irksome to us, were integrated into the total scheme of living and were accepted as normal. So fully accepted were they that they still remain vivid in the unwritten history of peoples who, under foreign control, remember their virtues and forget their shortcomings.

IV

Those who study native patterns of living scientifically probably come closest to being able to understand how the native regards the colonial system. This is very different indeed from the impression given the government official who deals with the daily events of native life. In West Africa, for example, the colonial system has brought many benefits to the natives, as the natives themselves will readily admit. This is especially the case in the British colonies. The native has personal security as never before. He has a higher standard of living than he did in the days of autonomous rule. Health conditions have been greatly improved. Native horizons have been widened in many directions. Only freedom is lacking. Hence, despite all the benefits bestowed, one rarely encounters a native who does not speak with nostalgia of "the time when we were free" and who, if he speaks frankly and without fear, does not say he looks forward to a day in the predictable future when he will be liberated from foreign control.

This raises a question which troubles many who seek a wise decision regarding the place of native peoples in the postwar world. Can the native be granted his own way of life, they ask, if this means that the world society must countenance Melanesian cannibalism, Borneo head-hunting, African slavery? Or can it allow autocratic controls, rigid social stratification, intra-tribal economic inequalities? The problem must be faced squarely and without subterfuge. One type of answer—never very satisfactory—is the *tu quoque*. Have Borneo head-hunters taken the heads of as many persons in long generations as we, for all our boasted culture, kill in automobile accidents in a single normal year, or in a single skirmish in modern warfare? Arguments on this level, however, lead us nowhere. Nor is it useful to be sentimental, to picture native peoples as having lived formerly in a golden age and to think they should retain their aboriginal ways merely because these are picturesque.

Where different peoples come into close contact changes are bound to occur. The point is that the changes must not be imposed, but induced on the one side and accepted on the other. Native folk are just as quick to see and seize upon material advantages as we are ourselves, provided these are not forced on them or presented to them as an integral part of a system which in its totality is incomprehensible. To do so affronts their dignity as adult human beings. Here the student of primitive cultures can be of service by suggesting transfers of interest which easily and naturally wean a tribe away from practices that will handicap it in assuming its place in a world organization. Many traditions will wither and disappear of themselves as a result of changes in the economic bases of native life. Others will never be resurrected from the tribal past even if the opportunity should offer, because those who would be harmed by them will not, once they have been freed of their disabilities while under colonial rule, countenance a return to the previous status.

A principle well known to students of culture suggests the proper general approach—namely, that while no body of customs is static, any new element which is successfully introduced either from within a group or from without must be cast in terms of preëxisting patterns. Innovations arising within the group are taken up or discarded according as they can or cannot be harmonized with established beliefs and habits. So are innovations introduced from outside, as long as the group is in a position to determine for itself what it will accept and what reject. That is why changes arbitrarily introduced from without "for the good of the people" are resented, no matter how enlightened the intent of the would-be benefactor. And that is why the problem of "educating the native" has proved so baffling. If new political or cultural patterns cannot be integrated with the old ones they will be rejected. Controls which "train for self-government" are thus as little acceptable to natives as would be educational attempts based on a recent interpretation of the Atlantic Charter, which was held to impose an obligation on Europeans and Americans to free the native from the "fears" presumably arising out of his "primitive superstitions."

v

Once again it must be emphasized that the hands of the historical clock cannot be turned back. Native peoples cannot be returned to their aboriginal isolation. The effects of their contact with Europeans cannot be erased. Practically speaking, then, it must be recognized that any abrupt withdrawal by the colonial Powers, even if it could be brought about, would result in chaos. Native political systems long suppressed would not function as they did in pre-colonial times. They could not govern if they were catapulted into control. Nor, in the main, are native peoples calling for the abrupt withdrawal of the colonial Powers. Those of their number who have knowledge of the world as it is recognize the need for outside protection against aggression—economic no less than political—until such time as experience has taught the art of self-protection and has provided the means. Most such individuals, as well as the mass of the peoples concerned, would be quite content if they knew that they were being accorded protection until, at definitely stated terminal periods, or according to some fixed procedure, they could achieve complete control over their own ways of life.

There are many fields, however, in which the natives can and should be left to themselves. These include local economic arrangements, forms of local government, marriage forms, social structures, religious beliefs and moral codes. Only in that way can the occupying Powers remove existing irritation or hostility. Most native folk have preserved their customs well enough so that they could easily achieve cultural autonomy of the kind suggested. Only such peoples as have been transplanted to reserves, or whose aboriginal habitat has been invaded by foreigners in large numbers, or who have been compelled to live under conditions that prevented key elements in their cultures from functioning, would find it impossible to exercise even local cultural control over their own societies. But they would be the exception in the colonial world rather than the rule—they would present the sort of situation which has arisen in North America or the Union of South Africa, for example, rather than in Java or the Gold Coast. The difficulty lies in our unwillingness to admit the worth of native ways of life, to refrain from passing judgment upon their values and traditions merely because they differ from our own.

The next step, after we have accorded native peoples local and cultural autonomy, is to *induce*, not impose, such changes as will integrate them successfully into the postwar world. We should proceed entirely realistically. It would be folly, for example, not to recognize that regardless of the degree of cultural autonomy native peoples may be privileged to exercise, they still will continue to occupy land and possess manpower and influence the production of commodities which are essential to the functioning of the modern world's economy and hence are of general political concern.

Education is indeed needed; but it is needed not only for natives, but for those who wield world power as well. The first lesson to be learned, if successful progress is to be made, is that native custom must be fully and continuously taken into account in all plans for integrating a given people into the world scene, and that their sensibilities must be given as much weight as the sensibilities of the outside dominant group. Secondly, it must be remembered that native collaboration is a minimum requirement. We shall merely perpetuate the existing points of irritation under a new name if we continue to regard native peoples as groups for whom we must make decisions, who are capable of executing plans only under our direction, whose customs are to be respected only if they are not in conflict with our own standards. We must shed the assumption that if there is to be a world order it must be organized wholly on the European and American model. Equally important is the realization that definite periods must be set in which autonomy, or some phase of autonomy, is to be achieved. In some instances, of course, there will be justification for stating that a considerable interval must elapse before even cultural autonomy can be granted. The main thing is to establish a timetable.

Special techniques must be devised to attain the above objectives. An example is the manner in which the Office of Indian Affairs of the United States has used the device of incorporation to permit tribal matters to be placed in tribal hands. The right solutions will be hard to find, for the problem is highly complex. But it is urgently necessary that the search be made and that it succeed, for in native discontents are foreshadowed renewed conflict on a world scale and in the critical form of struggles between races.

With sufficient good will, mutual respect and ingenuity the conflict can be avoided. But the premise of any satisfactory solution, it must be stressed again, will have to be the recognition that no people can speak or plan for another permanently, that every group not demoralized by the long operation of outside controls is capable at least of local self-government, and that those groups not immediately capable of participating largely in world affairs will be able to do so in time. "Education for self-government" thus should mean adopting a procedure which will bring home to native peoples the advantages of participating in the world economic and political order and make them desire spontaneously to adapt their ways of life to its requirements.

Note

BRITISH AIMS IN AFRICA
BY ELSPETH HUXLEY

October 1949

Ever since Mary Kingsley swept through the bush and jungle of West Africa—her Victorian skirts dragging in mosquito-infested swamps where no European had been—Africa has attracted more than its fair share of brilliant and sensitive women who have served as scholars, interpreters and uninhibited lovers of that strangely seductive continent. Two of them are included in this section and their appearance back to back is the more interesting because each reflects a viewpoint that is highly informed, sympathetic and yet frequently at odds with the other. During World War II, Elspeth Huxley and Margery Perham conducted an extended correspondence on the future of East Africa and the white man's place and purpose in it. Their debate afforded such a clear and useful delineation of the issues which would have to be met in the postwar period that they were persuaded to publish it under the title, "Race and Politics in Kenya." Their differences, so much a product of their separate backgrounds, are less sharply drawn here, but the dissimilarity of their approach is yet evident.

Miss Huxley is a Kenyan with an abiding affection for the country where she was born and has lived all her life. Although she shares many of the views of her fellow Europeans in that colony, hers is by no means the typical "settler mentality." Her novels—especially "Red Strangers," about the reaction of the Kikuyu to the first coming of the white man to Kenya—demonstrate unusual knowledge and understanding of the African, not merely as servant or squatter or educated politician, but as a member of a tribe whose way of life she respects.

Though her judgments of the African often seem harsh, her essential view is that the Europeans have destroyed what was good, or at

114

least harmonious, in African culture without being given time to put anything stable or constructive in its place. Her skepticism about the capacity of the African to find his way without a further period of European tutelage is as profound today as it was when this article was written 14 years ago. To leave the African in his present limbo, she sincerely believes, is nothing less than a crime.

Miss Huxley served in 1959 as a U.K. independent member of the influential Monckton Advisory Commission which made recommendations for the future of the Central African Federation. She has a degree in agriculture, and as the following article demonstrates, she has maintained an interest in the subject as it applies to Africa.

British Aims in Africa

by ELSPETH HUXLEY

Three times in history has an empire sloughed off into independence from the British Isles: America first, then the four white Dominions, lastly the four new Asiatic nations. Now attention is directed toward the fourth and last empire, which lies almost wholly within the tropics and mainly in Africa. It is to Africa that Britain must look for that field for investment, source of raw materials and expanding market which she needs in order to survive, and she must win it quickly from the swamps and forest and highveld of the last continent to be pioneered.

The drive to "open up" this treacherous and fascinating land has in fact begun. Nor is Britain the only nation concerned. France, Belgium and Portugal have big stakes in Africa's future and are turning more to development, as yet with very limited coördination and in pursuit of at least three different policies. But the fundamental fact is the same. For centuries, indeed millennia, Africa slumbered. Held in their rigid tribal mold, men lived as their ancestors before them, neither striving after nor desiring change. Now the mold is broken, the old ways are dying, and African man is suddenly conscious of a new, bewildering, turbulent world and faced with the colossal task of building a new society from the ruins of the old. Seldom in history, if ever, has change struck at a continent so swiftly and with so little mercy, allowing no time for adjustment and no room for compromise, and confronting the four western nations with the obligation so to shape their policies as to bring material prosperity to the land and spiritual hope to the people. Can it be done? That is today's enigma in Africa.

II

We must note first that we are dealing here only with that half of the continent lying within the tropics. North Africa was opened up 2,000 years ago by the Romans and still forms part of the Mediterranean world. South Africa was colonized over a century ago, first by the Dutch and then by the British, and forms a self-governing Dominion, independent of the western nations. It is the great "black belt" stretching some 3,000 miles from the Atlantic to the Indian Ocean with which we are concerned—Negro Africa, occupied by more than 100,000,000 people of many different races and tribes, and speaking more than 700 different tongues. In area, it is about three times as large as the United States and in resources it is almost as varied.

It is the minerals that have so far been most thoroughly exploited. Gold and coal enrich the Union of South Africa and, with thriving chrome mines, sustain also the British colony immediately to the north, Southern Rhodesia. North of that again lies the central African copper belt, shared between British Northern Rhodesia and the prosperous Belgian Congo: a strange outcrop of modern industry and huge labor camps in the heart of barren, dry, monotonous bush, and probably the world's greatest deposit of copper-bearing ores. To the northeast lie unexploited lead and coal fields and the largest single diamond mine in the world, discovered as recently as 1941 by a Canadian geologist. To the west lie the gold and diamonds of the Gold Coast and the tin of Nigeria, and underground, everywhere, mineral deposits still unsuspected or untapped. As yet, no oil fields have been discovered.

In matters of agricultural production, the colonial Powers follow two opposite policies, in some cases simultaneously. There is the plantation system, developed to its highest pitch in the Belgian Congo, where land is leased for long terms to big companies such as Unilever and used for the scientific production of export crops such as oil palms, rubber, cotton, coffee, tea. Sisal, too, is grown by these methods in Tanganyika and Kenya, both under British control. Such up-to-date plantations are but small islands dotted about a great ocean of peasant proprietorship, the prevailing system throughout the colonial section of the continent; in British West Africa no European company is allowed to buy or lease land. In the Gold Coast, half the world's supply of cocoa is grown by Africans on their own small farms, and in East Africa a great deal of coffee. In both cases, Africans themselves are considerable employers of labor, and some fortunes are made. A few Gold Coast Africans have been assessed for taxation at incomes of over £10,000 a year, and in Uganda there are one or two Baganda landowners drawing revenues from estates of more than 50,000 acres. The cattle lands lie mostly on the highveld in the east and east-center. Development has scarcely yet been started, save in the Kenya highlands where British settlers have imported English cattle and improved both breed and pastures. Disease, poor grass and lack of water have hitherto conspired together to hold back a great area of potential stock-raising country from easing the world's shortage of proteins.

Such a cursory and incomplete sketch of tropical Africa's resources would seem to support the current belief in the potentialities of this last undeveloped land—"Tomorrow's Continent," as it has been called. Some consider that Britain's best hope of a solution to her dollar crisis lies in building up there alternative sources of supply. And it is true that the basis for reciprocal trade does exist between Africa and not Britain only but all Western Europe: on the one hand, a raw-material-producing region crying out for capital development and manufactures, on the other an industrial area in as dire a need of markets.

This is the dynamic behind the now rather notorious groundnut scheme in Tanganyika, the largest single project launched by the British since the war. The idea is imaginative: to open up with mechanized equipment nearly 3,000,000 acres of uninhabited or sparsely inhabited bush, nearly all infested by the tsetse fly and without communications; to build railways, a modern port and new cities in the wilderness; and to raise, by scientific means, large tonnages of groundnuts to help meet the world's fat deficiency. It was always admitted that the project would be expensive, but owing to top-heavy administration, lack of knowledge and sheer bad luck, it is to cost the British taxpayer about three times as much as he bargained for. This scheme was overambitious and has been badly handled by the Overseas Food Corporation, the government agency responsible; but the idea is nevertheless sound.

This is only one of several planned developments. In general, these are of two kinds. There are those, like the groundnut scheme, designed to increase the economic wealth of colonial Africa and ultimately to pay their way. Others of this nature include the damming of the Upper Nile and the generating of cheap hydroelectric power to serve a large and thickly populated region round Lake Victoria. A further hydroelectric scheme is proposed for Northern and Southern Rhodesia, and a project to open up the coal and lead deposits in the remotest corner of Tanganyika, the United Nations Trust Territory administered by Britain. Other proposals are as yet more nebulous, but could add greatly to the wealth of equatorial Africa, at present so lightly and patchily exploited that this whole vast region contributes less than 3 percent of the total amount of world trade.

At present Southern Rhodesia, for instance, supplies rather over one-fifth of Britain's consumption of tobacco. Given encouragement, east and central Africa could probably produce nearly all of it; hitherto the taste of the British public and the interests of American producers have prevented such encouragement. Much of the cotton and many of the fats could be raised in Africa, and, in time, a good deal of the meat. A new discovery made by chemists working for Imperial Chemical Industries has, for the first time, made feasible a great increase in meat production. This is antrycide, a drug believed to offer almost complete protection against diseases carried by tsetse flies. If it succeeds, several million square miles of bush will ultimately, though not for some time, be fitted for the raising of cattle.

A second set of projects falls under the head of "welfare," and includes such urgently needed benefits as roads (almost everywhere primitive), schools, mass education projects, hospitals, dispensaries, cheap literature, better markets and—perhaps of all things most important—a great extension of afforestation and soil conservation. These good works cannot yield an immediate return in cash, but their advocates expect them to pay a long-term dividend in greater human productivity, contentment and skill. Since most of colonial Africa is rat-poor, they are being paid for in part, though not wholly, by the British taxpayer, who has voted a sum of £120,000,000 for the purpose, interest-free.

Inevitably, this new drive to open up Africa—significantly an affair of large, costly government schemes and not, as in the past, of the heroic, predatory and often picturesque forays of individuals—will encounter difficulties, some of nature's making and some of man's. Of the two, the first set are probably the easier to deal with. Drought, disease, distance—those dragons in the path of progress can, with vigor, resolution and expense, be conquered; the scientist and the engineer will see to it. More difficult, more complex are the problems set by human nature; and it must be said that, as yet, very little progress has been made towards their mastery.

III

These problems may be roughly summed up thus: advance in Africa is impossible without the full and eager coöperation of the African people. And hitherto, in spite of many obvious benefits derived and others promised, they have shown increasing distrust for the white man's intentions and growing reluctance either to believe what he says or to play their full part in working with him toward economic prosperity.

At first sight this seems absurd, and indeed it is often a nose-cutting operation. A voluntary campaign to terrace badly eroded land is, with scientific supervision, launched by the government and carried through at first by the people; enter the native politicians, and in a few weeks the scheme is abandoned, the chiefs who have helped to work it threatened with violence. Those who suffer are the people themselves, whose crops fail and who go hungry. Or the cocoa trees which support the whole economy of the Gold Coast contract "swollen shoot" disease, and the only way to stop infection spreading is to cut them down. At first this is done; then, once more, enter the native politicians; and in a very short time the cutting of trees—for which compensation is paid—has to be abandoned. Again, it is the native cocoa farms that suffer. It would be a mistake to suppose this attitude universal; on the contrary, all over Africa a great deal of solid, unobtrusive work toward bettering health and agriculture proceeds with full coöperation between white and black. Nevertheless—and this is what is disturbing—it is on the increase, and most in evidence not among backward peasants but among the more sophisticated and educated folk.

The reasons for this deterioration are in the main political and social. To take the second first: we do not always realize how much must be destroyed in order to rebuild, or how drastic that destruction must be to the human beings involved in it. The customary way of life of the African, that is, the life of the tribe, is incompatible with westernism. It must go, and in places is going quickly. The question is, what will replace it?

European administrators talk of "preserving what is best in the old" to blend with "what is best in the new." In other words, they want the best of both worlds for the African—a natural and human wish, but one never likely to be satisfied. You cannot change societies selectively, picking out the plums and throwing the rest away; the whole pudding must be remade. In deliberately destroying what was "bad" in tribalism the white man is breaking also most of what was "good." And the "good" includes discipline, loyalty, faith and the sense of community, of working together for common ends, which was one of tribalism's strongest features. The result is a generation which sometimes seems—these generalizations are of course by no means universally valid—all froth and no body, easily led, ignorant yet arrogant, undisciplined, above all self-seeking and unstable. In practical ways this means, with other things, that young men do not seem willing to put in the hard work needed to build a new country. You cannot open up a continent just with fine speeches and good engineers. People must work, and work very hard, and there is no evidence that Africans, in the mass, have realized this.

The great majority work not for settlers or mines or governments but for themselves, on their small and crudely farmed plots. The first and most urgent need of Africa is to raise the pitifully low productivity of these peasant holdings and to arrest a hastening decline of soil fertility which will, at the present rate, soon threaten the whole continent with starvation. In the past, tribal agriculture was inefficient, but it got by because there was plenty of land, and soil could be rested under bush for long periods and at frequent intervals. Epidemics kept cattle and human populations down to a level where the dry pastures and the soil could support them. Today, in most places there is not plenty of land, because populations are everywhere going up by leaps and bounds, thanks to medical services and to the grip of law and order. The most terrifying single fact about tropical Africa is that in most parts the population will, at the present rate of increase, double itself in 30 years. Where is double the food to come from, and more than double? This is a nightmare that keeps conscientious officials awake at night, and so far there has been no answer.

Part of the answer, at least, must be the greatly improved productivity of land already under cultivation. That it could produce far more, properly farmed, is undeniable. It boils down to the question of how to get the African to farm it properly without using the methods of coercion employed, for instance, by the Russians when faced with a similar problem among their own peasants, methods repudiated by the Western Powers.

On the face of it, persuasion would seem easy. If you put side by side two plots of cotton, one grown by ordinary native and the other by scientific methods, and if the yield from the scientific plot is four times higher than that from the native, almost any African, you might say, would see the point and follow the new methods, none of which is complicated or costly. But that does not happen. I have visited an experimental station where this has been done for 15 years, and Africans whose land marches with the station's, who can see the difference by looking over a fence, still follow the old ways. Superstition, suspicion and conservatism are formidable, and there is something else also, a factor to which the name "tropical inertia" has with good reason been given.

Some hold tropical inertia to be a matter of health and diet only: remove the debilitating diseases that ravage the African—in some places hookworm and malarial infestations reach almost 100 percent— and feed him on a properly balanced diet, and he would be as pushful and alert as the next man. No one questions that real improvements in the shockingly low standards of health in the tropics would make great differences, but doubts are growing as to whether this is the complete answer. There is also the climate to be reckoned with, the whole soft, enervating feel of the tropics. Nowhere in the world, perhaps, is it so easy to exist and so hard to excel. Readers of Toynbee will recall that of the 26 civilizations believed by him to have arisen in the world's history, not one has ever come into being within the tropics. And they will find the reason in his theory of "challenge and response." The challenge can be too tough, as in the Arctic, or too feeble, and that is Africa's case. It may be that no virile civilization is likely to form and thrive in lands without winters to stimulate hardihood and forethought (e.g. the storage of food).

This is a theory only, and history may disprove it; in the meantime, it is a fact that Africans on their own land do not work as men of other races do, and that much which is being done for them by benevolent governments, in the form of free social services and famine relief in bad seasons, weakens rather than sharpens the stimulus to labor. This matter was reduced to a set of telling figures at a small-holding experimental station in Kenya. The average cash income of the inhabitants of this region, derived from the sale of surplus produce, is 50 shillings a year. On the experimental plots, by the use of a few cheap and simple practices like rotations and manuring, yields were increased tenfold, and the cash income of families cultivating six-acre plots raised to 200 shillings yearly.

Continual propaganda is carried out to convince the surrounding people that, by following the methods suggested, they too could increase their income fourfold, greatly improve their diet and save their deteriorating land. Very few have responded. In the opinion of the officer in charge, the main reason is because, in order to enjoy the higher output, an eight-hour working day is needed; whereas "improvidence, laissez faire and indolence, combined with the general peasant tendency to enjoy life to the full and visit every burial, beer drink and market, reduce the average working day to five hours." And it was found recently on a group of East African sisal estates that the average working week was 23 hours. The day's task was normally completed by 11.30 A.M. and all inducements by way of bonuses to put in overtime rejected.

Many Europeans, sweating in the stifling heat of a tropical afternoon, wonder if, after all, the Africans are not wiser. Better to lie in the shade, idly gossiping at the market, than to strive in the sun for extra reward to go, perhaps, on a shirt, a pound of tea or a term's schooling for one of the children; better to go without than to sacrifice leisure. And, in valuing leisure, are not Africans chiming in with the modern trend in Europe and America toward shorter hours and less toil? Who are we to tell them to work harder when we make a principle of doing less ourselves?

Africans may be right so to value leisure, but that is not the way to open up a continent. No country ever has been developed save by the hard, unremitting and prolonged labors of the mass of its citizens, nor will it ever be; until this is known and acted on, many of the schemes being so hopefully canvassed will never reach maturity. Already a shortage of manpower holds up some projects and impairs the efficiency of others. It is the very low output, due to the irregularity and the inefficiency of labor, that creates the shortage, and the fact that many active men scarcely work at all, leaving most of the field labor to their wives, whose universal task it is, throughout tropical Africa, to raise the food crops, while the husband takes care of crops like palm-oil and cocoa which bring in money.

IV

Paradoxically, European rule has in some ways made the problem harder. In the past, men obeyed their chiefs and elders without argument. No young man, for instance, was normally allowed to drink liquor, and drunkenness among those below the status of elders was almost unknown. Now there are parts where drunkenness among young men is so common that it seriously interferes with production. The problem is not merely to make people work harder but to replace the dying discipline of the tribe with some new system of belief and order. It is a question of giving men an object to work for, a purpose in life.

This brings us to the last obstacle in the path of Africa's development: the political factor. The declared aim of British policy is to bring about self-government in the shortest possible time. These black lands are seen as the last inheritors of those principles of freedom which have created as independent nations Canada and India, Burma and Ceylon—last because they are, by all standards, the most backward, and because the European ferment has been at work in them only for some 50 years.

When this goal was proclaimed, the process of achieving self-government was seen as one of gradual evolution, allowing time to learn from experience and to build up a healthy economy and a sound, well-informed public opinion. Estimates of the time needed for this were shunned; but as it had taken Britain more than a thousand years to evolve her political and economic system, it was universally assumed that the pace would be a slow one. And a second important assumption was made. Education could not, for practical reasons, be provided immediately for all; the policy was to concentrate first on training the few, who would then become leaders of the many. So, with no little difficulty and struggle, a new élite was created out of primitive tribesmen: an élite educated in western fashion to be schoolmasters, doctors, lawyers, engineers, traders, clerks, civil servants—and politicians. The assumption was that this élite would remain, on the whole, loyal to the European connection and anxious to help raise the general level of their backward fellows: that from the white man's point of view they would be coöperators, not opponents.

The plan has gone wrong in two important ways. First, the time to be allowed for the period of political training has been drastically cut. People no longer think in centuries but in decades, or even in single years. African politicians, new-hatched and raw, repeatedly told that self-government is to be "pressed on with" at the quickest possible speed, naturally start to demand it not for their children but for themselves, here and now. And when white authority, a little taken aback, starts to point out some of the difficulties, the colonial politician immediately supposes that this is part of a subtle plot to postpone indefinitely the day of freedom, which for him is also the day of power.

And so the second assumption, that the élite will remain coöperators, is exploded too. A considerable number, cut off by education from their own society and background and yet not integrated into the European's, are turning sour and losing no chance to inject the venom of suspicion and race-hatred into the minds of their less sophisticated fellows. Since these young men are the natural leaders of the still ignorant and illiterate masses, looked up to almost as gods because they have in their hands the coveted magic of education, their powers to influence opinion, aided and abetted by the British tradition of free speech, are almost monopolistic.

The rising tempo of events has so hastened matters that political developments which might have been spread over a century have been crammed into the last three years. In that time Nigeria has had two new constitutions, each making long strides toward self-rule. Nigeria and the Gold Coast now have African majorities in the legislature. In the Gold Coast, political riots were followed by the promise of African ministers to preside over government departments and a policy of "Africanization" of the civil service which will quickly and drastically reduce the number of Englishmen in high places.

Some observers feel that too much is made of the difficulties of self-government in these raw countries. Having got so far, they urge, the best course is to press on to the conclusion, taking with faith and courage a leap in the dark that the good sense of the African will, in good time, justify. This may well be true; since retreat is impossible, a bold advance may be the wisest policy. Yet it is also true that history has much to say of the results of handing over to a small —a very small—minority of privileged persons (as the educated African is privileged above his peasant brother) all the powers of government before a fairly considerable body of citizens with critical judgment and independent views has been formed to keep them in check. While there is no reason to suppose that Negroes are less intelligent, given the same opportunities, than anyone else, there is equally no reason to suppose that they are far more virtuous. And only a community of angels could withstand the temptations which would lie in the path of a small native oligarchy, to whom power would be surrendered, in countries where the proportion of the even barely literate to the rest of the community is seldom higher than one in twenty. This is the road not to democracy but to tyranny.

And even if Africans were angels, they would still be unable, at the present time, to muster a sufficient body of trained and seasoned men to carry on the government, the technical services and the necessary development, and to steer a transitional society through the shoals and maelstroms of the modern world. They have not the unity, the resources, and above all the experience. Britain may be blamed for having done too little between the wars to produce them, but this does not alter the fact that an adequate corps of trained and able men is not there, and cannot be manufactured overnight. It takes 15 years to educate a person and at least another 15 to equip him with the experience needed in political leadership. And, meanwhile, a new factor has intervened. This is Communism, the refuge of the disgruntled, the restless and the ambitious.

There has probably been some exaggeration about the Communistic threat, but there is no doubt that contacts have been made with certain African political leaders. The truth probably is that Communists do not at present need to come into the open, being content to ally themselves with the various nationalist bodies which have sprung up everywhere to press for quicker political advances, and with the embryonic trades unions. Leadership of these bodies can then, by degrees, be gathered into Communist hands, following the well-tried and now almost universally applied technique of the Party.

In the Gold Coast, for instance, an African trained in London was sent out to take over the secretaryship of the largest political body there, the United Gold Coast Convention; and within a few months the first serious rioting took place since the pacification of the country. Another cheap and easy way for Communist influence to infiltrate is through African students sent to British universities, and there is no doubt that a deliberate attempt has been made to gather into the fold many of these young men. In presenting themselves as friends and allies in the struggle for freedom against British imperialism, Communists have cleverly linked themselves to the strongest political force in the colonies, the newly-awakened fervor of nationalism, no doubt with full confidence that they will be able to direct and control it for their own ends.

This, then, is the position: on the one hand the need and some of the potentialities for an economic forward drive, and on the other political and social factors which hold back, and may even frustrate, that advance. It is a pull devil, pull baker affair, and there is no man living who can say which way events will fall out.

v

The truth is that Britain in Africa is pursuing two opposite and contradictory aims. On the one hand is, as we have seen, the aim to develop, to open up and expand; on the other, to give political freedom to countries at present too immature, backward and unstable to use it wisely. The two aims are incompatible. The danger is that quick self-government will lead to chaos and perhaps Communist influence, and thence to the wiping out of economic gains, to the loss of invested capital and possibly even to the strategic encirclement of the west.

What is to be done? Abandon Africa or repudiate self-government? The first is impossible if the West wishes to survive. The second would entail breaches of faith, reproaches by foreign Powers, and colonial disturbances on a scale too great to be contemplated. Nor is the British public by any means convinced of the need. It holds to the comfortable hope that somehow or other Africa will survive her "growing pains" and learn to work self-government satisfactorily, that appeasement of the nationalists will lead to happier relations. Thus it seems most unlikely that any drastic change in British policy will occur.

Is there, then, no hope that the economic program will be carried through to success? To admit this would be to plunge too deep into defeatism. There is hope, but perhaps it is justified only if certain things are done, or not done, to overcome the social and political dangers.

The first is a slowing up in the tempo of political advance until time has allowed the emergence of more seasoned leaders and the development of a more alert public opinion, combined with a firmer tone throughout the British administration. If this is to come about, there must be sympathy and understanding from other non-Communist nations, above all from the United States. This understanding of the issues, it is fair to say, has not yet been in evidence. Americans who support any move to liquidate the "British imperialism," which has for so long been a bogey, need to realize that imperialism's heir is less likely to be a series of prosperous Negro democracies than the return of chaos, as for example in Burma, which plays straight into Communist hands.

A slowing down in the tempo of political advance is not, of course, in itself sufficient. It is a playing for time. Vigorous efforts are needed also to save the soil from destruction, to dispel the people's ignorance, to convince them of the truth of the ancient saying that God helps them who help themselves, to enlist their loyalty and enthusiasm in the task of building their own countries, and to restore on a new basis some of the discipline and community spirit that has perished.

Discussion of how all this might be done would need a book, and a Solomon to write it. One can say only that it must be done if hopes of economic advancement are not to beckon us, like an Irish traveller, ever deeper into the bog. "Except the Lord build the house, they labor in vain that build it." Today the identity of the Lord may be clouded but the words are as true as when they were written; and we have still our golden calves whose worship leads to perdition. We have still the human element to reckon with; and one of the crucial questions of our time, for ourselves no less than Africans, is whether, in this age of centralized bureaucracies, our rulers, no longer lords or bankers but great impersonal departments, have not, under mountains of protocol and paper, buried the human touch too deeply.

Note

THE BRITISH PROBLEM IN AFRICA
BY MARGERY PERHAM

July 1951

Among British Africanists, Margery Perham holds a place of special distinction. Eloquent in arguing for greater opportunity and responsibility for Africans, clear-eyed in seeing through the self-decep-
tions of her countrymen, she has undoubtedly had a real though
largely indirect influence on British policy. In this essay, written in
1951, one senses a drawing back in fear that the pace of evolution
may be getting out of hand, that all the British have worked to
achieve may collapse in chaos. Yet ironically, she vastly overestimates
the time remaining to Britain to impart that degree of competence
in affairs of state which she feels is necessary for self-government and
independence.

What is most interesting about this article, then, is that so sympathetic and informed an observer, writing less than ten years before
virtually the whole continent was emancipated, could take so gloomy
a view of the Africans' capacity for self-government. That her worst
fears have not been realized should not lead one to dismiss her estimate of the situation; other Congos are still possible and the severest
tests still lie ahead when the joys and satisfactions of independence
give way to the frustrations of creating modern states out of poor and
ill-educated clusters of tribal people. In view of the attention that
Miss Perham gives here to East Africa, it is worth noting that the
ugly Mau Mau rebellion broke out only shortly after this article was
published.

Miss Perham is Fellow in Imperial Government, Nuffield College,
Oxford, with which she has been associated for most of her life. Early
in her career she studied problems of race and colonial administration
in North America, Polynesia, Australia and the West Indies, but most
of her mature life has been devoted to Africa. Her major works in-

clude "Native Administration in Nigeria" (1937), "Africans and British Rule" (1941) and a two-volume biography of Lord Lugard, completed in 1960. (See also p. 114.) When the African Studies Association of the United Kingdom was formed in July 1963, Miss Perham was elected its president.

The British Problem in Africa

by MARGERY PERHAM

The Gold Coast elections of February 1951 have sent a shock right through Africa, or at least that Africa which lies south of the Sahara. To white men who have made their home in the African continent the shock has come as a perhaps only half-formulated question: "Is this the beginning of the end for us?" And every African who has heard the news—a number no one can exactly estimate—has felt a thrill of joy, and of the sudden, almost incredulous hope: "Is this the beginning for us?"

There can be no doubt that the first assumption of ministerial office by elected Negroes in a British colonial territory makes 1951 an important date in the political history of Africa and a very proper date at which to take stock. For this event in the middle of the century means that Britain is committed in act as well as in word to the speedy promotion of self-government in her African colonies. It is just 50 years, from the occupation of the interior, since British rule over these territories began; and it is not a very bold speculation to believe that they may become fully self-governing nation-states by the end of the century. It almost seems as though future African writers of history books may thus be able very neatly to sum up the first half of the twentieth century as the age of imperialism, and the second as the age of liberation.

When, however, our glance is extended from the Gold Coast to the rest of Africa, or even if it is confined to British territories, the possibility that African self-government will spread surely and smoothly appears much less certain. Developments in Asia, which may give cause for optimism to some who are anxiously looking for reasons for optimism in the stern conditions of the day, are not easily comparable with those of Africa. Even if they were, the great issues in Asia are far from being decided in favor of the West. The two great conflicts of our world—the political issue between the Communist and democratic nations, and the division of race or, less inaccurately, of color—are in danger of converging. At present, the Chinese excepted, the great majority of the colored races lie within the orbit of the Western democratic Powers. But in Africa this is because they are still under the political control of these Powers; and in much of Asia it is because they have just emerged from that control and are still linked to the West by many economic ties, and marked—who would confidently assert how deeply?—with the impress of Western civilization.

The task of helping to develop these peoples, and of holding them in partnership, is not the same in Asia as in Africa. In Asia, though the divisions which are called communal are deep and cut across the demands of national solidarity, there are nonetheless great areas of cultural and religious unity, and of common pride based upon the inheritance of ancient civilizations. These peoples have brought their historic cultures through centuries of subjection to Western influence with their deepest elements still inviolate and they are resolved to reassert the validity of their cultures in the modern world. The special offer of the West must therefore be the possibility of a free association of differing cultures, instead of the crushing monolithic system offered by Communism. The meeting of the West with Asia, for all the present disparity of material power, will have to be between equals in status. It will have the nature of alliance rather than assimilation.

The dealings between tropical Africa and the West must be different. Here in place of the large unities of Asia was the multicellular tissue of tribalism: instead of an ancient civilization, the largest area of primitive poverty enduring into the modern age. Until the very recent penetration by Europe the greater part of the continent was without the wheel, the plough or the transport-animal; almost without stone houses or clothes, except for skins; without writing and so without history. Mentally as well as physically the Africans were helpless before a European intrusion all the more speedy and overwhelming because it came at a time when science had given Europe such immense material power. Yet the African peoples on the whole, as slavery proved, are tenacious and adaptable. The revolutionary changes which Europe has imposed upon tropical Africa within 50 years have evoked from them a positive and vigorous reaction which was lacking in some Amerindian and Pacific races. Yet it remains true that in losing their thousandfold tribal past Africans must grow into the general shape of the civilization which has been brought to them, whatever color they may in time give it from their own character and physical setting. Thus, for the next half-century or so, the relationship between the West and Negro Africa must be assimilative in the broadest sense.

If the West is to win and to hold Africa, the effort needed is thus different from that needed in Asia. But it is no less great. As in Asia, it will be a race with time. The process of enfranchisement from European control has been so hastened by a combination of forcing influences that these least-civilized peoples are likely to have the shortest period of tutelage. They may therefore break prematurely out of a recently imposed framework of unity and order into conditions of chaos or stagnation. If the primitive poverty of this vast area is to be raised there has to be massive application of capital accumulated through the energy and restraint of other peoples; managerial skill will be needed on a vast scale, with large numbers of experts discovering the lessons of science and applying them in campaigns for the betterment of life—human, animal and vegetable—and of the earth which carries this life.

If plans devised in London, Washington and other centers are not to be put through with coercive direction, but are to win the intelligent coöperation of Africans, each must be accompanied by sociological study and patient educational effort. The trained Africans now ready to play any but a subordinate part in these great schemes of betterment are to be numbered in hundreds rather than thousands. Even fewer have the wide knowledge which allows them to recognize their need of European planners, still less to play a part in drawing up the plans. While Africans outgrow the suspicions produced by sheer ignorance, a new political suspicion takes their place and this can be overcome only by political measures aimed at producing a common will between Africans and Europeans.

II

The main political question that we must answer, as we try to look into Africa's next 50 years, is whether the promise of political emancipation which Britain has made on the west coast can be fulfilled and then extended to her eastern and central colonies. The answer will depend largely upon the assessment of the strength of the influences which have prompted this policy of political emancipation. The first is to be found in the character of Britain's parliamentary institutions. By their very nature they could not be confined within her borders and were carried overseas by her own emigrants. The evolution of the white Dominions followed, and their institutions were extended, with hesitation and difficulty, to Asia, and with even more hesitation to Africa. But this does not account for the sudden advance in Africa, during the last ten years, toward an end which, with much justification, was thought to be very distant.

The reason for this acceleration, which has come as a surprise to many people even in Britain, is to be found in a convergence of many different factors just before, during and after the Second World War. Among them was the natural maturing, especially in west Africa, of an educational system which by the thirties had begun to turn out graduates with the training and confidence to occupy responsible positions, and the ability to define and voice their political discontents. The town dwellers and wage earners increased in numbers, and since they were detached from their tribal systems, they became increasingly responsive to the new leaders. Then as the British Labor Party grew in strength it encouraged, by the force of example, the new proletarians who were beginning to develop political consciousness and to call themselves "underprivileged;" and it encouraged them directly by giving a new urgency and completeness to the promise of self-government. At the same time the uncompromising doctrines of Communism which damn imperialism and capitalism and exalt the "toiling masses" began to influence Africans, even though they did not consciously accept the doctrines or even identify them. A further factor which speeded up the process in the years before the Second World War was the effect of the demand of the Germans for the retrocession of their former colonies, since it forced Britain to emphasize the contrast between her own program for colonial freedom and the doctrine of racial supremacy put forward by the Herrenvolk.

When the war brought a period of extreme danger for Britain, strenuous economic and military services had to be asked from the colonial peoples, upon a basis of willing coöperation. And with the coming of peace, Britain's relatively greater weakness in the world subtly altered her position as a ruler of colonial peoples. Thus the heat of war forced the growth of self-government; and the favorable temperature was kept after the war by pressure from the United Nations in general, and, from their very different points in the political compass, from Russia and the United States in particular. The colonial peoples had behaved with great steadiness and loyalty, and they expected to be rewarded. Their leaders were few in numbers, but they were quick to take advantage of the relaxation of the imperial grasp which had allowed the liberation of India, Ceylon and Burma. Moreover, new and flamboyant leaders emerged. The social and economic life of the colonies had been deeply shaken by five years of war, and, especially in west Africa and the West Indies, Negroes eagerly absorbed those millennial hopes which are born so strangely out of ruinous conflicts. Instinctively seeking to exploit the unifying forces of discontent and of indignation generated by an almost universal inferiority of status of their race, the leaders directed the restlessness of their followers against their foreign rulers. Under the protection of the old British civil liberties, a large part of the immature native press, especially in west Africa, treated every act of the Government, good, bad or indifferent, with unvarying but highly spiced denunciation.

With one of those rapid assessments of a critical situation of which they are capable after a long blind period, the British quickly decided that, since it had become morally impossible for them to answer this agitation by repressive force, there was no alternative to ungrudging and immediate cession of what had so long been promised. Hence the open-handed gestures in Asia were followed by the large installments of freedom in the West Indies and Africa. In these regions Britain revised almost every constitution between 1944 and 1950, some of them more than once, to introduce or increase native participation in the central colonial governments. Many other measures in the interests of the native people were introduced in the spheres of local government, finance, economics and social services. The recent events in the Gold Coast, the most politically-advanced African territory, by which Africans have drawn up their own constitution, carried out a general election, and put an imprisoned leader and his extreme party in power, are only the most striking results of this policy.

III

If this is the policy, and these the pressures which have produced it, this would seem the line upon which Britain must go forward. But when the situation in all of Africa south of the Sahara is considered, certain factors appear which are not merely unfavorable to the rapid development of African self-government but even hostile to it. The British Commonwealth countries in this vast area fall into three parts: the territory in the west, South Africa, and the eastern and central territories. It is not difficult to describe South Africa's place in the political picture, as that country is now and as it apparently intends to be in the future. The Union of South Africa is a stratified society. A minority of 2,500,000 white men are absolutely dominant—politically, economically and socially—over some 8,500,000 Africans and the smaller Indian and colored communities. No one can judge the policy of the white group who does not try to enter into the tragic dilemma in which their history has placed them. They feel themselves obliged to defend their domination by principles of racial superiority which are an absolute denial of those upon which Britain is acting in her tropical colonies. The Gold Coast election has brought this contradiction into dramatic conflict, and it is not surprising that the fiercest denunciation of the Gold Coast experiment has come from Dr. Malan, the Nationalist Prime Minister of the Union. If other native territories followed this example, he said, "it meant nothing less than the expulsion of white men from practically everywhere between the Union and the Sahara." What that would mean was not a matter for conjecture. However, he comforted himself with the assertion that the experiment would undoubtedly fail, since a wrong application of the principle of democracy had made it ridiculous.

Dr. Malan was prompted by the very understandable fear that hangs over white South Africa. Even so, he was only putting into extreme terms the doubts about the Gold Coast election, and the promise of an immediate similar experiment in nearby Nigeria, which have been widespread among the white colonists in Africa. Even in England this advance is thought by many to be a leap in the dark. The fact is that the west of Africa, and the south, are moving in opposite directions. Even a partial failure on the west coast will strengthen the determination of the Union to follow its own system, and will deepen the uncertainty that hangs over the large British block of colonies to the east.

These fears about the Gold Coast experiment (which are Dr. Malan's hopes) are not groundless. There is no precedent for the sudden grant of the parliamentary franchise to a large, illiterate, tribal population, utterly remote from the political experience of the Western peoples. It is unnecessary to list all the contrasts between the development, setting and character of the British parliamentary system and the conditions in the arbitrarily demarcated region of Africa into which it has been exported. A perilously small fraction of the African people have any knowledge of the arts or sciences by which the modern welfare state they demand is conducted. With an electorate at once so ignorant, so expectant and so racially sensitive, and with none of the conditions present for the development of a party system, the invitation to demagogy seems certain to be accepted. It remains to be seen whether the restraining advice of the colonial government, the powers which it has reserved, and the long-established substructure of local government based upon tribal organization, will succeed in containing the full tide of this very new democracy. No hope of easy achievement should be cherished. But it is now in the interests of Britain, as well as of the peoples of these territories, to exert every effort to make the experiment succeed. The direct results of failure would fall first upon the inhabitants who are entirely African, but the results of a breakdown would also discourage and anger the Negro peoples throughout the world. It would harden the caste system of the Union of South Africa and would deeply influence the still undecided future of east and central Africa.

Because of the emigration of European and Indian colonists to east and central Africa, and the strains set up by the competition for power among these groups and between them and the native majorities, the situation here is even more sensitive. The tension runs from one territory to the other, affecting even those areas which have no immigrant groups. And it goes down from them to the Union, and then overseas to excite the interest and support of the nations from which the emigrants came. The conflict of power represents in microcosm, in one of its most intractable forms, the world tensions between white and brown, and white and black. The situations vary in the several territories and it may be useful to remind ourselves of the racial distribution in the countries which lie southward from Ethiopia.

To understand the full meaning of these figures it should be remembered that the Union of South Africa is a completely independent Dominion, and that Southern Rhodesia has full, responsible self-government, subject to some formal reservations by Britain over native matters which in practice are never used. All the other territories are administered directly by Britain, though Tanganyika is under United Nations Trusteeship. The penetration of the temperate highlands of these tropical dependencies by white colonists is not the only point of contrast between them and west Africa.

RACIAL POPULATIONS IN EAST AND SOUTH AFRICA

	Africans	Europeans	Indians & Pakistanis[2]	Arabs	Colored
Union of So. Africa[1]	8,347,000	2,620,000	323,000		1,030,000
Basutoland	540,000	1,700	340		547
Bechuanaland	290,000	2,300			1,700
Swaziland	181,000	3,200			
Southern Rhodesia	1,960,000	129,000			
Northern Rhodesia	1,849,000	36,000			
Nyasaland	2,455,000	3,800	5,250		2,000
Tanganyika	7,332,539	10,648	46,254	11,074	1,335
Uganda	4,914,211	3,448	35,215	1,475	643
Kenya	5,218,232	29,660	97,687	24,174	964

[1] These figures exclude South-West Africa which according to the 1946 census had 259,000 Africans, 10,500 Bushmen, 38,000 Europeans, 44,500 Colored.

[2] These figures include a small number of other Asians.

Most of the peoples of eastern Africa were far less advanced in their political organization and in their culture, and were much more sparsely distributed. The chief exception was the fertile and populous region around Lake Victoria, with its large chieftainships. An additional contrast, which still further explains the relative political immaturity of the eastern Africans, is their much later contact with Europeans, and indeed with the outside world. Uganda, which contains the advanced and prosperous kingdom of Buganda, is free from white settlement, but it is closely bound to Kenya through which run its communications to the sea, and its peoples watch the white colony there with deep anxiety.

Individually and as a group, these territories confront Britain with difficult decisions. Here the principles of democracy do not fit the situation: numerically insignificant white minorities have built up the Western economies which are in operation; and they have been the dominant element politically as well. The African tribes have hitherto shown little sense of solidarity, and little interest in public affairs. Only in the last few years has there been much sign of political vitality, and that has been confined to some of the more advanced tribes, such as the Ganda in Uganda, the Kikuyu in Kenya and the Chagga in Tanganyika. In Northern Rhodesia the copper belt has attracted a mixed and restless African proletariat which is beginning to organize itself effectively in defense of its interests. The Indians are in the main confined to the towns: they are traders, large and small, and they own much of the urban property in the main cities. They are resentful of their inferior political status in Kenya, where they have smaller political representation than the Europeans, though they are more numerous. The present split between Hindu and Moslem, reflected from their homelands, has divided their leadership.

What kind of constitution should Britain try to fit upon this patchwork of races? Partition within mixed territories, the current treatment for the irreconcilables, is ruled out. Although there are large tribal areas, the Europeans and Africans outside them are interlocked in a capital-labor, master-servant relationship, while the Indian occupies an uneasy intermediate commercial position. If there were no white settlement Britain would, as in west Africa, concentrate without doubts or distractions upon the all-round development of the Africans. As it is, she faces a problem only less sharp and embittered than that of South Africa. For more than a century in South Africa she was involved in a painful attempt to regulate the seemingly irreconcilable clash between white colonist and native African; it has left the three High Commission Territories embarrassingly upon her hands. History has shown how difficult it is for a relatively detached imperial government to mediate between its own people and the weaker groups which they have subjected. The United States experienced this difficulty in a special form when it found that victory in a bloody civil war did not enable the Federal Government to enforce its principles of justice and equality fully upon the Southern States. Britain's attempt at enforcement in South Africa lasted a century and may be said to have failed. Since the establishment of the Union, and still more since the Afrikaner Nationalists gained power, she has seen the vestiges of her equalitarian policy rooted out one by one until African subordination has been made complete.

The same problem has now presented itself in Kenya and the Rhodesias, though in less advanced form. Kenya may be chosen to illustrate the apparent insolubility of the constitutional question. The immediate introduction there of full parliamentary democracy would put control into the hands of some 5,000,000 Africans, of whom not 1 percent have any knowledge of the working of the modern state or the economy which has been built up over their heads. It would also put them in control of those small groups—British officials, white settlers and Indian traders—who are politically and economically the dominant and dynamic elements in the colony. A few people are led by humanitarian emotion or political doctrines to advocate this as an immediate policy, but even those most confident of the necessity of the new steps in the Gold Coast cannot show that Kenya is at present in a comparable position. Even if it held no immigrant groups Kenya would not be ready for such a policy. African unity and experience would have to grow very much stronger before the Kenya settlers would be ready to relinquish the position they have secured, and the imperial government willing to coerce them and to imperil such a vital strategic area.

With so much to lose it is not surprising that most of the white settlers agree with the South African Government that the racial situation permits no middle course: that if they grant something, they grant everything. This seems the logical short-term answer; it is also the shortsighted one. The humane and long-term answer is surely that to treat people, whose potential equality has been proved in so many individual instances, as something less than men is to demoralize both those who give and those who suffer this treatment, and to harden society so that it cannot grow and must some day break. The alternative course seems to be to continue in the face of all fears and doubts with the present slow and difficult British policy of obliging the impatient white colonists to mark time politically, while actively assisting the advance of the uncivilized race and making gradual adjustments to accommodate its advance.

IV

But there is some choice of political direction as well as of pace. The British constitution, with its concentration of sovereignty in one of its legislative chambers, a system developed gradually by one of the most united and mature nations in the world, is obviously unsuited to east Africa. Nor does it seem likely that any superficial adaptations of this system, for example by way of communal voting with racial allotment of seats, will do anything but exacerbate political conflict. The aim should be to distribute rather than to concentrate power. This method runs counter to modern tendencies, but its value in absorbing racial shocks and in widening political education outweighs its easily enumerated defects. The aim might be carried out through a somewhat rigid federal structure for the whole of east Africa, with extensive powers resting in large provinces. Their boundaries should be drawn to attain the utmost possible homogeneity, but even so some of their councils would contain representatives of all races, and they would thus allow coöperation at a level where the major political fears need not haunt the proceedings. At the center there could be a distribution of many social and economic functions to temporary or standing boards. The practical character of their work would be realistic and unifying, while the relative privacy of their proceedings would discourage any playing to the racial gallery. In a government for eastern Africa constructed upon this pattern, with the rights of minorities and the powers of provinces within the federal structure guaranteed by the imperial government, it might be possible for the several races to learn to modify their fears of each other, and thus valuable time for the experience of coöperation might be gained.

This result will not be obtained easily. In Kenya, above all, dissensions have been sharp for 30 years, and political attitudes have crystallized. But there are encouraging signs even there, for some Europeans have faced the hard truth that though they built their original privileged position upon African weakness and inferiority, such a foundation is not immutable and preliminary steps must be taken now for its gradual reconstruction. This explains why at least some of the settlers have accepted African and Indian representation in the quasi-federal East African High Commission and in the Kenya legislature, and have even also embarked upon some experiments in interracial social contact. All of this would be impossible in South Africa.

The racial situation in central Africa takes a somewhat different form. There is no Indian population of any importance, and in the Rhodesias the whites are less overwhelmingly outnumbered by the Africans than in the three northern territories. Southern Rhodesia, advancing at breakneck speed today through white immigration and industrial development, is almost a Dominion. Northern Rhodesia, with little more than 1,000,000 Africans, is dominated politically by the white settlers. The copper mines govern the economy of the country. Nyasaland, small and isolated, is a mainly African territory, but is bound by economic ties to the Rhodesias.

There have been many years of vacillation about the relationship of these three territories. In recent years, following a measure of coöperation through a central council, the Europeans of the two Rhodesias have drawn more closely together and demanded some form of federation. The Gold Coast election has now startled them into angry alignment like the crack of a whip. "The feeling is growing among the European community," declared Mr. Welensky, leader of the Northern Rhodesian colonials, commenting on the election, "that the Government of the United Kingdom is not going to judge self-government for the colonies on the ability of the people to govern themselves: the whole thing will be a matter of political expediency. To the British Socialist Government, the ills of the colonies are dispelled by the provision of the ballot box and a trade union. This is a travesty of development." The Prime Minister of Southern Rhodesia has said with equal bluntness that sticking to mere numbers in a constitution might turn democracy to mob-rule in Africa.

However, while the leaders condemn Britain in these terms they also dissociate themselves from the racial policy of South Africa. They claim to be following a middle way between Britain's dangerous surrender to an unready majority and the Union's policy of repression. Britain's reason for refusing hitherto to permit amalgamation of the central African territories has been that the native policy which she has followed in the two northern Colonial Office territories is not compatible with the less liberal system of Southern Rhodesia. Native opinion, just beginning to express itself through a few voices, emphatically endorses this view. Southern Rhodesia hangs unhappily between the Colonial Office territories on the north and the Union on the south. Devotedly British in their allegiance, the white colonists recoil from the increasingly assertive Afrikaner nationalism of the Union. Yet, when they look north, they are repelled, and indeed alarmed, by the native policy Britain is following. At this moment, the delicate problem of their future affiliation has just been discussed in a private official conference which has endeavored to find some form of closer union which will square all the circles presented by race and politics. If Southern Rhodesia could be attached to the northern colonies without Britain's paying too high a price in concessions at the expense of the African, then a boundary might be drawn along the Zambesi against the northward advance of the Union policy.

v

In all these African issues, west, east and central, Britain is obliged to play a leading part as ruler or arbiter. She cannot simply sit back and allow matters to take their course: the forces generated by European intrusion into primitive Africa are too disturbing to be left to work themselves out. Yet, though Britain must play the leading part, and must, if she is true to her principles and professions, take up the Union's challenge with growing boldness, she is not, of course, the only influence even in tropical Africa. Great regions are under Portuguese, Belgian and French rule. But in the development of African self-government, Britain is without doubt the formative influence. Portugal and Belgium have, so far with success, sealed their territories against "unsettling" ideas. France is deeply engaged in inducing her colonies to fulfill their political ambitions as parts of a great French Union, rather than as autonomous nations. None of these Powers regards British policy with a friendly eye. Britain must reckon also upon the increasing intervention in Africa by America and the United Nations. The relations of each colony are no longer limited to contacts between it and the imperial ruler: many influences are at work to draw Africa together physically and mentally, to link its peoples to the world and to awaken them to the world's growing concern about their affairs. International intervention, which has pushed through plans for the speedy independence of Libya and Somaliland, and which plays chiefly but not exclusively upon the Trust Territories, quickens the political pace by reinforcing colonial nationalism.

Africa is indeed becoming part of the world. This vast raw continent which lies so close to Europe has, apart from that northern strip which has for so long been the southern fringe of Europe, been locked away from the influences of civilization. It is now fast being drawn strategically and economically into the Western sphere. Tropical Africa was at first little more to the Western nations than a coast line; then it became a hunting ground for slaves; next, it was parcelled up as the property of Western nations and its people regarded primarily as their supply of labor. And now the West has new and urgent economic and strategic claims upon the continent. In other words, Africa and Africans have been the instruments of other nations. Now, as a result of the civilizing influences brought consciously and unconsciously by the West, Africans are at last demanding the right to state and to follow their own purposes. The difficulties before them, mainly inherent in the physical conditions of the continent and in their own history, or lack of it, are immense. And the West faces equal difficulties in trying to find a way of harmonizing its own interests with those of this awakening Africa. The seeds have been sown for a racial conflict that will weaken, if it does not ruin, the attempt to develop the people and their continent at the speed which the impatience of Africans and the world situation demand. The West has the desire, the science, the energy and the capital to develop Africa. Africa has a desperate need of all these things. The question is whether Africans will be able to accept them. Their poverty and weakness allowed (it might almost be said to have necessitated) a subjection so complete that when Africans became aware at last of their history and position in the world, the discovery created a deep bitterness. It finds its natural object in the colonial Powers which have brought Africa at once subjection and civilization.

The civilization is, however, in its very earliest stage, and it is impossible to foretell whether, Africa being what it is, the process could be carried on if that subjection were suddenly brought to an end. The white colonists say "no." But they are deeply interested parties, and the Africans and their supporters reject and resent their opinion just because it is theirs. The very fact of the presence of these white settlers, above all in the form which it takes in South Africa, makes it difficult for many Africans to consider reasonably any proposition about their future relations with the white man. The British policy of a gradual transfer of powers, so logical and defensible as the compromise between two extremes, thus runs against the opposition of black and white in Africa. It is too quick for the whites; it is too slow for the Gold Coast Africans today and will be too slow for those of Kenya tomorrow. Yet, since there is no alternative to this policy, Britain will be obliged to continue with it, and she must not despair if only a fraction of success is achieved. For the stakes are very high. Analogy between peoples and individuals can be misleading, but both do seem to have this in common, that their characteristics are formed very early in their development. The Western nations have grave reason to know what the Romans' failure to impose their civilization over the whole of Europe has meant to that continent: within the next 50 years, or even less, it may be decided whether Negro Africa will be won or lost to the religion and society of the West.

Note

THE NEW AFRICAN PROFILE
BY CHIEF H. O. DAVIES

January 1962

"The truth is," James Baldwin has written, "that there is something unutterably painful about the end of oppression—not that it *has* ended yet, on a black-white basis, I mean, but it *is* ending—and one flinches from the responsibility, which we all now face, of judging black people solely as people."

Understandably, it has been easier for the African to blame the colonialists than to examine his own failures and limitations. There are signs that this is changing, but the following article is one of the earliest examples of critical analysis of Africans by an African who is not a political refugee, but an active participant in the building of his native country—in this case, Nigeria, which has done better than most in preserving democratic institutions.

The central question to which this essay is relevant is how to achieve a workable and satisfying synthesis of Western values and African traditions, of Western political institutions and tribal customs—a synthesis which preserves the essential rights of individuals while recognizing that "democracy" has never had a chance to evolve in Africa but was imposed by men who did not always honor its tenets. This synthesis is being sought in an environment rife with tensions between those who glorify whatever is indigenously African and those who believe that modernity can be achieved only by destroying African custom and tradition; between those who romanticize the African past and those who see it only as a cause for shame; between those who have become so Westernized that they have lost touch with their people and those who belligerently defend tradition for its own sake; between those who want to adopt only the technology of the West, leaving all the rest, and those who believe they will have failed if their governments are not perfect replicas of those in London, Paris or Washington; between those who feel that Africans are incapable of making democracy work and those who take this view to be a mortal insult.

What is particularly poignant is that these conflicts—oversimplified and perhaps exaggerated as they are presented above—exist not only between groups and individuals, but within them. Thus they are in a constant state of tension. The wonder is that with all these stresses, with a history that is so short on recorded achievement and so long on humiliation, the African generally acquits himself with so much dignity.

Chief Hezekiah Oladipo Davies, Q.C., was—next to Dr. Nnamdi Azikiwe—the best-known Nigerian nationalist during the decade of the forties. Kwame Nkrumah was one of his lieutenants in the West African Students' Union, of which Davies was a principal founder in London. He was educated at King's College, Lagos, and the London School of Economics, where he graduated in 1936 with a degree in Commerce. He later studied law and was admitted to the bar in 1946. In the forties he was Secretary-General of the Nigerian Youth Movement and founder of *The Daily Service*, the official organ of the movement and subsequently the newspaper of the Action Party in Western Nigeria. He helped to defend Jomo Kenyatta in 1952, and was made Queen's Counsel in 1958. While a fellow at Harvard's Center for International Affairs in 1958–59, he wrote "Nigeria: The Prospects for Democracy."

The New African Profile

by CHIEF H. O. DAVIES

The revolutionary transformation of the African continent from a congeries of passive, dependent territories into an association of active, sovereign states attained its climax in 1960. At the end of 1959, there were only nine independent states on the continent; a year later there were 27. Even without the additions that occurred during 1961, sovereign states became the majority on the African continent as against a minority of colonial or quasi-colonial territories. The revolution of African independence had become an objective fact.

After a year, the question may be asked: How are these new states faring in their independence? How are their constitutions working out in relation to the needs and aspirations of their people? What is the pattern, if any, of the constitutional system which is evolving and what is the shape of the African profile that is emerging? A comprehensive answer to these questions would require a review not only of the political activities of the new states, but also of what they are doing in economic, social, cultural and spiritual realms. Although this obviously cannot be undertaken here, we may find a partial answer by examining some of the problems, contradictions and inconsistencies bequeathed to us by colonial rule, or created by independence itself, and the manner in which they are being solved or reconciled.

Perhaps the most fundamental problem that has confronted the newly independent states is the difficult task of fitting their people to the alien constitutions which have been adopted. The colonial powers have greatly influenced the former colonies in the making of their constitutions. The educated élite in the colonial territory and the representatives of the metropolitan country who negotiated and drafted the constitutions had both been bred in the climate of the metropolitan constitution and were *ad idem* in the belief that a carbon copy of that constitution was all that was required. Little did

147

they realize that their outlook on life generally was completely foreign to that of the ordinary citizens of the colony. In the end, the constitutions that were made were not only alien to the nature and needs of the ordinary citizens of the new states, they were so advanced and complicated as to be completely misunderstood. The net result is that, in the absence of constitutions suitable for the people, the people have to be suited to their new constitutions. This arduous process is still going on.

In the British territories, for example, after some 30 years of colonial rule, only a handful of Africans had exercised the vote and this was restricted to people with specified incomes in a few important towns. The masses lived more or less the old traditional life of uncritical obedience to their chiefs and to the expatriate administrative officers, for the system of indirect rule perpetuated the old method of government by limited leadership. The Obas, Emirs, Asantehene, chiefs and district heads were the leaders of the people and commanded their unflinching loyalty. Contrary to the misconception of the uninformed critics, these leaders were not autocrats ruling by whim and caprice. They had their councils of distinguished chiefs and elders with whom they discussed issues and constantly consulted. The authority of the leaders devolved on a hierarchy of lesser rulers from the national level to the remotest village. Every ruler, great or small, was advised by his own council which gave him its loyalty. Both the leader and the council members were selected either on hereditary qualifications or on the merit of their past performance in the community.

With the coming of self-government, however, the alien system of parliamentary democracy, as practiced in the metropolitan country, was introduced, as it were, overnight. In the English-speaking states, party politics, electioneering campaigns, universal adult suffrage, secret ballot, parliament, ministries, the cabinet, the Speaker and the Opposition all sprang into existence as if by the magician's wand. The obvious underlying assumption was that a constitution which was good for Britain, and the facsimile of which had kept the United States, Canada, Australia and New Zealand together, must be good enough for everybody else. It was assumed that the greatness achieved by the colonial power had been due to the constitution under which it was governed and that the colonial peoples must submit to complete transformation if they wished to attain greatness.

Elsewhere, the constitution followed the French Presidential system. Chieftaincy, on the whole, had suffered a decline in the French-speaking territories, for there the colonial rulers believed in "direct" rule and paid relatively little attention to African political tradition. To this extent, the impact of an imposed alien constitution, introduced suddenly upon the attainment of self-government, was somewhat moderated.

Generally speaking, however, these facsimile constitutions have not been a tremendous success anywhere. The ordinary people do not understand party politics, except as a call to war against the members of the rival parties. The martial spirit in the people, which had become moribund or latent with the abolition of the slave trade and the stoppage of raiding expeditions, seems to be suddenly aroused by the coming of party politics. The truth about human nature is that adventure and war are more exciting and therefore more welcome than a life of drudgery and peaceful inactivity. The stimulus of a new world to conquer has throughout the ages evoked enthusiastic response. The unsophisticated citizens of the new African states mistake party slogans for a clarion call to war and they go into it with zest. The result is that the people who enjoyed peace and unity during the colonial days are now divided into political warring camps, sniping at each other and sometimes engaging in violent encounter.

The alien system of government by party politics opened new vistas of wealth and power to a people who had literally been starved of them. Everybody who could, therefore, has sallied forth along the road to political and plutocratic eminence. Those who found themselves in power have used every stratagem to keep themselves there, while for those in the minority no weapon has been too mean to employ in an effort to encompass the downfall of the government and to attain power. In Ghana and in some parts of Nigeria, supporters of rival political parties are constantly in conflict, beating each other up and wounding and sometimes killing. Nigerian national newspapers are regularly full of stories of partisan clashes which often result in casualties.

It is a source of constant complaint in Nigeria that the customary courts and Tax Assessment Committees which have been established in the Regions are manned wholly by members and supporters of the government party and that they use their position to victimize their opponents, imposing upon them arbitrary and excessive tax assessments. In default of payment, the victims face prosecution and imprisonment without just cause.

One would like to be able to say that these tactics are a passing phase and that, as political education and experience spread, normal relations will soon be established. Unfortunately, the politicians show no interest in encouraging such political education as might enable their supporters to overcome prejudices which so far have operated to their own advantage.

A careful analysis of party politics suggests that the evil is probably in the method of choosing the people's representatives. Under the indigenous African political system, the most common criterion in the selection of the leader or chief is heredity. However inequitable that method may be, it at least makes for stability. Once the leader is chosen, he functions for the whole of his life, subject to good behavior, and he therefore has no cause to curry favor with his fellow citizens. Any dispute about succession that may arise is narrowed down to which of rival candidates is the most entitled, and this is an issue of status. Once that is settled and the leader accepted, that is the end of the matter. Until he dies or is removed by higher powers, he continues to function without the fear of being defeated at the next election.

The system of parliamentary democracy, on the other hand, rests on the unproven theory that every citizen or taxpayer has a right to be represented and that he should exercise that right by direct vote for the candidate of his choice. No prerequisite qualification of behavior, ability or performance is demanded of the parliamentary candidate and everybody, literally speaking, is entitled to put himself forward. In an unenlightened community, it thus becomes expedient, if not legitimate, for any aspirant, conscious of his limitations and the electorate's lack of judgment, to use all methods available to get himself into office. Thus the two-party system of election lends itself to bribery and corruption on a large scale, and encourages hooliganism, and the invocation of tribal, racial and religious prejudices. These stratagems are indulged in by political parties and their candidates notwithstanding the written law which forbids them. And since elections are periodic, those who get into power want to stay in power; they resort to the use of patronage and nepotism in favor of their supporters and to creating an atmosphere of frustration around those who do not give them their support.

On the use of violence in furtherance of party interests in Ghana, Kwame Nkrumah wrote: "A campaign of violence developed in

Ashanti where the situation became so desperate that hundreds of Ashanti C.P.P. men and women were forced to leave their homes and to seek refuge in other parts of the country." [1] In Nigeria, similar charges have been constantly made by various political parties about the plight of their members and supporters in the Regions where they are in the minority. The parties in power were accused of using such strong-arm methods against members of the Opposition that several of them were forced to leave their Regions and find temporary refuge elsewhere.

In this "War of the Roses," the party in power, having all the organs of government at its disposal, has almost invariably come out victorious. It is a matter for serious doubt whether any party in power in any African state can ever be defeated in subsequent elections. In the older states like Liberia or Ethiopia, the governments of President Tubman and Emperor Haile Selassie seem to run on incessantly. In Ghana, the methods used by Dr. Nkrumah and his party, the C.P.P., to liquidate the Opposition were a ruthless and arbitrary exercise of powers by a government which had overwhelming support. The excuse that the Opposition were resorting to methods unfavorable to unity seems very poor justification for arresting and imprisoning members of the Opposition, without trial, under the Preventive Detention Act. In Sierra Leone, which attained independence in April 1961, the members of a minority opposition party, the African Peoples Party, were rounded up and locked in jail during the independence celebrations in order that they might not wreck the ceremonies, as they were alleged to have threatened to do.

Broadly speaking, the African parliamentarian does not understand the meaning or function of the Opposition. He believes that once a leader has been elected, he is in for good and everybody must accept his leadership. He tends to regard the opposition member as a saboteur who should be hounded out of the political arena. The only place throughout West Africa where the Opposition appears to be happily accommodated is in the Federal Parliament of Nigeria. This is due, in large measure, to the federal character of the legislature. But the personality of the Federal Prime Minister, Alhaji Sir Abubakar Tafawa Balewa, a thoroughbred democrat, and the willingness of the people to accept compromise, both make a significant contribution. All things taken into consideration, however, the emergent

---

[1] "Ghana: The Autobiography of Kwame Nkrumah." New York: Thomas Nelson & Sons, 1957, p. 216.

profile of the African politician appears to be that of the leader who has no use and no sympathy for the Opposition.

Another serious defect of the two-party system, as it is applied in Africa, is its wastefulness in human and material resources. Owing to party antagonism, a government in power is never inclined to rely upon the administrative or technical skill of members or supporters of any rival party. In most places, the applicant for a government post is disqualified immediately if he belongs to or sympathizes with a rival party. Thus one sees the paradox of a country which suffers from want of managerial and technological skill, and which has embarked upon ambitious plans for development, excluding qualified citizens from service simply because they belong to a different political party.

The practice of parliamentary democracy itself is terribly expensive, especially under a federal system. Nigeria, for example, has eight legislative houses, which are likely soon to be increased to ten. She has one Governor-General and three governors; one Prime Minister and three Premiers; over 100 ministers, about the same number of junior ministers; and myriad legislators. The expense of supporting the formidable array of institutions and instrumentalities which are called into active play is enormous and it is doubtful whether Nigeria, with its comparatively slender means, can shoulder the burden for long. Each government, regional as well as federal, slavishly imitates the structure and forms of parliamentary practice of the metropolitan country. The result is that the citizens of Nigeria, who number less than the population of the United Kingdom, are called upon to pay four times as much for their administration as the British people. This is a crippling burden that threatens to overwhelm a young state.

There are one or two other constitutional problems which may be briefly mentioned. Since the powers of the different legislative and executive organs of the new states are set out in written constitutions, the task of interpreting the constitution falls upon the judiciary.

Both in the British and the French African states, provision is made in the constitution for safeguarding the independence of the judiciary, which is regarded everywhere as the guardian of the freedom of the individual. To place the judges above influence and corruption, their salaries are made bounteous. Appointments, promotions, dismissals and the general welfare of judicial officers are normally removed from governmental interference and left in the hands of an independent Judicial Service Commission or Superior Judiciary

Council. In some of the constitutions it is provided that judges may not be removed from office.

The politicians assail this security in several ways. In Ghana, for example, by legislative adroitness the Judicial Service Commission was abolished and some of the judges are now appointed, in effect, by the President of the Republic. In Nigeria, some of the legislatures frequently exclude the jurisdiction of the courts by express provisions in the acts they pass. Also, new courts of a subordinate character, *e.g.* the customary courts in Nigeria, have been created, and these are generally placed outside the control of the Judicial Service Commission and under a politician, usually the Minister of Local Government. In these ways, the safeguards provided in the constitution are often bypassed and the courts are sometimes made an organ of political action.

In Nigeria and Sierra Leone, several fundamental human rights are imbedded in the constitution and a clause provides that any law which is inconsistent with the provisions of the constitution shall be void to the extent of that inconsistency. Here lies an ever-present opportunity for serious friction between the judiciary and the legislature, some of whose members cannot understand why any limitations should be placed on the sovereignty of Parliament, or why an individual judge should be set above the collective wisdom of the legislators.

The contradictions and inconsistencies which independence itself has brought have created additional problems for the new states. Every citizen wants to be completely rid of all vestiges of colonialism. He is very sensitive to anything which savors of the old relationship. The slogan throughout the African world appears to be: "Away with neo-colonialism."

For this reason, each state takes early steps to Africanize its administrative service, sometimes at the expense of efficiency and almost invariably upon the payment of heavy compensation to the expatriates relieved of their employment. This really is as it should be. The continuance of an expatriate citizen in a strategic administrative position would be expected to arouse a nationalist's suspicion that colonialism might be returning by the back door. He therefore insists that the expatriate servants of the government and corporations should be replaced by Africans. Since no government can afford to ignore the views of the nationalists, "ization" [2] has become a cardinal

[2] A suffix to words like Nigerian, Ghanaian, Sudan, etc., and indicating the process by which expatriates are replaced by nationals. The initial letter "i" undoubtedly stands for

policy of all new states, subject only to the proviso that it should not be implemented at reckless cost in efficiency.

What really frustrates "ization" is the patent fact that the new states are poor, and that they lack capital, technological know-how and managerial skill. Conscious of the vital importance of economic development, they have to look to the old source for expertise, and they fully realize that economic aid, whether by way of loan or gift, would appear to come more gracefully from the pocket of the erstwhile colonial power, which may feel a sense of obligation to see the young state well on its feet.

There is, however, a lingering suspicion that such aid will carry with it some obligations which may amount to a return of imperialism in a new guise. So the nationalist in the new state shouts at the top of his voice for "Aid without strings!" and "Freedom to borrow from any source!" But as time goes on, it becomes increasingly obvious, even to the least observant, that such slogans overlook a simple political truth. Altruism does not have any place in international relations. As this fact becomes more evident, the young state unobtrusively returns to the old friend. He then accepts the truism that it is better to treat with the devil that one knows. Thus Britain and France continue to play a leading role in aiding the economic development of their former colonies. The United States is strongly identified with these two powers and it is for that reason that the new states have no hesitation in seeking and accepting American aid. Furthermore, in spite of an avowed policy of neutralism, and the abhorrence of "neo-colonialism," the "British" African states seek membership in the British Commonwealth, and the "French" African states retain their comradeship within the *Communauté Rénovée*.

There is an ever-present danger of overdoing "ization" of the administrative service. Where this has happened, and there has been a breakdown in efficiency, the new state has had to rehire expatriates on much less favorable terms than were available initially.

One may now attempt an answer to the last questions posed above: "What is the pattern, if any, of the constitutional system which is evolving on the independent continent? What is the shape of the emergent African profile?" Ghana, Nigeria and Sierra Leone, being ex-British colonial territories, started independence with two-party parliamentary democracy patterned on the British system. The

India, where the effort to replace expatriates with indigenes first started as a national policy.

"French" African Republics, on the other hand, adopted the presidential system and seem to have preferred the one-party rule. Even in places like the Ivory Coast and Senegal, where more than one political party contested election, the electorate returned the government party to power with virtually a 100 percent victory.

Apart from the defects and unsuitability of the two-party system already noted, it is a matter for comment that fewer upheavals have bedevilled the French African states which have one-party systems of government than have disturbed the British African two-party governments. It seems the former have avoided the instability which characterized the earlier French Republic, by adopting the governmental system established by General de Gaulle.

Nigeria has not yet had occasion to amend its constitution. Ghana, on the other hand, has altered her own beyond recognition and has noticeably drifted toward a one-party system of government almost from the beginning. There is now no Opposition in Ghana worth
- talking about and the powers assumed by the President are as wide as, if not wider than, those of any French-speaking African state. For instance, the appointment of Ministers by the Ghanaian President does not require the approval or ratification of the National Assembly. Also, if a bill is vetoed by him, it cannot be sent back later for his assent by the Assembly. What stands out preëminently is the fact that Ghana, like the majority of African states, is practically committed to a one-party system.

It has been widely suggested that Dr. Nkrumah is rapidly heading toward dictatorship. He has taken every conceivable opportunity available to deny it. It is only fair to grant him *bona fides* and to accept, as he has always claimed, that he does not eschew democracy. It is at least clear that, without expressly declaring for a one-party system, he seems to have been concerned with the obvious defects of two-party democracy and to have proceeded to cure them on his own terms and to his own advantage. He has carried the reforms of the Ghanaian constitution to the point of annihilating the Opposition.

Since Dr. Nkrumah attained power under a two-party system of democracy, one would have preferred that, if he found that system irksome or the Opposition intolerable, he should seek the mandate of the people to alter the constitution before he destroyed the Opposition, not after. The issue of a one-party as against a two-party system is not only important, it is fundamental. To have won election under a two-party constitution and then to proceed to exterminate the Opposition without the people's mandate was to break faith with the electorate of Ghana. By his ruthless use of his majority, he has derogated the sovereignty of the people of Ghana and has equated the authority of the members of the Convention Peoples Party to that of the whole nation. His challenge to that sovereignty reached its climax when he clapped into jail under the Preventive Detention Act his Presidential rival, Dr. J. B. Danquah. So long as Ghana is still ostensibly committed to the two-party system of government, this can only be interpreted as disregarding the rights of the minority whose will and number were expressed in the votes cast for Dr. Danquah.

Sierra Leone, like Nigeria, entered independence with a coalition government. In the case of Nigeria, coalition was enforced by the nature of the election results. In Sierra Leone, however, the coalition is in the nature of a national front, formed in acknowledgment of the unsuitability of a two-party system for a young state newly emerged from colonial rule. Perhaps Sierra Leone decided to benefit from the experience of other states.

The pattern of the constitution which is evolving on the African continent is therefore "democracy with strong leadership." It is the African equivalent of the "guided democracy" of President Sukarno of Indonesia and the authoritarian military régimes of Pakistan, Sudan and, until the last election, Burma. Africans obviously believe that the commencement of independent life calls for a united and disciplined people under a strong and dedicated leadership. Nkrumah of Ghana, Sékou Touré of Guinea, General Aboud of Sudan, President Nasser of Egypt—this is the profile that is emerging in independent Africa. The stress is not on "the people" but on "the leader" and the leader unmistakably speaks with the tongue of the millions of his people.

Part IV

African "Isms"

Note

PAN-AFRICANISM: A DREAM COME TRUE
BY PAUL-MARC HENRY

October 1959

Pan-Africanism remains one of the driving political forces in Africa. Every politician pays it at least lip service; some work for it strenuously. What it means or how it is to be accomplished are not easily defined, but the desire of the Africans to draw closer together is real. They see it as a means of achieving power and greatness, of marshaling the forces to remove the last vestiges of white domination in Africa, of resisting neo-colonialism, of expressing their growing sense of identity as Africans. Moreover, they are impressed by the European example of integration and by economic arguments for forming larger markets. But the obstacles are enormous. Apart from the normal fears and rivalries that would exist in any comparable situation, the new African states have emerged with different colonial inheritance in terms of language, political institutions and ways of doing things. They are savoring the first delights of power and prestige—a voice at the United Nations, red-carpet treatment of their leaders in foreign capitals. It is not easy to sacrifice these and other prerogatives to a unified or federated African state embracing all or part of the continent. (See below the articles by Senghor and Olympio.)

In the title of the subtle and analytical essay that follows, there is more than a touch of Gallic irony. Writing on the eve of Africa's "year of independence," the author seems to be saying: "Pan-Africanism as an objective or an ideology has become nearly universal, and to that extent it is a dream come true; but mark well the practical problems." Among these, he gives emphasis to the differences between the former French and British territories of West Africa in respect to language, culture and experience. It will have come as no surprise to the author of this article that the closest and most developed association of African states which emerged after he wrote, and the one which most stubbornly refused to dissolve after the formation of the Organization of African Unity (see below), is that of the former French territories organized in the U.A.M. (*Union Africaine et Malgache*). Other important groupings which arose after independence were the Casablanca powers (Ghana, Guinea, Mali, Morocco, Algeria, Libya, U.A.R.) and the more conservative Monrovia grouping, consisting of Nigeria, Liberia and most of the former French territories; but these are now defunct.

For in 1963 all 32 independent states of Africa (excepting only Togo, which was not invited) came together in Addis Ababa and formed an Organization of African Unity, patterned on the Organization of American States. Overruling President Nkrumah, who was alone in fighting for a real surrender of sovereignty, the leaders nevertheless drafted a charter providing for extensive coöperation in politics, economics, education and defense. A secretariat is being established in Addis and a Commission on Mediation and Conciliation has been created to help settle intra-African disputes. A Council of Ministers meets every six months and heads of state and government meet annually. Although it is too early to tell how effective the organization will be, this first successful effort of the independent African states to draw together on a continent-wide basis appears to be a remarkable accomplishment. It is likely to play a particularly important role in the struggle to remove the vestiges of colonialism in Africa.

At the time this article was written, M. Henry was head of the Division of Africa South of the Sahara in the French Ministry of Foreign Affairs, and thereafter became head of the Division of International Technical Coöperation. Following previous service with the United Nations, he is now with the Special Fund. From 1952 to 1957 he was Secretary General of the Commission for Technical Coöperation in Africa South of the Sahara (C.C.T.A.) and of the Scientific Council for Africa South of the Sahara (C.S.A.). He has taught or lectured in France, Britain and the United States.

Pan-Africanism:
A Dream Come True

by PAUL-MARC HENRY

Few were the French-speaking delegates who could hear, even less understand, what the grand old man of pan-Africanism, Dr. W. E. B. Du Bois, had to say at Accra during the All African People's Conference last December. Some, however, may have recalled that the first Pan-African Congress ever convened took place with the permission of the Prime Minister of France, Georges Clemenceau, in 1919, at the Grand Hotel in Paris. It is difficult to find any trace or report of the event in the French or Anglo-Saxon press, which was then busy with what were known as "more important things," such as the fate of the Middle East, the Balkans and an obscure bunch of conspirators called the Soviet Communist Party somewhere in Moscow.

Last December Dr. Du Bois was describing to much younger and more successful generations of African politicians his various efforts to convene the second, third and fourth Pan-African Congresses, none of which actually took place in Africa. Were these young men moved by his account of the struggles of the pan-African movement? And were some disturbed by Dr. Du Bois' rather equivocal conclusions? "Your nearest friends and neighbors," he said, "are the colored peoples of China and India, the rest of Asia, the Middle East and the Sea Isles, once close bound to the heart of Africa and now long severed by the greed of Europe. Your bond is not mere color of skin but the deeper experience of wage slavery and contempt. So too, your bond with the white world is closest to those who support and defend China and help India and not those who exploit the Middle East and South America."

English-speaking Africans may have read and meditated the re-

161

markable book by George Padmore (now Advisor on African Affairs on Kwame Nkrumah's personal staff) entitled "Pan-Africanism or Communism?" It is unlikely that many of the French-speaking delegates had done so. They were more likely to have known the remarkable Senegalese, Blaise Diagne, usually represented as a symbol of a successful assimilationist policy, but in fact one of the most active supporters of the pan-African movement, as represented by Du Bois. It has been said that "Diagne was not without his critics, some of whom were sincere and others motivated by jealousy. He was called by some a traitor for having brought the Africans to fight for France and a tool of the rich white colonial interests. Others, however, praised him as having done more than any other to strengthen the position of colored peoples in the French Empire." [1]

Europeans would do well to cease underestimating the practical stimulation which can be derived by efficient African politicians from the intelligent use of ideological weapons. As seen from Paris, politics in French Africa has appeared to be merely an extension of party politics as played in the rather special atmosphere of the Palais Bourbon. It was "unrealistic" and slightly treacherous to reinterpret some of the attitudes of French-trained African politicians according to criteria which found their origins outside the magic and closed system of French politics. Yet Diagne, the most important actor of the first Pan-African Congress, was not alone in being drawn into activities which had nothing to do with French political parties. A quarter of a century later, another French-trained deputy, Sourou Apithy, from Dahomey, took a prominent part in the conference which followed the fifth Pan-African Congress (held in Manchester in 1945), and which was supposed to set up a permanent institution to be known later as the "West African National Secretariat." It was there he met Dr. Nkrumah, then a rather penniless postgraduate student in London.

This individual participation by two leading French Africans is important and significant, but not decisive. For between 1946 and 1958 one does not find any trace of activity by any French-speaking politician in the various stages of the pan-African movement, as interpreted and operated by Mr. Padmore and Dr. Nkrumah.

This chasm materialized clearly when Dr. Nkrumah took the initiative in organizing the West African delegates into the West African

[1] J. A. Rogers, "World's Great Men of Colour," as quoted by Padmore, p. 121.

National Secretariat. Later events were to take Dr. Nkrumah even further away from his self-appointed task of organizing a movement which would cover West Africa as a whole. From 1947 to 1957, the year of Ghana's independence, it is fair to say that the dream of pan-Africanism, though alive, was second in priority to the immediate task of establishing self-government and then independence.

It is surely significant that during the same period the French territories of West Africa went through somewhat the same evolution but devoted their efforts to obtaining within the rigid framework of *la République une et indivisible* enough autonomy and self-government to be able to stand on their own and develop their personalities without for the time being considering independence as a prime objective.

Meanwhile it has become a fact that the vigor and inspiration of pan-Africanism, stripped of any excess of American-Negro influence as expressed by black zionism or Garveyism, has taken roots in the land of Africa under the active and skillful leadership of Dr. Nkrumah, political secretary of the fifth Pan-African Congress held in Manchester in 1945. As a movement which was conceived in America and which blossomed in West Africa, pan-Africanism remains essentially an English-speaking movement, a delayed boomerang from the era of slavery as practiced on the West African coast two centuries ago. It is significant that, linguistically and ethnically, most of the American Negroes in North America came from the coastal areas on the Gulf of Guinea, and only a few from the interior areas of Senegal and Niger.

The Prime Minister of Ghana has been thoroughly consistent as far as pan-Africanism is concerned. According to him, "the independence of Ghana will have no meaning unless it is strengthened with the total liberation of Africa." Ghana, in other words, is to be as Piedmont was to an amorphous Italy—Accra the Mecca of pan-Africanism. Not to accept implicitly or explicitly the basic leadership of the Prime Minister of Ghana is in fact to reject the basic tenets of pan-Africanism, as defined by the small team which has followed the Prime Minister since his early days in London.

II

One may wonder why so little attention was paid by the leaders of Ghana as well as by foreign observers to the very important changes which were taking place simultaneously in the French-speaking territories nearby. The barrier of language is one explanation, but not sufficient. One difficulty was that the French-trained politicians were far more interested in what was happening in Paris and in their constituencies than in neighboring Ghana and Nigeria. The road to freedom was to be found through a free negotiation between the French territories in Africa and their Metropole and not through some kind of local arrangement with a neighbor, even though that neighbor in fact had to deal with the same problems and tackle the same difficulties. Therefore, pan-African propaganda for a short time fell on deaf ears.

The same was true, however, in Nigeria where the several provinces were far too busy negotiating their own differences to worry about the gigantic problem of West African unification. It can even be said that the more Ghana claimed a special position of leadership in Black Africa, the more Nigerian and French territories became aware of the need to evolve their own plans for some kind of loose confederacy which would eliminate the risk of personal power without rejecting what seemed both unavoidable and useful. In other words, pan-Africanism as an ideology was growing fast, but not as a uniform and well-disciplined movement. The problem was basically how to establish contact between French-speaking and English-speaking areas.

The history of the next few years, perhaps of the next few months, will show if the Prime Minister of Ghana considers himself first and foremost a national leader or an international one. In some respects he finds himself in a position similar to Napoleon the Third, who as Emperor of the French was responsible for the welfare and peace of France, but was also committed, through his past activities and connections, to the liberation of the captive nationalities of Western Europe, such as the Germans and Italians. Nkrumah, like Napoleon III, and some of the more contemporary European leaders, is committed to a revisionist policy. As the fifth Pan-African Congress observed: "The artificial divisions and territorial boundaries created by the imperialist powers are deliberate steps to obstruct the political unity of the West African peoples." Echoing this basic view, the All African People's Conference, meeting in Accra last year, held that "the great bulk of the African continent has been carved out arbitrarily to the detriment of the indigenous African peoples by European imperialists, namely: Britain, France, Belgium, Spain, Italy and Portugal."

As the spokesman for African revisionism, Nkrumah has no challenger. Together with his advisor, George Padmore, he is the *doctrinaire* to whom all nationalist movements in Africa south of the Sahara are looking for example, support and guidance. He is fast becoming the elder statesman of Black Africa. Apart from the heads of the independent states of Liberia and Ethiopia, who had to carry in isolation their own struggle for survival, he has contributed more than anybody else to the promotion of the "African personality" which is to play so important a role in world politics during the next decade.

Students familiar with the story of the rise of European nationalism in the nineteenth century will find many differences between the national struggle of, say, Germany and Italy to build up their political unity and the various brands of African nationalism. However, the emotional fervor is the same and is certainly to be found in the spiritual leaders of pan-Africanism. In this vein, Nkrumah expressed the hope in Accra that the African continent will not see a repetition of the petty quarrels and the constant disagreements, wars and national disasters which have marked the history of the other continents.

To an outside observer therefore, pan-Africanism, as interpreted and expounded by Nkrumah and his team, is a political Janus. One face is looking towards more effective power at home, that is, in Ghana and on the African continent. The other is looking outward upon a world in which a reborn and reunited Africa will play a most important role in the promotion of peace and progress.

To a next-door neighbor, like Félix Houphouet-Boigny, political leader of the Ivory Coast, or Sylvanus Olympio, Prime Minister of the Republic of Togoland, pan-Africanism is apt to look like a convenient smoke screen for very precise and down-to-earth territorial ambitions. To a distant colleague in "world government," like Mr. Nehru in India, it must clearly be the other way round: pan-Africanism is indeed a movement of world-wide importance and the petty affairs of Ghana are to be left in their parochial context.

III

The fate of Africa will be the result, however, of a concrete interplay of local forces in a regional framework and not of an abstract generalization. As the heartland of pan-Africanism is, after all, in West Africa, and is surrounded on all sides by French-speaking territories, it may be profitable to find out how these French-speaking territories have so far reacted to this so-called "universal doctrine"—a doctrine which may very well be for them as abstract as the theory of the Covenant was to Georges Clemenceau or, conversely, the theory of collective security to President Hoover.

The story of "nationalism" in French Africa is basically different from the story of African nationalism in British-dominated territories. From 1946, the date of the constitution of the Fourth Republic and the year in which French citizenship was granted to all the inhabitants of French Africa, to 1956, when the hotly debated *loi-cadre* was adopted, the political élite of French Africa had to express itself *within* the framework of the French political system, the center of which was the National Assembly in Paris. There is hardly a politician now responsible for the fate of the new autonomous republics and federations who has not been closely involved at one time or another with the intricacies, contradictions and excitement of the French parliamentary game. Votes of the African members of the National Assembly were sometimes decisive factors in a fragile governmental majority. African *députés* and *sénateurs* learned their politics, not in the narrow confines of territorial problems, but in the strange and stimulating world of the French parliament, where every issue in contemporary history was discussed thoroughly, albeit inconclusively.

One could argue that the world as seen from Paris is rather distorted. French deputies themselves were not always aware of the real factors of power politics. The continuous presence of friendly and able African colleagues led them to believe that there was no such thing as African nationalism in French areas, that the idea was a foreign import and, in some cases, one of those notorious plots against Franco-African community and its spiritual achievements.

On the other hand, there was no better school for intellectual and political sophistication than that of the French parliament of the Fourth Republic. The high level of debate in the congresses of the *Rassemblement Démocratique Africain* and the *Parti du Regroupement Africain* shows how deep the Paris influence went. During the recent discussions in Africa, between the *Fédéralistes* and the *Territorialistes*, the most demanding of constitutional advisors could not have found any flaw in the legal reasoning involved.

Such is the result of more than ten years of direct participation of the African élite in the French political game, to which must be added the close connection existing for more than eight years between the trade-union movement in France and the trade-union movement in French Africa. Also, France, like Britain, carried out during this period a systematic policy of promoting university and higher education with a massive program of scholarships in French universities. As in Britain, and perhaps more so, the African student has picked up eagerly the rhetoric, the logic and the *Weltanschauung* of his fellow students of the postwar period, who were ready to reexamine the basic postulates of political life. In Paris, existentialism, Catholicism, "progressivism" and Communism were the abstract intellectual categories which dominated the thoughts of the young and enthusiastic African.

Political leadership in French Africa is therefore of the most "modern" kind. In this process of assimilating new values and destroying old ones, the French-trained Africans found great support in their innermost spiritual being. The fundamental process of eliminating any "inferiority complex," which was done in North America and in English-speaking Africa by a quasi-mystical pan-Africanism and black zionism, was carried out in France through entirely different methods.

The American public did not pay much attention to the Congress devoted to *la négritude* which took place in Paris in 1957, under the sponsorship of that vigorous group, *Présence Africaine*. Many prominent Negroes from the New World and from Africa participated. Very few English-speaking Negroes were present, with the important exception of Richard Wright, now living in Normandy. This gathering showed clearly, however, that French-speaking Africans (and for that matter French-speaking West Indians) were claiming not merely redress for the untold harm done by European slavery and colonialism on the African continent. They were asking for full recognition by European cultures of the essential contribution made by Black Africa to what is known as Western civilization. In the fields of history, music, poetry, plastic arts, their contribution was said to place Africa, and therefore the African himself, on a footing of equality with Europe. There was no denial of the positive contribution of Western culture to Africa, provided it was recognized by all concerned that Africa can give and had already given much in exchange.

Obtaining spiritual equality is in a sense far more important than the immediate achievement of political and constitutional equality. The quest goes beyond the more theoretical aspiration for "liberty, equality and fraternity." This is where the English-speaking African politicians and those of the pan-African "school" have made a basic mistake. They considered the rather empty phrases of the 1789 vocabulary as one more "trick" of the French colonialists to exorcise the temptations of black nationalism. This belief seriously underestimates the depth of the spiritual revolution which has taken place in French Africa. Most of the French-trained African politicians are simply not interested in a doctrine which has been evolved by small teams of theoreticians who have derived their experience from the very special situation of the Negroes in America or of the constitutional struggles in British crown colonies. The same words, including "African unity," may have very different meanings. One suspects that this basic misunderstanding may dominate the trend of events in West Africa during the next few months, if it has not already emptied the much publicized Ghana-Guinea union of any real significance.

IV

If French-trained African politicians are relatively immune to the seduction of pan-Africanism, one may wonder why it was a former French territory, independent Guinea, which took the first concrete step toward the pan-African program, that is, the Union of West African States. How is it possible, in the first place, that the vast Federation of French West Africa, which once embraced in one administrative, economic, financial and cultural union the eight territories of Mauritania, Senegal, Guinea, Sudan, Ivory Coast, Upper Volta, Niger and Dahomey, was broken into component parts in less than two years? The answer lies in the *loi-cadre* itself, which deliberately selected the "territory" as the basic unit within which the process of transferring power would take place. But individual governments led naturally to growth of local patriotism which was hostile to any form of interference from outside.

Territories became used to discussing their individual problems directly with the metropolitan authorities concerned. The only common instruments which crossed territorial boundaries were in the fields of customs, federal finances, investments, defense and foreign affairs; these were left to the representatives of France which, through parliament, were indirectly controlled by the African members of the National Assembly sitting in Paris. This uneasy compromise between the power of the basic unit and the semi-federal powers exercised by the Metropole was a transitional one. Within the parties and the trade-union organizations like R.D.A., P.R.A. and the *Union Générale des Travailleurs d'Afrique Noire*, of which the Prime Minister of Guinea, Sékou Touré, was vice-president, there was a strong movement toward a new formula of federation. This would have a joint all-African executive and would, in fact, restore the federation as a purely African instrument rather than as a projection of the metropolitan bureaucracy. When the referendum was organized, the decision was taken to count the votes *by territories* and not by federation or by overseas territories as a whole.

Territorial sections of inter-territorial parties, like the R.D.A., were given the freedom to vote as they wished. Thus it was possible for Sékou Touré, who happened to be vice-president of the R.D.A., to ask for a negative vote and for Houphouet-Boigny, who is the president of the same party, to vote affirmatively. Similarly, certain sections of the R.D.A., in the Sudan for instance, are in favor of a West African Federation, although the R.D.A. of the Ivory Coast is dead set against it. Through this procedure, French West Africa ceased to be an organized block of French-speaking territories as soon as one territory, at least, could vote no, and did so, taking the opportunity offered by General de Gaulle to become immediately independent.

One may argue about the basic reason for Mr. Sékou Touré's negative vote. It is likely on the basis of his own statements that it was a tactical move to give himself a better bargaining position in future negotiations with France and with the neighboring French territories, and in the hope of eventually setting up a new West African Federation on his own terms. Instead, he was thrown into the whirlpool of pan-African politics at the very moment when Mr. Nkrumah was looking for an opening into French-speaking territories after having largely failed to get his foot in the door of Nigeria.

It is rumored that when Mr. Sékou Touré was presented with a first draft of a treaty of union between Ghana and Guinea he disliked the spirit of the whole thing, which was little more than the offer of a merger under the leadership of Ghana. The first draft was therefore much watered down, so that the final result was a statement of intention rather than an actual act of union. The final declaration is limited to a statement of principle. Subject to the ratification of the respective National Assemblies, the two Prime Ministers "have agreed to constitute their two states as the nucleus of a Union of West African States." It is, however, made clear that "the action taken with a view to achieving a Union of West African States is not, in any way, designed to prejudice the present or future relations between Ghana and the Commonwealth, on the one hand, and the Republic of Guinea and the French Community, on the other."

Dr. Nkrumah and Mr. Sékou Touré also made it clear in later statements that the joint declaration had practical possibilities in the fields of communications, foreign affairs, monetary, financial and economic matters, which would be studied and implemented in due course. The Union had also more general aspects of value for the rest of West Africa. It was an "open union" in which any other West African state was invited to participate. It was, Nkrumah told the Ghana National Assembly, a step "towards the establishment of the African community which will have its own distinctive outlook and African personality."

What is important here is that the two states wish to keep their own separate personalities and are anxious not to prejudice their respective relations with the Commonwealth and the French Community. From now on, pan-Africanism will have to leave the ground of "utopian romanticism" and, in Nkrumah's words, "will be guided in the creation of the African community upon which we have embarked by the realities of the actual situation."

Pan-Africanism has therefore entered a new phase. Like every successful ideological movement, it has had to transform itself. Its basic theses are now common ground for all African politicians in the same way as the European ideal is accepted by all nations of Western Europe. Emerging Africa will raise many new problems that Dr. Du Bois, Dr. Padmore and Dr. Nkrumah could not have imagined within the limited context of American Negro experience and the British West African experiment with parliamentary democracy. French Africa has been through its own type of revolution. French-trained African politicians have different traditions. Their view of a united Africa is apt to be at the same time more intellectual, more Western and somewhat more Marxist than the concept evolved by the small team responsible for the success of the fifth Pan-African Congress and the two recent Accra Conferences.

Such as it is, pan-Africanism is a dream come true. It will soon be taken for granted, at the very moment when it will be transforming itself into something more complex and more powerful. The change will probably be in the direction of a general ideology rather than a practical political movement based in Ghana, and led by a ruling few.

Note

THE COMING SHOWDOWN IN CENTRAL AFRICA
BY N. M. SHAMUYARIRA

January 1961

The Federation of Rhodesia and Nyasaland was formed in 1953 against the wishes of the Africans concerned. Ten years later the Federation was dead—destroyed by mutual fears of Africans and of the largest white settler community outside of the Union of South Africa.

Economically the Federation had made sense and was successful. The joining of relatively developed Southern Rhodesia with copper-rich Northern Rhodesia and poor but heavily populated Nyasaland offered opportunities and advantages to each of the regions. But politically the union of the self-governing territory of Southern Rhodesia with the two British protectorates to the north made sense only if the white minority fulfilled its promise to establish genuine "partnership" with the Africans. After ten years the Africans, who from the first feared the dominance of the substantial white minority in Southern Rhodesia, were more certain than ever that what they had obtained was "the partnership of horse and rider."

Today, Northern Rhodesia and Nyasaland are both governed by African majorities and are soon to be independent. The British Government has yielded to virtually irresistible pressure to permit each of them to withdraw from the Federation, leaving it a hollow shell. The question remaining—and it is one of the most crucial in Africa—is what will become of Southern Rhodesia, which has been self-governing and wholly under white domination since 1923? With a 16 to 1 superiority in numbers, the Africans are certain to control the government in time; the only question is whether this will be achieved without violence—a possibility that seems increasingly remote as settler opinion moves stubbornly to the right.

It is probably too late for the white settlers to learn what *The Economist* once called "the art of being submerged without actually drowning." Southern Rhodesia has a new constitution which makes few concessions to the Africans, and it is governed by a party determined to maintain European dominance. Despite some relaxation of the color bar in recent years, Southern Rhodesia seems more and more to be slipping away from the professed objective of partnership to something more nearly approaching the policies of South Africa. Severe security laws have been passed and much of the limited African leadership is in exile. If Southern Rhodesia should obtain independence under a white government, her African leaders have warned that they will set up a government in exile and declare war—a war that would be likely to involve South Africa and then other African states. Meanwhile, white settlers have been leaving at the rate of 600 a month and the economy has been floundering.

The showdown in Central Africa, then, is not over, and the issues which Nathan Shamuyarira here describes are very much alive, even though federation is dead. At the time this article was written, Mr. Shamuyarira was Chief Editor of African Newspapers, Ltd., of Salisbury, which publishes the *African Daily News* and six weekly newspapers. He resigned in 1962 over differences of editorial policy and for a short time was editor of the *Central African Mail*, a weekly published in Lusaka, the capital of Northern Rhodesia. He is now a teacher at the Institute of Adult Education at the University College of Rhodesia and Nyasaland.

The Coming Showdown in Central Africa

by N. M. SHAMUYARIRA

After the Congo and Algeria, the next trouble spot in Africa is likely to be the British-controlled Federation of Rhodesia and Nyasaland. Flanked on the south by Dr. Verwoerd's racist Republic of South Africa, on the east and west by Dr. Salazar's undeveloped provinces of Mozambique and Angola, and on the north by strife-torn Congo and self-governing Tanganyika, it is a major battleground between the protagonists of white rule in Africa and the surging tide of African nationalism. On the eve of a Constitutional Conference which will determine the shape of events in the immediate future, racial tensions have mounted dangerously. The riots in Southern Rhodesia last summer and the repressive legislation which followed, the Monckton Commission report calling for fundamental changes in the Federation, and the British decision to grant legislative majorities to the Africans in Northern Rhodesia and Nyasaland have all contributed to a sense of grievance in one group or another.

Rhodesian Europeans seeking to rally support for Sir Roy Welensky, the Federal Prime Minister, are putting stickers on their car windows bearing a large letter "W" (for Welensky—or possibly White supremacy). Their comparatively few white opponents apply the stickers upside-down, showing an "M" for Macmillan, Macleod and Monckton. But by far the strongest opposition to Sir Roy Welensky within the Federation comes from Dr. Hastings Banda, the Nyasaland leader of the Malawi Congress Party, and Mr. Kenneth Kaunda, leader of Northern Rhodesia's United National Independence Party, who want to secede from the Federation.

In the Federation, there are in general three schools of thought. First, there are those who want Federation to proceed basically unchanged but with minor alterations to the prompt attainment of full independence. The chief spokesman of this opinion is of course Welensky. Sir Edgar Whitehead, the Prime Minister of Southern Rhodesia, agrees, but under pressure from the more segregation-minded Opposition adds that Southern Rhodesia may choose to secede if full independence is not granted. Secondly, there are those who think that Federation is economically of such importance to the three territories that they are willing to pay a considerable price politically to maintain it. Variations in this body of opinion range from those who want to see a liberal white government in which Africans play an increasingly prominent part to those who advocate a black federal government with safeguards for white interests. Considerable weight has been added to this opinion by the far-reaching recommendations of the Monckton Commission, presented in October. In brief, the Commission recognized the need for economic ties among the three territories, but advocated increased representation of Africans in the 59-member Federal Parliament, the right of a territory to secede after a further trial period, the return of certain powers to the territorial governments and the need for a wider territorial franchise, especially in Southern Rhodesia. The third viewpoint, which is held strongly by the Africans themselves, is that the present Federation must be broken up.

It is clear that the Federation cannot continue in its present form without widespread and severe violence, comparable in scope if not in character to the Mau Mau Emergency in Kenya. Hostility to Federation among Africans, particularly in the two Northern territories, is intense and not altogether unfounded. It is built on and buttressed by the mistakes of the Federal Government in the last seven years, the speeches of its leading spokesman and the actions of its officers.

The first major failure was in the implementation of the policy of partnership or multi-racialism on which the Federation was founded. After seven years, senior positions in the Federal Civil Service are still occupied exclusively by whites; there is only one African Parliamentary Secretary in a Cabinet of nine men; the Federation's government-owned airline employs Africans only as janitors, drivers and the like; and, with the exception of doctors and some nurses, the principle of equal pay for equal work is by no means honored, even by the Government. In matters for which the territorial governments are responsible, discrimination is still extreme, especially in Southern Rhodesia, aptly referred to as the "nigger in the woodpile" of Federation. There the Civil Service can be entered only by Europeans (an amendment has been promised); residential segregation is so sharp that even the African Cabinet Minister could not be accommodated in the white suburbs where other Ministers live; African businessmen cannot trade in the center of the main towns; passes are still enforced; wages are disproportionate; cafés and restaurants are closed to non-whites. Several breaches in the color bar have been made in respect of common services in post offices, in trains and at airports, and at the University College at Salisbury. But the fundamental issues of the land and the vote have not been tackled, although the evils of the land policy in Southern Rhodesia have at last been acknowledged by an investigating committee of the legislature.

The major blow to African hopes of partnership came in 1955 when the Federal Government rejected a motion by an African Federal Member of Parliament from Northern Rhodesia, Mr. Dauti Yamba, to the effect that discrimination should be outlawed in public places. Sir Roy Welensky, speaking for the Government, said the solution to this apparent human problem could be found only in economic progress—a point of view he has reiterated on many occasions. At about that time, a Cabinet Minister, pressed by angry white farmers at a meeting in Bindura to state whether partnership meant an alteration of the status quo, likened it to the partnership of a donkey and its rider—obviously with the same goals, travelling on the same road, but not equals.

As a result of segregation and the absence of communication between the two races, particularly in Southern Rhodesia, the Federal Government has been out of touch with African opinion, and Federal Ministers out of touch with African leaders. Although Dr. Banda, Mr. Kaunda and Mr. Joshua Nkomo, all Presidents of the largest African political parties in their respective territories, have discussed the Federal situation variously with Mr. Macmillan, Mr. Macleod and other British M.P.s, they have not exchanged a single word on the same problems with Sir Roy Welensky or his strong Cabinet colleagues, Sir Malcolm Barrow and Mr. Julius Greenfield. None of these Federal Ministers has had an African in his home for an evening, although Sir Roy has an "open stoep" for all his old friends in the all-white Rhodesia Railway Workers' Union, and others, most Sunday afternoons. It is important to emphasize this human aspect which has been so sadly neglected in Federal affairs, hampered as they are by law and traditional prejudices. Confidence and understanding, so necessary in negotiating a new constitutional agreement, cannot be achieved in such circumstances.

In 1957 a further blow was dealt to African confidence in federation when the Federal Government enacted a franchise law, the intent of which was obviously to keep power in the hands of 3.7 percent of the population, namely the whites. (There are 300,000 Europeans and 8,000,000 Africans in the Federation.) By setting high income and educational qualifications, it has been possible to keep 97 percent of the Common Voters' Roll in white hands, although it is supposedly non-racial. Africans see no possibility of ever having a decisive influence on this roll, for as their wages rise and education becomes more widespread they have no doubt that the qualifications would be raised, as has been done in Southern Rhodesia twice in the last ten years.

Africans throughout the Federation cannot see why such stringent requirements should be set for them, when in India illiterate men and women vote by symbols, and in Nigeria they vote merely by throwing a stone in a bucket below a party symbol they recognize. White Federal politicians lay much emphasis on the need for voters to be responsible and civilized, but Africans interpret this as a mere device to deprive them of political power and influence—the more so as these arbitrary standards of civilization and responsibility can be raised whenever the white man feels his political control is threatened.

Last but by no means least important, Africans in the Federation cannot and will not crouch in submission with arms folded when all around them they can see their fellowmen governing themselves. The advent of Ghana, Nigeria and other states as free and independent nations, represented at the United Nations, and of Tanganyika as a self-governing state, is obviously an exciting idea to every African. Southern Rhodesia boasts of the highest literacy rate south of the Sahara; it has more than 100 university-trained Africans. But, paradoxically, it has not a single African in its 30-member legislature, and not one has entered the Territory's Civil Service in the 37 years since self-government was granted to Southern Rhodesia. This applies even to the Department of Native Affairs which looks primarily after African interests.

Americans often ask whether the Federation has trained Africans who can do better than the Congolese, if given self-rule. In Northern Rhodesia and Nyasaland, which are British Protectorates, the Colonial Office policy of "African Paramountcy" has led to a more serious effort to train Africans for the Civil Service. There are now several

Africans in top executive posts, and four are in the Executive Councils (Cabinet). It is Southern Rhodesia that is perpetuating conditions similar to those of the Congo before June 30, although it has the largest number of Africans equipped for administrative responsibility.

The third and most popular viewpoint toward Federation—that of unqualified opposition—stems from the Africans' fear that the policies and attitudes of Southern Rhodesian whites will be permitted to dominate the larger political association. In principle, Africans certainly do not want Africa to be balkanized. Kwame Nkrumah, the leading exponent of Pan-Africanism, said recently, "African States must federate and survive, or remain divided and disintegrate." George Padmore's books preach endlessly about the dream of a United States of Africa. The objections to the present Federation are not, then, based on opposition to the concept of unity but on the understandable dislike of the retrogressive racial policies of Southern Rhodesia. The Monckton Commission established this point beyond doubt. It discovered that the most vocal critics were those Africans from the north who had visited Southern Rhodesia to find work, and had been forced to carry passes on big tobacco farms owned exclusively by white settlers.

The economic argument for Federation is, however, a valid one, although many Nyasas and Northern Rhodesians do not want to admit it lest they weaken their strong political position. If the Federation were broken up, the economic consequences would be extremely grave, except perhaps for the Northern Rhodesians. In unity, Northern Rhodesia's coppermines, Southern Rhodesia's growing industries and Nyasaland's labor force complement each other's needs. The Kariba Dam has been built at a cost of neary $660,000,000 which must be repaid by the territories either jointly or singly if the Federation is broken up; customs tariffs for manufactured goods have been lowered; and direly needed transportation is being expanded on a Federation-wide basis.

If more development money is to be found, the confidence of monetary institutions like the World Bank, the largest investor in Africa, will have to be maintained, and if possible increased. It is hard to imagine how this can be done if the Federation breaks apart entirely. Further, we will have lost the opportunity to plunge straight ahead with the development of what is one of the very few states in Africa with a broadly based industrial economy. The pressing problems of unemployment, low wages, health, transportation to exploit more natural resources, and lack of technical skills—problems which will be with us even at the end of the century, regardless of political status—would be accentuated if the Federation is dissolved.

What the forthcoming London Conference must agree to is that Africans shall have a decisive political influence in the Federation. Three measures are required. First, the franchise must be made broad enough so that Europeans no longer predominate at the polls. If universal adult suffrage is rejected, the purpose could be accomplished by establishing six years of education as the only voter qualification. Second, a Bill of Human Rights should be enacted to ensure the safety of the person and property of every individual in the Federation. Such a Bill would be of immediate advantage to the Africans, but in the long run it will be of tremendous advantage to the Europeans. Under this provision, the individual territorial governments would be compelled to outlaw many forms of racial discrimination which now exist. Third, the two northern territories, which have already been assured African majorities, should be placed in a position of political equality with Southern Rhodesia so that they can object effectively to arrangements they find restrictive and distasteful. One bargains best from a position of strength.

A Federation in which Southern Rhodesian Europeans were no longer dominant in the Federal Assembly and Cabinet, in which the obvious economic advantages were combined with a universal (or broadly qualified) Federal franchise and civil rights for all—such a Federation would, I believe, be acceptable to African opinion, even in Northern Rhodesia and Nyasaland.

What chances of success has such a plan? Nil, at present, because of massive resistance from the Europeans of Southern Rhodesia who are afraid of losing their jobs, land and general position of privilege. Politicians like Sir Roy and Sir Edgar have gone far to promise the white electors that there will be "no retreat" and "certainly no sellout." Several African Uncle Toms support them in this contention, thereby giving the tough line a semblance of African support. For its part, the British Government is afraid of a Boston Teaparty on the Zambezi or Lake Nyasa. Yet it knows that, unless the plan emerging from the London Conference is far-reaching, Africans will reject it out of hand, thereby threatening a more prolonged and violent "teaparty." Soon Dr. Banda and Mr. Kaunda will have Legislative Council majorities. They will then be in a position to resist effectively Federal connections with race-conscious Southern Rhodesia.

Who, then, can initiate the drastic constitutional reforms so necessary even to begin meeting the mounting aspirations of the African people? The answer, of course, is the British Government. It must act decisively and courageously if violence is to be avoided and if today's moderate African leadership in the Federation is not to be replaced by more radical men, who may even lean to the East. Fortunately, Mr. Macmillan and Mr. Macleod enter the difficult negotiations with one big advantage—the confidence of the African people; Dr. Banda has repeatedly poured glowing praise on the Colonial Secretary, who has clearly had the Prime Minister's full support. Further, in recent months when Belgian policy in the Congo has been under heavy fire, British colonial policy has benefited by comparison and has frequently been praised. After Mr. Macmillan's high-flown declarations about colonialism in reply to Mr. Khrushchev in the United Nations, the British Prime Minister cannot now afford to do less than his utmost to save the situation in Central Africa.

A showdown with Welensky and Whitehead seems inevitable. In the final analysis, the resolution of the Federation problem depends entirely on the ability to deal with the Southern Rhodesian Europeans, who form the strongest single political force in the country, electing as they do both the Federal and Southern Rhodesian Governments. If they feel that the changes being made are too drastic, they will attempt to secede. However, the fear that Southern Rhodesia might join the Union of South Africa is unfounded. This threat is being used by Europeans as a stick with which to beat the British Government into acceptance of their policies. But it is out of the question, particularly since South Africa voted to become a republic. Afrikaaner domination would be as objectionable to most Southern Rhodesian Europeans as black domination. Furthermore, it is quite improbable that South Africa would agree to add a hostile English-speaking bloc and 2,250,000 rebellious Africans to its already acute racial problems. The most that Southern Rhodesia can do is to try to go it alone.

The 200,000 Europeans of Southern Rhodesia are now engaged in a last-ditch struggle for the maintenance of white supremacy. The all-white administration and legislature have sent police to occupy the African townships, 20 lives have been lost, and 550 Africans have been arrested under an increasing volume of security legislation which has led to the resignation of the Federal Chief Justice, Sir Robert Tredgold. Rhodesian-born and widely respected, Sir Robert may lead a new liberal political party; one hopes that his fate is not that of Garfield Todd, a former Prime Minister who is now in the political wilderness. It will take far more than a Tredgold, a Todd or further African rioting to convince Rhodesian whites to make the necessary concessions. Only the British Government can accomplish this, and to do so it may have to go so far as to remind Sir Edgar Whitehead and his colleagues that it still has powers to suspend the Southern Rhodesian constitution, as was done in recent years in Malta and British Guiana.

Yet many fears of the consequences of an African majority are groundless. It cannot be overemphasized that Africans do not intend to drive Europeans away or dispossess them arbitrarily. The doctrine of "Africa for the Africans" has long been abandoned, and replaced with "one man one vote" or—more tellingly—"government of the people, by the people and for the people." We know that each skilled European who comes into any part of Central Africa creates eight jobs for Africans. Therefore, no African Prime Minister in his proper senses would squeeze Europeans out lest he be faced with a grave unemployment problem. Contrary to the alarmists' view, Europeans will be encouraged to stay in the Federation and others will be urged to come, as has been the case in Ghana where the white population has doubled since independence. Dr. Banda, who was painted as an arch-enemy of Europeans, now wants Europeans to fight the next election under the banner of his own party; Mr. Kaunda could be expected to behave in the same way once his goals are achieved in Northern Rhodesia. The struggle is against the régime, not against Europeans; Africans ask only for equality—at the ballot box, on the land and in terms of opportunity. Only then can the much-publicized concept of a multi-racial state succeed in Central Africa.

Note

COMMUNISM AND NATIONALISM IN TROPICAL AFRICA
BY WALTER Z. LAQUEUR

July 1961

In many respects, Black Africa has seemed to be ideal ground for Communism. The colonial experience has predisposed the African to resent and suspect the leading powers of the non-Communist world. Where independence has not yet been achieved, there is bitterness and fear; where it has been achieved, there is frustration at the failure of the millennium to appear and at the generally slow rate of development. Yet Communism appears to have made fewer inroads than one might have expected. Despite Africa's poverty, Communist ideology and doctrine are not particularly relevant, and Soviet spokesmen in Africa have been unadaptable if not downright inept. Indeed, the Soviets, and to a lesser extent the Chinese, have often seemed at a loss as to how to deal with a society which is virtually classless, which shows a certain immunity to discipline of the Communist type, and which is extremely jealous of its new-won independence.

The most dramatic example is afforded by Guinea, on which the West turned its back so resolutely after independence that Guinea was forced into the arms of the Soviet Union, yet has resisted its exclusive embrace with a growing awareness of the dangers and a growing disillusionment with unfulfilled promises (see page 314). Although ironically the very failure of the Soviet Union in this instance has to some extent reassured other African nations that they can do business with the Russians and Chinese without undue risk, the greatest danger of Communism appears today not in the independent African states but wherever the white man is still in control and professing to be defending the free world against Communism—as in Southern Rhodesia and South Africa.

In the following article, one of the keenest students of Communism analyzes not Soviet or Chinese performance in Africa but rather the ground in which they seek to sow their doctrine. He finds that even where Communism has penetrated Africa it has been shaped into something quite different from the Marxism-Leninism of the European and Soviet brand. A prolific and articulate writer, Walter Z. Laqueur is editor of *Survey*, A Journal of Soviet and East European Studies, published in London, and his articles have appeared throughout the world. His books include "Communism and Nationalism in the Middle East" and "Young Germany: A History of the German Youth Movement," and he edited "The Future of Communist Society" and "Soviet Attitudes Towards Africa." He has been a visiting professor at the Universities of Chicago and Johns Hopkins and a fellow of the Russian Research Center at Harvard.

Communism and Nationalism in Tropical Africa

by WALTER Z. LAQUEUR

Almost overnight Communism in Africa has become an international problem of the first magnitude. Ten years ago, or even five, all that was known, or needed to be known, about the subject could be stated in two or three sentences mainly of a negative character. Now, in 1961, Africa has replaced the Middle East as the world's chief trouble center, and it is likely to remain the main area of contest between West and East for many years to come. On the African continent the Soviet bloc and China have succeeded in gaining important footholds within a very short space of time. The Communist states are represented in most of the newly independent countries and their envoys are untiring in their exertions. There is a constant stream of cultural and trade missions and other visitors between Moscow, Peking and some African capitals. These activities undoubtedly constitute a serious challenge to the West; but even more important are the efforts of local pro-Communist or national Communist groups to gain the upper hand in the struggle for the future of Africa; one can hardly exaggerate the implications of the outcome of this struggle.

Discussion of the problems facing Communism in tropical Africa (meaning Africa south of the Sahara excluding the Union of South Africa) is frequently hampered by the absence of reliable facts. To give but one example: On August 2, 1960, the existence of a Congolese Communist party, with a central committee headed by M. Mwamba-Mukanya, was announced in Leopoldville; it was said to have been in existence for the past decade. This was the first and the last to be heard about this party and its central committee. Shortly afterwards M. Mwamba-Mukanya was introduced to the Soviet pub-

184

lic as no more than a Congolese public figure; his party had apparently vanished into thin air. It would be unwise to assume that such practices are designed merely to confuse the outside observer. There are good reasons to believe that Russian, Chinese and other Communists are at least as bewildered as everybody else by the frequent upheavals and the changing allegiances on the African scene.

But it is hardly less difficult to arrive at a realistic appraisal of the political forces in Africa that are commonly defined as "Communist" or pro-Communist. If Soviet and other official Communist sources have so far applied this term in Africa only sparingly, perhaps more so than was really warranted, it has been bandied about rather freely by some Western observers, for whom a trip to Moscow or Peking undertaken by some African leader has seemed sufficient evidence to that effect. Since Communism and nationalism (and/or Pan-Africanism) are very closely intermingled in the political make-up of most of these African groups, it is not at all easy to find a fitting label for their aims and general political orientation. To stress these distinctions is not mere hair-splitting; a correct analysis of African political movements is of the greatest importance for the appraisal of their future development, and, of course, for the shaping of any effective Western policy.

According to official Communist sources, there are no "Marxist-Leninist mass parties" at present in Africa south of the Sahara—with the sole exception of one on the island of Réunion.[1] The only political party considered to be very close to Leninism is the P.A.I. (Parti Africain d'Indépendance) in West Africa; it is headed by Majhemout Diop, a Dakar bookseller who has spent several years in Eastern Europe as a member of the secretariat of the International Union of Students (I.U.S.). There are, of course, individual Communists in many African countries, and the intention to establish Communist parties at some future date is clear. It is apparently thought, however, that at present Communists should work through other political movements as well as through front organizations and trade unions. In present circumstances, the existence of official Communist parties would probably be more of a handicap than an advantage, given the reluctance of Africans to get involved with super-national movements and ideologies. Moreover, there are probably no more than a handful of Communists in the whole African continent whose polit-

[1] *Afrikanische Gegenwartsfragen*, (East) Berlin, 1960, p. 12.

ical education and judgment come up to Moscow's requirements. In view of the many past disappointments with African fellow travellers, who for a while coöperated with the Communists but then turned against them, or simply drifted away, it is thought preferable to delay the recognition of official Communist parties until more evidence has been received about the quality of the candidates for Communist representation and leadership.

Communism in 1961 means different things to different people. Afro-Communism as it now emerges has not very much in common with the theories of Karl Marx, not even in the modified form in which they have been applied in politically and economically backward countries. Afro-Communism represents above all a means of gaining political power for a small group of intellectuals. In foreign policy its protagonists stand for close collaboration with the Soviet bloc and/or China. On the domestic scene it implies agrarian reform, frequently a foreign trade monopoly and central planning, a one-party dictatorship and the gradual indoctrination of the population with some kind of official ideology. It hardly needs to be demonstrated that such revolutionary technique may be very efficient both in gaining power and in maintaining it; of this China will serve as an example. But it is equally obvious that the net result is a system that has very little in common with Marxism as it was originally conceived. It is in effect a new political phenomenon that can be only partly explained by reference to developments in the past, or in other parts of the world.

Clearly Afro-Communism cannot be equated with Communism as known in Russia or the West, but there are also important differences between Afro-Communism and Communism in Asia. The leaders of the Chinese, Korean or Indonesian parties were closely connected with the Comintern or Cominform for decades; they have had a thorough training in the essentials of Leninism, they have acquired the specific mental make-up of leading members of a very powerful sect, and they subject themselves to party discipline and "proletarian internationalism." In short, leaders like Mao or Ho Chi-Minh modelled themselves on the "ideal type" of the Russian Bolshevik of the 1920s.

The representatives of Afro-Communism, on the other hand, belong to a much younger generation. They grew up at a time when Communism had become much more powerful, but its ideological and psychological impact much lighter—and when various centers of

Communist power had come into being. Their familiarity with the theory of Marxism-Leninism is often superficial, restricted in most cases to some knowledge of its more practical aspects such as political organization and planning, and of course a nodding acquaintance with the Leninist theory of imperialism. These are not the strong and silent heroes who had to fight for many years in conditions of illegality. Independence and power came to them on the whole rather easily; as in Guinea, they sometimes received it on a platter. Their beliefs are, in short, less deeply rooted and they are very unlike the intransigent "Old Bolsheviks" with their iron discipline and their unending ideological squabbles. The rudimentary political training they have received may give them an advantage over their political rivals and competitors, but it does not make them Communists in the sense of the word accepted in the West; at most they are Communists of a new type. This is not to split theoretical hairs or to stick unduly to ideological niceties; it has important and far-reaching implications.

It means, for instance, that nationalism, Pan-Africanism and even racialism play an important part in the attitude of these leaders. In Moscow their *nationalisme communisant* is regarded with great indulgence as a transitional phenomenon that will in due time give way to the real thing. (No such tolerance is shown to Tito, an old Comrade who ought to know better.) But it is highly doubtful whether this "transitional phenomenon" will really end as the Communists expect. The Afro-Communists have their own ideas about what ought to be done in their continent, and they are not overawed by the authority of Lenin or the experience of Communist régimes outside Africa.[2] They regard themselves as the founding members of a new third group, the African ex-Colonial International; "People of the Colonies Unite," Kwame Nkrumah wrote in one of his articles.

The name of a half-forgotten precursor of this ex-Colonial Communism, Sultan Galiev, has frequently been mentioned in recent years in this context. He was a Soviet leader of Tatar origin, at one time Stalin's deputy as Commissar of Nationalities. He was expelled for "nationalist deviations" and disappeared in the purges. His theories were, briefly, that Marxism had been mistaken in concentrating its hopes on the industrialized people of the West rather than the

---

[2] As Sékou Touré once put it, discussing dialectical materialism: "Philosophy does not interest us. We have enough concrete tasks." Sékou Touré, *Texte des Interviews accordées aux Représentants de la Presse.* Conakry, 1959, p. 108.

colonial peoples of the East, who are progressive, in as much as they constitute the proletarian nations on the world scale. Since all classes in these countries had been subjected to Western rule and exploitation, the class struggle there is of much less importance. His ideas culminated in an appeal for the establishment of a new Colonial International. On some points Sultan Galiev went even farther, as in his demand for the establishment of the dictatorship of the ex-colonial peoples over the metropolitan nations.

Some of Sultan Galiev's basic notions are now generally accepted throughout Asia and Africa; to a certain extent they have even superseded the Leninist theory of imperialism, though Lenin is remembered and the name of Sultan Galiev forgotten. There is abundant evidence that the Communists are perfectly aware of the dangers involved. Commenting on the general attitude of some of his compatriots, M. Achufusi, an African Communist now teaching in East Germany, recently wrote: "Their experience in the capitalist world has strengthened the Africans in their belief that world political problems have a racial character. . . . They think that Africa is the proletariat while Europe constitutes the bourgeoisie. They demand a specific African philosophy and ideology in order to liberate the Africans spiritually. . . . They equate the workers of Europe with the exploiters and thus violate the canon of proletarian internationalism. . . . Such a trend leads to playing down the class conflicts inside Africa." [3]

Afro-Communism is taking only its first steps, and predictions about its future developments are probably premature. In view of the conflict of ambition and interest between its leaders, it seems rather doubtful whether any unity of action will be achieved in the near future. What can be stated now with near certainty is that, though strongly influenced by some tenets of Soviet ideology, Afro-Communism is showing marked political independence. This does not make it more friendly toward the West. But it is not willing to take orders from the East either; its apparent ambition is to emerge as an independent factor in world politics.

II

The observations made so far apply in varying degree to most supporters of Communism in Africa. But supporters of Communism in

[3] *Geschichte und Geschichtsbild Afrikas*, (East) Berlin, 1960, p. 222.

Africa are a very heterogeneous group—among them left-wing nationalist elements and orthodox Communists, with the great majority somewhere in between. It is doubtful whether much significance should be attributed to vaguely pro-Communist declarations made from time to time by leading nationalists. Most African political parties are in favor of some form of socialist planning, all are anti-imperialist, and traces of the Leninist theory of imperialism can be recognized in their views. This hardly makes them Communists, for the theory has in the past and present found many adherents (including Chiang Kai-shek) both in Asia and Europe, in circles otherwise very much opposed to Leninism. Such leaders may frequently follow the Soviet lead in the United Nations or participate in conferences convened by Communist-front organizations, but a closer analysis usually shows that they are radical nationalist rather than Communist in character.

Of greater interest in this context are such para-Communist groups as Sékou Touré's P.D.G. (Parti Démocratique de Guinée), one part of the Camerounian U.P.C. (Union des Populations du Cameroun), as well as the more radical sections of the ruling parties in Ghana and Mali. That these groups have certain features in common with the Communists is well known and need hardly be elaborated in detail. Apart from their enmity to the West (particularly pronounced in the case of Guinea and the U.P.C.), they have borrowed from Leninism the concept of "democratic centralism" and of the state party as a revolutionary vanguard. According to Dr. Nkrumah, "Once a majority decision is taken we expect such a decision to be loyally executed, even by those who might have opposed that decision. This we consider and proclaim to be the truest form of Democratic Centralism . . ."[4]

The adaptation of Communist ideas and methods has been in some cases very extensive. Guinea has been called the country in the world closest to Communism without actually belonging to the Soviet bloc, and Dr. Félix Moumié, the late leader of the Cameroun U.P.C., is said to have been criticized by Mr. Khrushchev for "infantile extremism." The U.P.C. has taken much of its inspiration and guidance from China in its six-year-old guerrilla war. In conversation

---

[4] *Accra Evening News*, June 16, 1959, quoted in Thomas Hodgkin, "A note on the language of African nationalism," in *African Affairs*, No. 1, London, 1961, p. 34. The "majority decision," needless to say, is more often than not the decision of the leader or leaders of the party.

with a Swiss journalist, Dr. Moumié stated that he had discussed with Mao at great length the Chinese leader's writings on the strategy and tactics of partisan warfare. Moumié then produced a copy of Mao's book, first published in 1936, with a personal dedication by the Chinese leader, and said, "Here you'll find out what is going to happen in Cameroun." [5]

All these groups have received Soviet bloc support but none has been recognized as a Communist party. While Sékou Touré has called his country the "most advanced democracy on earth" and pointed to a specific Guinean road to socialism, Communist observers prefer to talk about "the Guinean experiment." They think that Sékou Touré's party has a "proletarian kernel," but not more than that, and they see a danger in the "swollen-headedness of the leaders as a result of imperialist flattery and the respect shown and homage paid to Guinea by the great powers of America, Europe and Asia" (sic). Another possible pitfall in Communist eyes is the reluctance of the Guinean leaders to "arm the working classes and the masses of the people generally with the knowledge and understanding of Marxist-Leninist theory." In order to leave no doubts of any kind, it is added that only with the emergence of a strong Communist party could a return to capitalism be definitely ruled out. [6]

President Sékou Touré, on the other hand, has more than once asserted his belief in a specific African socialism and his objection to any interference by Russia and China in what he considers his own parish. In a declaration in April 1960 he said that he refused to allow his party to follow the ideological line of Communism. If certain people wished to found a Guinean Communist party they should realize that the P.D.G. would oppose them under Sékou Touré's leadership, for Communism was not the way for Africa. The class struggle was not possible for there were no classes, only social strata. The fundamental basis of Guinean society was the family and the village community. On yet another occasion Sékou Touré expressed the view that, while dialectical materialism denied the existence of God, one would not find anybody in Africa, and particularly in Guinea, who did not be-

[5] *Neue Zürcher Zeitung*, January 13, 1961.

[6] *The African Communist*, April 1960, p. 26. This is the (clandestine) periodical of the (illegal) South African Communist Party, formerly published in Capetown, now in London. It is of particular interest because it is the only periodical in Africa that deals with African affairs in an orthodox Leninist spirit; it is written by Communists and for Communists.

lieve in God. Mr. Sékou Touré has recently been to Mecca as befitting
the head of a predominantly Muslim country.

Guinea has been praised in Communist publications as an example
to all the oppressed and exploited; and yet there are, as these illustra-
tions have shown, considerable differences of opinion between the
Communists and the African régime considered closest to them.
There are other dividing lines between orthodox Leninists and the
Afro-Communists. Many of the latter hold strong opinions about the
central role of the African intellectuals as the pioneers and leaders of
the national liberation movement; the orthodox Communists, on the
other hand, disparage the role of the intelligentsia. But the central
issue on which opinions widely diverge is the question of the specific
character of Africa. The Leninists do not deny the existence of pecu-
liarities in the historical development and present state of Africa, but
they maintain that all the basic tenets of Marxism-Leninism are applicable in Africa and that to disregard them would lead to dangerous
nationalist deviations. The Afro-Communists, on the other hand, are
much more selective in their approval of Leninist theory; while bor-
rowing with much enthusiasm some of the tenets of this body of doctrine, they have emphatically rejected others. Some of their more
sophisticated spokesmen who have read the young Marx consider
Communism in Europe the natural reaction against a society in which
the individual has been alienated, in which money is the supreme
good, and in which spiritual values count for little if anything. Africa,
in their view, is different; it may be economically backward but it is
not a society with its values in process of disintegration; it still has
a human richness, warmth and spontaneity sadly lacking in both
West and East. These convictions are shared by a majority of African
intellectuals and incidentally by quite a number of White missionaries
who have called for the "Bantuization of Christianity." On the
cultural level these convictions have given rise to the concept of
négritude; on the political level they have found their reflection in the
movement of Pan-Africanism.

Orthodox Leninists are bound to reject both *négritude* and Pan-
Africanism as romantic petty-bourgeois nationalist deviations. They
try to do so with the maximum of tact, for they realize clearly that
this rejection brings them into conflict with the great majority of
African political leaders and intellectuals, who all share these views to
some degree. For obvious tactical reasons, the orthodox Communists

want to prevent a split with the Afro-Communists, but in the long run they cannot afford to compromise, for without clearly defining their own views they cannot hope to make much headway in the future. They face a dilemma which they probably will not be able to resolve, for the prevailing political climate is overwhelmingly in favor of nationalism and Pan-Africanism. The situation in this respect is not dissimilar to the state of affairs in the Middle East a few years ago. The Arab Communists tried very hard to evade, or at any rate to delay, a head-on clash with Pan-Arabism as represented by President Nasser. It is doubtful whether orthodox African Communists will be more successful in postponing the outbreak of what seems otherwise an inevitable conflict.

III

The orthodox Leninist camp, to which reference has so far been made only in contradistinction to the Afro-Communists, includes a handful of party stalwarts who underwent training in East Germany, Czechoslovakia and Hungary, as well as the P.A.I. mentioned above. Founded in 1957, the P.A.I. publishes a daily newspaper, *La Lutte*, in Dakar, but its influence in terms of votes is as yet minute; at last year's municipal elections in Senegal it received 300 votes. It is debatable whether to include in this category also the radical wing of the Camerounian U.P.C., founded by Ruben um Nyobe, a trade unionist trained in Prague who was shot during a guerrilla engagement. His successor, Dr. Moumié, was poisoned last year in Switzerland; one faction of the U.P.C. under Matip seceded, renounced terrorism and became the Cameroun parliamentary opposition, but another section still fights on. This wing of the U.P.C. seems, however, to be under the influence of Peking rather than Moscow. A third, comparatively orthodox group is the P.I.M. (Parti de l'Indépendance Malagache), founded in 1959 originally as a coalition of radical-nationalist and left-wing groups which quickly fell under the influence of its Communist wing. This Leninist party has the unique distinction of having a priest as its president—the Reverend Richard Andriamanjato. It has gained control of the town council of the capital of Madagascar, Tananarive, but has done rather badly elsewhere. Communist factions are also reported to exist in the Congolese "Parti du Peuple" (headed by Alphonse Nguvulu, who was minister of planning in the Lumumba government), and in PUNGA (Parti de l'Unité Nationale

Gabonaise), an opposition party in Gabon. By no stretch of the imagination, however, can any of these parties be regarded as a Leninist mass party.

The main problem that has faced all these groups during the past decade, and their main dilemma at the present time, is the stand to be taken vis-à-vis the national movement in their respective countries, or, in Leninist parlance, the problem of the "national bourgeoisie." Up to about 1955 the Communist attitude, briefly summarized, was that the leaders of the national movement could not be trusted, that their struggle against colonialism was a sham, and that sooner or later they would betray the national cause. They were incapable of any consistent struggle and inclined towards compromise and collaboration with the imperialist enemy.[7] There was considerable mistrust of the movements that had won, or were about to win, independence for their countries. Such independence, it was argued, could not possibly be genuine; it was "only a more skillful hidden form of continued association with imperialism," as the leading British Communist theoretician, Palme Dutt, put it at the time.[8] Among those attacked were Dr. Nkrumah's Convention People's Party in Ghana and Dr. Azikiwe and his supporters in Nigeria. The R.D.A. (Rassemblement Démocratique Africain), the leading political party in French West Africa, fared no better; it had "unmasked itself," made a "shameful deal with the colonizers," and its "treason" had allegedly caused tremendous anger among the toilers of Africa. It would be tedious to prolong this list, which included virtually every political leader and party in Africa at the time.

In 1955, however, attitudes towards the African national movement were substantially modified, and for a while it seemed that the Communists were willing to collaborate with practically everybody in Africa. The general assumption was that the West was the main enemy and that anti-Western sentiment in Africa should be used to constitute a common anti-Western front. But it is doubtful whether the basic attitude towards the African nationalists has really changed. African Communists believe that the support of the "patriotic elements" is essential for a speedy victory over colonialism, to quote a recent authoritative comment. But, they argue, the "national bour-

---

[7] For a more detailed review of Soviet and Communist attitudes towards the African national movement see my "Soviet Views on Africa" in *Soviet Survey* (London), April 1959, p. 37 *et seq.*

[8] *Allies for Freedom*, London, 1954, p. 25.

geoisie" is a very unsatisfactory leader of the national movement: "They are apt to be narrow, selfishly hidebound and conservative. They are apt to be guided not by the interest of the masses but by their own special, minority class interests. Often they are parochial, chauvinistic, tribalistic, and lacking a broad vision. They are usually opportunistic, tend to compromise with the colonialists for small gains at the sacrifice of principle, because they fear the revolutionary activities of the masses of workers and rural people." [9] According to a more recent statement, the "national bourgeoisie" is a "counter-revolutionary force to socialism." [10]

Do these formidable strictures apply to left-wing intellectuals such as Dr. Nkrumah or Sékou Touré, who cannot possibly be regarded as representatives of the "national bourgeoisie"? The Communists are willing to give them their due: "They have been the founders of our national liberation movement and have carried the spark of enlightenment and rebellion from one end of Africa to another." [11] But handsome compliments are about all these revolutionary nationalists can expect, for in the future, as the Communists envisage it, there will be no room for them at the top of the national movement. "In conditions of modern society, the intellectuals occupy a middle position between the rulers and the ruled, the bourgeoisie and the proletariat. . . . Many of these intellectuals vacillate between one camp and another, are always swinging helplessly between the oppressors and the oppressed. . . . We must remember that it (the intelligentsia) as a group is inherently unstable and unfit for leadership." [12]

The intellectuals, in other words, cannot be relied upon, unless they join the Communist movement. If this is the comparatively restrained language of ideological analysis, there is no reason to be surprised by the much sharper attacks, in propaganda organs, on African leaders such as Tom Mboya, Alioune Cisse (Senegal), or Macrae (Uganda), all leading trade unionists, or on leading West African Socialists such as Léopold Senghor and Mamadou Dia. Clearly, for the orthodox Leninist, there are narrow limits to collaboration even with "progressive intellectuals" of the Afro-Communist brand; their leading position in the national movement is apparently to be challenged in the not-too-distant future.

[9] N. Numade, "Marxism and African Liberation," in *The African Communist*, April 1960, p. 32–40.
[10] F. Kumalo, "Socialism in Africa," in *The African Communist*, January 1961, p. 36.
[11] *Ibid.*
[12] *The African Communist*, April 1960.

It has been attempted in the present article to review the problems now facing Communism in Africa; a systematic survey of Communist activities in the trade unions and various kinds of front organizations would require lengthy and detailed studies of a specialized character. But even a cursory examination of the African scene establishes a number of facts of considerable political importance: above all, perhaps, the great difference between, on the one hand, radical leaders and groups who have adopted some of the ideas and much of the language of Communism, but who have remained essentially left-wing nationalist and Pan-Africanist; and on the other, the orthodox Leninists whose number and influence are quite small. The former, the "Afro-Communists," may be as extreme as the latter in their hostility to the West; they may even on occasion be more intransigent. Nevertheless, there are basic differences and it would be a great mistake not to differentiate between them. There certainly is a great temptation to judge them all alike, because of the widespread and indiscriminate use of quasi-Leninist slogans among the radical nationalists in Africa. It is a temptation that should be resisted.

It could be argued that some Afro-Communists may move at some future date towards full acceptance of the Leninist credo. This, of course, is not unthinkable. But it is equally possible that the orthodox Communists will become "nationalist deviationists." Ten years ago there could be no doubts and hesitations for a Communist: there was but one center for the faithful, Rome and Mecca in one. The situation in 1961 is much more confusing from the point of view of the orthodox believer; this is the age of polycentric Communism—the time of infallibility and of the Russian monopoly of the means of grace has irrevocably passed. If Moscow and Peking proclaim rival truths, and if Belgrade preaches yet a third way to paradise, there will have to be room ultimately for a fourth and fifth independent center. In the transition from the age of proletarian internationalism to the era of schism, we will do well to encourage independence of mind and to avoid confusing radical nationalism or Afro-Communism with orthodox Marxism-Leninism.

Part V

Dead End in South Africa

Note

RACE QUESTIONS IN SOUTH AFRICA
BY PATRICK DUNCAN

January 1927

One of the most scarifying problems in the world today is the racial conflict in South Africa. Of all the major points of tension in the world, what distinguishes the South African problem is that (a) it is the only one that can be resolved without the coöperation of the Communist world, and (b) it seems the most likely to blow up in the next ten years. In the event of a race war between 3,000,000 well armed whites and 11,000,000 blacks supported by all the independent states of Africa, and many in Asia, where will our loyalties lie? Will we actively support our "white brothers," who by then may appear not as oppressors but as the underdog victims of terrible savagery? If so, the implications for our political position in the world, for our moral leadership and for our own race problem are beyond reckoning.

One would have to look far to find a better introduction to the race problems of South Africa than this article, written in 1927 by an active South African politician who was later Governor-General of the Union. All the basic elements of the problem are here set forth, and the alternatives considered—"repression," "assimilation" or "segregation." The author calls for a rational and humane policy that falls between the second and third alternatives, and in doing so reminds us that the policy of apartheid and the machinery of oppression required to make it work were not inevitable in the situation, but the conscious acts of men to whom more reasonable alternatives were open.

Today, such freedoms as are still exercised in South Africa—by whites as well as blacks—are by sufferance, not by right. South Africa is a nation living in fear and in fatalistic resignation to the violence that is already an everyday occurrence, and the much greater violence that lies ahead.

Patrick Duncan went out to South Africa from England at the age of 31—a fact which helps to account for the objectivity he was able to bring to the political and racial problems of his adopted country. British born and Oxford educated, he was working in the Inland Revenue Department when he attracted the notice of its Board Chairman, Lord Milner, whose private secretary he became. When Lord Milner returned to South Africa in 1901 to become Governor of both the Transvaal and the Orange River Colony, he persuaded Duncan to go with him. The year after the Union was formed in 1910 Duncan was elected to Parliament, and subsequently became Minister of the Interior, of Education and of Public Health—posts in which he had only recently served when he wrote the following article. Later he returned to the Government of the United Party, and for a time it seemed likely that he might become Prime Minister of a coalition government. In 1936 he was made Governor-General of the Union, the first South African to be appointed to that post. Sir Patrick, as he then became, fought hard and effectively during World War II to keep South Africa engaged on the side of the Allies, but died in 1943 before the outcome was known.

The population of South Africa has more than doubled since Sir Patrick wrote. As population figures for the various racial groups are important in any consideration of South Africa's political problems, it may be useful for the reader to have more up-to-date figures. They show, among other things, that, despite white immigration, the African population is growing relatively faster than the white. According to the 1960 census, there were: 10,907,789 Bantu; 1,509,258 colored; 477,125 Asians; and 3,088,492 whites.

Nearly four decades after this article was written Sir Patrick's son and bearer of the same name wrote for *Foreign Affairs* an article which shows how far South Africa has since moved in the direction of "segregation" and "repression." See page 250.

Race Questions in
South Africa

by PATRICK DUNCAN

The main problems confronting the Union of South Africa in respect of its colored races and peoples, and of their relations with the European population, are peculiarly complex. They call with increasing insistence for the reconsideration and readjustment of our political and industrial policies.

Our non-European peoples fall into three main groups. First and most important, both in regard to existing numbers and future potentialities, comes the native population. Then there are the people known in South Africa as "colored," who include colored people of mixed race and also a small community of Malays settled for the most part in and near Capetown. The Malays were introduced by the Dutch East India Company before the British occupation of the Cape, and have long since lost all connection with their country of origin, but retain their Mohammedan religion; their numbers are insignificant for the purposes with which we are concerned, but they are grouped for administrative and other purposes with the "colored" population. (This term, it must always be remembered, has a peculiar connotation in South Africa, in that it is used to distinguish the South African colored man of mixed race—including the small Malay community just mentioned—from the native.) The third racial element is the Asiatic, consisting for the most part of British Indians, some of whom are traders or the descendants of traders who have come here from India, but the great majority of whom are persons or the descendants of persons who were brought over from India to work as laborers in the tea and sugar plantations of Natal.

The native population at the last census (1921) numbered 4,699,-433; the mixed and other colored races numbered 545,548; and the

201

Asiatic 163,896. The total of the European population at the same census was 1,519,488. If we add to these figures the population of the territories adjacent to the Union and now administered directly by the British Government, but which may one day be included in the Union, the effect would be to add approximately 5,500 to the European population and 750,000 (all but a few of whom are natives) to the non-European. We at once see South Africa's peculiar position. She stands somewhere between the two principal types of countries where the white and colored races of the world are clashing.

In one type of country, of which British India is the best example, white men are there as the governing power, but do not claim that their stock will permanently take root and occupy the land. They are governors, soldiers, officials, business and professional men, but they are a small caste amidst a native population overwhelmingly larger in numbers, a population whose gradual rise in education, in the material equipment of civilization, and in political and administrative capacity will inevitably, whether sooner or later, entitle them to emerge from a state of tutelage. Such a country the white man can never claim as a "white man's land." Where he rules he does so admittedly as a trustee. Where he is living as official, trader, or professional man, he has either cut himself off from his own race, or he is there as a bird of passage with his eyes turned homeward. He does not think of the land of his residence as one with whose fortunes the future of his children is irrevocably bound up.

The other type is exemplified by the United States of America. There a population of about 12,000,000 negroes gives rise at many points to social and industrial and political friction. But, grave as are the questions which spring from these causes, they do not interfere with the sense of security with which the white citizen regards the future of his country. They do not arise from, and are not aggravated by, any feeling of doubt or fear as to whether his children or the children of his stock are in danger of seeing their place and the outlet for their energies in the country gradually encroached upon by the rising tide of a colored race. For as far ahead as he can see the effective occupation of his country will be by the white races, and the control of its destinies in their hands.

South Africa, as has been said, is in a position somewhere between these two types. Since the European first made effective settlement on its shores, about 270 years ago, he has gradually extended his hold upon the land. He has introduced his civilization, broken the power of the savage tribes who disputed his occupation, reclaimed the land to agricultural and pastoral uses, established mining and manufacturing industries. He has made the land his home. Its civilization came with him, and could not even now continue without him. And yet he sees this very civilization being turned against him by the descendants of those barbarous tribes among whom he had to win his way through many years of warfare. He has abolished the famines and inter-tribal wars which formerly kept a check on the growth of the native peoples, and these peoples are strong enough to withstand the physical degeneration which contact with civilization so often spreads among savages. They do not die out. On the contrary, they increase and multiply. They take their part in the white man's industries and learn in the schools and educational institutions which he provides for them. It is no more than natural, therefore, that he should watch their gradual rise in civilization, slow though it may be, with some measure of apprehension for the future of his own race. As they turn to habits of industry, monopolize (as they almost do) the unskilled labor of the country, begin to push their way into skilled trades and even professions, the white man not unnaturally has fears that they may in time so encroach upon the field which his race has hitherto regarded as its own, as to prevent its normal expansion, reduce its numbers, and in the end threaten its political supremacy.

This fear lies at the root of what is called the "native problem" in South Africa. It is responsible for much of the narrowness of outlook and intensity of feeling with which in the past the problem has usually been envisaged in South African politics.

The other two racial groups—the "colored" and the Asiatic—give rise to problems of their own, serious in their way, but the issues between them and the white man are not so far-reaching as those involved in the white man's relations with the native. In the case of the "colored" man the tendency is to associate him more and more with the European, and to draw the line, not between white and colored, but between the European, including the mixed race, on the one side, and the native on the other. Socially, it is true, the line of division is for the most part one of color. In hotels, in theatres, in trains, the color line is enforced—in the northern provinces with absolute strictness, and in the Cape, at any rate in Capetown and its surrounding districts, with a little more latitude. In the Cape the trade unions admit the skilled colored worker to membership on equal terms. In the northern provinces he is excluded, and indeed he is not regarded by his white fellow workers as having any right to be a skilled worker at all. But there can be little doubt that the present trend of policy is to find a place for the "colored" man in the ranks of the European. This finds expression in the recent proposals laid before the country by the Prime Minister for a complete readjustment of the relations of the European and the native. The underlying principle of these proposals is segregation of the native from the European, and the "colored" population for this purpose is classed with the European, although outside the Cape Province it is likely to be some time before full political equality is conceded to them.

The third group—the Asiatic—consists, as has been said, almost entirely of Indians, and they are confined in great part to the Province of Natal. The census of 1921 showed that of a total Asiatic population in the Union of, in round figures, 164,000, approximately 142,000 were living in Natal. These are for the most part people who were brought in as laborers for the sugar and tea plantations, and their descendants. A certain number of them return to India, and the Government encourages this movement by allowing them a free passage and a cash payment on arrival in India. Of those now in Natal, however, nearly two-thirds have been born there, and in their case naturally the idea of returning to India becomes less and less attractive as their connection with it becomes more remote. Since 1911 no more Indians have been brought in as laborers, and since 1913 the immigration of Asiatics into the Union has been completely stopped by the Immigrants Regulation Act of 1913, which empowers the Government to prohibit the entry of any person or class of persons deemed by them on economic grounds, or on account of standard or habits of life, to be unsuited to the requirements of the Union or any particular province thereof. By the exercise of that power Asiatics as a class have been deemed to be prohibited immigrants.

Even inter-provincial migration is forbidden to the Asiatic, with the result that, while the trouble arising from the presence of the Indian population has been localized to the Province of Natal, it is all the more acute there, because the impact has to be borne by a comparatively small European community. In fact the Indian population in Natal was, at the last census, slightly in excess of the European. In the other provinces the competition of the Indian traders gives rise to a certain amount of agitation on the part of the Europeans in the smaller towns who consider that his low standard of living gives the Indian trader an unfair advantage against the European, and leads to a gradual transfer of the petty retail trade into the hands of the Indian. In Natal, however, the clash of the two races is more serious. The children of the Indians who came in as laborers get education, and aspire to rise in the social scale. They become semi-skilled or skilled workmen, clerks and professional men. In Natal, therefore, what is called the "Indian menace" is a burning political question, and drastic action is demanded from the Government as necessary for the preservation of the white man and his western civilization. The census results, on the other hand, do not afford any evidence of restricted expansion of the European population. On the contrary, the census figures for 1921 showed an increase of about 40 percent in the European population of Natal as compared with the previous census of 1911—a much higher rate of increase than in any of the other provinces. A census of the European population of the Union, which was taken this year, shows an increase of the European population over the figure of 1921 of 15.6 percent, which again is a considerably higher rate of increase than in any of the other provinces.

The agitation against the Indians, however, is not likely to fade out in the cold light of census figures. In its extreme form the demand is for nothing less than the complete repatriation or expulsion of the Indians; but, as this is generally admitted to be an impossible solution, the demand has for its immediate object that Indians be prohibited from acquiring land, and that they be restricted from trading except in areas specially set apart for them. A conference is planned between the Union Government and the Government of India with a view to arriving at an agreed policy, which will reassure the European as to the maintenance of his western standards of civilization without imposing intolerable and humiliating restrictions upon the Indians. A conference such as this is quite a new feature in the long history of repressive legislation against Indians in South Africa, which goes back to the days of the Boer Republics before the Anglo-Boer War of 1899–1902. Formerly the British Government, as the superior power, endeavored to see justice done to the Indian, but its intervention usually had the effect of aggravating the Europeans without securing substantial relief for the Indians. Now the Indian Government and the Government of South Africa deal directly with each other, and Indian statesmen have for the first time an opportunity of meeting the South African Government on common ground.

It will be seen, therefore, that the questions which arise out of the relations of the white man with the two last-mentioned groups are side issues as compared with those arising between the European and the native. There is the real race clash.

There are certain fundamental differences between the position of the native here and that of the negro in the United States in relation to the population of European stock. In America the negro population is an alien element, which was introduced by the white community itself for the purpose of servile or unskilled labor, and which has gradually raised itself in civilization and efficiency. In that respect its closest analogy in South Africa is to be found in the Asiatic population, already described. But the native here in Africa is in his home. The white man found him here when he came, though it is probable that the Bantu tribes, who form the largest and most virile section of the native population today, made their appearance in what is now the Union of South Africa not very long before the white man. They spread over the land in nomadic fashion, subduing or exterminating the people whom they found there. They imposed themselves upon the land by superior organization and fighting power, just as the white man, when they met, did upon them; but their conquest was the conquest of savagery, not of civilization.

The other main point of difference is that the native population here is to a great extent still living under its primitive tribal organization. Its chiefs, of course, have not the powers of life and death over their subjects as they used to have, nor can they indulge in tribal wars or cattle raids. In many other ways, too, the contacts of civilization are undermining their old authority, and the whole system is slowly but surely breaking down. Economic pressure has driven the able-bodied men in thousands out to seek work in the white man's industries. Many of these retain their connection with their tribal home and in the end return there to stay. But many others break away from it and settle permanently in the towns and industrial centres. It is estimated that about 500,000 natives have become permanently de-tribalized in this way. Others occupy land on the white man's farms as labor-tenants. Others, in certain districts of the Cape Province, possess small holdings as peasants in individual ownership. But of the rest the vast majority are living under the old tribal conditions, subsisting on the produce of the tribal lands on the old communal system, supplemented by the earnings of those who go out from time to time for longer or shorter periods to work for the European.

It is now time to turn to the European's side of the picture and

see in what way the political and industrial conditions which he has
made for himself are affected by the gradual rise of the non-European
peoples in civilization and in industrial efficiency.

The Union of South Africa was brought into existence in 1910 by
the coming together of the four British colonies (as they then were)
of the Cape of Good Hope, Natal, the Transvaal and the Orange
River Colony. The two first were British Colonies of long standing—
the Cape for over a century, and Natal from its beginnings as an European settlement. The two others, formerly independent republics—
subject to an ill-defined claim of British suzerainty as regards their
foreign relations—became British colonies by annexation in the Anglo-
Boer war. At the National Convention, at which the new Union Constitution was drawn up, the idea of uniting on federal lines was deliberately rejected in favor of the principle of unification. The Constitution was drawn on that principle, and the four colonies, which
now became provinces of the Union, gave up to the new Union Government all powers of government except in regard to matters of local
and subsidiary concern.

The Constitution, however, which brought about unity in government and administration, could not reconcile the divergent policies
and outlooks which had prevailed in the different colonies in the matter of the native and colored races. It was again a case of a color line
dividing north against south. In the south the Colony of the Cape of
Good Hope, ever since its Constitution Ordinance of 1853, had drawn
no color or race distinction in the qualifications required for the exercise of the vote. Its franchise rolls were open to any man who was a
citizen and could fulfill a comparatively low property and education
test, whatever his race or color might be. But in the two northern
colonies a hard and fast color line ran right through all relations of
white and black. The old republican constitution of the Transvaal
had laid down as one of its fundamental principles that there should
be no equality in church or state between white and black, and this
principle was, in both, rigorously observed in every department of life.
When, after the British annexation, responsible government was
granted to the two new colonies, the franchise law preserved the old
color line, so that the people should have the opportunity of deciding
for themselves on so vital a question, and the right to vote was, as it
had been in the republics, based on white manhood suffrage. In Natal,
which when it received responsible government was a handful of
European colonists surrounded by a vast and uncivilized native popu-

lation, the native was not, in express terms, excluded from the franchise, but the conditions permitting him to be enrolled were such that only a few have ever qualified. The framers of Union found it impossible to agree on any common policy on this question, and, in consequence, it was simply left alone in the hope that time would bring about some approach to a common outlook. The old franchise laws were left in force, with the provision that the Cape laws were not to be altered so as to exclude persons on grounds of race or color except by a two-thirds majority of both Houses of the Legislature sitting together. That is where we stand today in the matter of the parliamentary vote. In the northern provinces the same color bar excludes any man of color from the right to vote for local and municipal councils.

The Union is now sixteen years old—a very infant among the nations—but, even in that short time, some progress is noticeable in the evolution of a common outlook on questions arising from the relations of European and non-European races. Where these questions affect the government of the country, they have to be dealt with, not as before in four separate and independent compartments, but as national questions by a parliament and government representing the whole people. The mere fact that the Legislature sits in Capetown has brought the members from the northern provinces face to face with a more liberal outlook. The advocates of the policy of equal rights for all civilized men have been led to understand more sympathetically the difficulties of its application in an environment quite different from their own. Moreover, the existence of the colored and native voter in the Cape province has had a potent influence on national politics throughout the Union. Low as are the qualifications for the franchise in that province, the number of colored and native voters actually on the rolls is not very great. The last registration showed a total of 36,853 non-European voters as against 156,884 Europeans, whereas the estimated population of that province in 1924 was 2,209,-671 natives, Asiatics and colored, as against 680,053 Europeans. But, though the number of non-European voters is small, they can in a considerable number of constituencies, if they vote solidly, exercise, if not a decisive influence as between rival political parties, at any rate an influence which no party with an election in view can afford to neglect or alienate. A government, therefore, is bound to take into account, in considering measures affecting natives in any province, what effect they may have on the sympathies of the voters in the Cape.

The contact of the white man with the native in the industrial field goes back to the beginnings of our industries. As soon as the superior force of the white man had established peace and security in the country, the native turned his attention from war to labor. The Europeans were few in number, and, both from habit and the exigencies of the climate, were averse to manual labor. In the native they found a man of strong physique, docile to authority, whose material wants were few. The two fell as if by nature into the rôles of master and servant. Before the discovery of the diamond mines of Kimberley and the gold mines of the Witwatersrand, the demand for labor was but small, and those natives who came to work on the white man's farms were not subjected to any serious break with their ancestral conditions. But with the opening up of the mines, South Africa passed by a rapid transition from a primitive pastoral state to one of highly developed industry. Thousands of natives were required for the rough manual work of the mines and the industries which sprang up around them, and the lure of money and the luxuries which it could buy was a powerful attraction. From the employer's point of view the native had many advantages as a laborer. He was easily trained, had an ingrained respect for the authority of the white man, and he worked under indenture, breach of which was punishable by law. Above all he was cheap. Coming to work as he first did, and still to a great extent does, only as an interlude in his tribal life, he could be housed in barracks or compounds, and his requirements as to food and clothing were of the simplest. His wage, therefore, was far below what a white man, living under civilized conditions, could possibly accept.

It is on this basis—namely, that all the unskilled labor is performed by natives under the conditions described—that the mining industry of the country has been built up; and today the gold mines of the Witwatersrand employ over 180,000 of them. Other industries have adopted the same principle as far as they could.

Three results have recently forced themselves on public attention. One is that the supply of native labor is inadequate for all industrial requirements. Another is that the growing class of natives who cut themselves adrift from their tribal homes and settle with their families in towns and industrial centers give rise to very serious problems in regard to housing, because their wage is inadequate to enable them to provide for housing themselves under civilized and sanitary conditions. The other is that there has grown up among the Europeans a class of "poor whites," as they are called—men who are unfitted for any occupation but that of unskilled or manual labor, but who cannot get it in competition with the native at the wage which the native accepts. Outside the field of unskilled labor, also, the native is beginning to come into competition with the European, and here again his docility in the hands of the white employer, and the low wage which he is prepared to accept, give him advantages which tell heavily against the superior skill and intelligence of the European.

The writer has attempted to present a general view of the contacts, political and industrial, which have been and are being established in South Africa between the European and the native. Slowly but inevitably, under the pressure of the white man's civilization, the native is becoming conscious of himself as an element in the community. Tribal barriers are breaking down. He is learning to organize himself industrially and politically, to realize his importance and to lay claim to what he regards as his rights. We must now try to see on what lines the European's policy, both in politics and industry, is adapting itself to meet his claim. Again this can only be done in broad outline.

Underlying all the ideas of the European as to his relations with the native, is the fundamental proposition that South Africa is to be a "white man's country," if not in the sense that its inhabitants shall be in number predominantly white, at any rate that its destinies shall be guided by his race and along the lines of European civilization. For the practical politics of today this may be taken as an axiom universally accepted. There is not here, as there is in India, a rival civilization, rooted in the soil, with a vital spirit of its own. Here the European represents civilization as against barbarism. Based on this fundamental proposition there are three main lines of policy, each of which has its advocates, and all of which from time to time, alternately or together, have combined to influence public policy in South Africa.

Of these three lines of policy the first may generally be described as that of repression. This policy adopts as its guiding principle "no equality in church or state," or, "the native must be kept in his place." The native is an inferior being, to be treated with fairness and humanity, but never allowed to aspire beyond his inferior status. His labor is an "asset" to the country, but the laborer himself must not use it so as to establish for himself an independent status. It must be used by the white man in strict subordination to his own ends. Political rights are denied. Carried to its logical conclusion this policy refuses to recognize the native or the colored man as a full member of the community. It goes back for its idea to the institutions of slavery or serfdom. The man of the subject race is denied the principles of citizenship, restricted in regard to his place of residence and movements, and confined by law, as regards his labor, to a certain status inferior to, and designed to serve the purposes of, the dominant race. It is perhaps the view which, if one took a poll of the European community, would carry the largest number of votes. It is, tacitly or avowedly, the view of the ordinary run of men who do not think very deeply about public affairs. It was the avowed policy of the two northern provinces before they came into the Union, and still finds its chief support there.

Another line of policy may be described for want of a better term as the policy of assimilation. That policy bases itself on civilization, refuses to recognize any difference in status or privilege based on race or color, and proclaims equality in political rights and equal opportunity in industry for all civilized men. This policy, in theory at least, was the policy of the Cape Province before Union and it stands as the antithesis of the policy of repression.

The third line of policy, and one which has been much discussed since Union, is the policy of segregation. Applied absolutely this would mean a line of territorial separation between native and European, the division of the Union into two areas reserved for the European and the native respectively. In this extreme form, however, it has few adherents, and is generally admitted to be impossible. In a modified form it has been put forward recently by the Prime Minister of the Union as the line on which a national policy should be built. Certain areas would be definitely set apart as native areas, within which no European would be allowed to acquire land, and conversely natives would be prohibited from acquiring land outside these areas. Natives who came into European areas to work would be subject to restrictions as regards competing with the European in skilled or semi-skilled occupations. The natives would not be allowed to be registered on the ordinary voters' rolls, but by a sort of communal franchise they would be allowed to elect a limited number of European members to the elected House of the Legislature with specially restricted powers. Inside their areas they would choose councils who would exercise advisory powers in matters of local interest and might in time be entrusted with certain administrative functions.

None of these three seems to afford in itself a basis comprehensive enough for an adjustment which is likely to be permanent and adequate for the needs of both races.

The first breaks down in practice because it runs counter to some of the deepest and most enduring elements of human nature. The dominant race inevitably falls a victim to a fatal infection from the very inferiority to which it condemns its subjects, and in the long run loses even the physical and material force necessary to keep the lower race down.

For the other line of policy, which we have called that of assimilation, it is sometimes claimed that there is no halfway house between it and that of repression. It is advocated especially by missionaries, and those who seek to apply the principles of Christianity as the final test of the validity of public institutions and policies. Looked at from the point of view of practical statesmen, the policy cannot safely be adopted in South Africa if it involves a grave risk to the fundamental principle of European supremacy. The European population, as has been seen, is vastly outnumbered by the native, and behind the comparatively small number of civilized natives is the great mass which is now and will for long remain in or near its primitive state of barbarism. The white man in South Africa looks on the question as one of race against race. Assimilation in the full sense of the word, involving social intercourse and in particular race admixture, is abhorrent to his instincts. Whatever biologists may say about race admixture—and they do not all say the same thing—he will have none of it. The lapses of individuals in this respect only serve to throw into clearer relief the strength of the general sentiment. And behind this instinct is the fact, admitted even by the most thoroughgoing champions of equality, that for as far as we can see in the future the supremacy of the white man is essential to the maintenance of civilization itself. Assimilation, even in respect of political rights, would before very long gravely imperil that supremacy.

The policy of segregation even in its modified form does not seem to take adequate account of the actual facts of the case. The lands which are now allotted, or can possibly be allotted, for native reserves are not now adequate for the support of the native population, and we have yet to see what would happen if part of these lands through mineral discoveries or otherwise should offer strong attractions for development by the European. Large numbers of natives even now who still cling to their tribal homes can only subsist by coming out to work for the white man for longer or shorter periods. Many of them, as has been seen—and their number is increasing—have become permanently de-tribalized. We have made the native, for good or evil, part of our industrial organization. It was inevitable that it should be so. But it would be unjust to him, and fatal in the long run to ourselves, to decree that if he comes amongst us as a worker, as he must do both for his own needs and for ours, he shall be confined by law, no matter what his abilities or his civilization may be, to the status of an unskilled laborer.

The peculiar conditions of South Africa seem to call for a somewhat different policy, something between the second and third of those just mentioned. The native should be segregated to the extent of being encouraged to remain on his tribal lands, and he should be assisted by training in agriculture to make these lands sustain a larger population than they now do. But he cannot be segregated to the extent of being put away in a sort of watertight compartment. We are one country. There is room only for one civilization—the European—and no artificial barriers will keep the two elements permanently cut off from each other. The native who comes to work in our industries must not be under a legal ban which prohibits him from utilizing, to such advantage as he may, his capacity for work, skilled or unskilled. But the employer should be prevented by wage regulation from exploiting the low demands of the native to undercut the civilized wage rate. If the native is to compete with workers who have to live as civilized men in civilized surroundings, he must be paid a wage which will enable him to do the same. The true protection for the white worker is not the repression of the native but the raising of the native's standard of living to something like his own. In politics the native cannot be permanently excluded from a voice in the government of the country, but his participation in political rights, as he rises in education and civilization, must be so graduated as not to endanger the hegemony of the European civilization and direction. With this must go effective measures for reinforcing the European population by encouraging the immigration of people who will assimilate with its stock and make a permanent home here.

Whether under some such policy South Africa can work out a peaceful and permanent adjustment in the relations of her European and native peoples is a question for the far future. There is no "solution" or short cut in problems such as these. Today we do not know adequately many facts which have the most important bearing on the question. We do not know, for example, what the comparative rates of increase of the two populations are now, still less what they will be as the native comes more and more completely in contact with civilization and with industrial conditions. Yet on that fact alone depends the validity of any forecast of the future.

Such, in broad outline, is the problem which confronts South Africa in regard to the relations between her European and non-European peoples. It affects more or less directly almost every important question of her public life. It is a problem almost unique in difficulty—that of holding together as organic constituents of a single state under the institutions of popular government a complex of races so diverse in conditions and so divergent in outlook. On her success depends her own existence as the national home of a European people, and with that are bound up issues of the gravest importance for the whole African continent and for the relations of the white and colored races throughout the world.

Note

FEAR IN AFRICA
BY SARAH GERTRUDE MILLIN

October 1949

When this article was written, South Africa had not yet frozen into its present rigid political mold. The rule of law as known in the West still prevailed. Although Malan had come to power, questions about how whites and blacks were to live in harmony could still be asked, if not always answered. There was room to hope that a reasonable accommodation might yet be found.

Since then, the policy of apartheid has been elaborated and every effort has been made to put it into effect. South Africa has been divided into nine parts—one white, consisting of 87 percent of the land, and eight black on the remaining 13 percent. The first of these Bantustans, as they are called, has already been set up in the Transkei, and although self-government is promised, it is a fiction at present. When and if plans are completed, more than 5,000,000 people will have been transplanted.

To enforce this separation and to control the opposition to it, the South African Government has pushed through a succession of laws and regulations giving it broad and arbitrary powers. The powers of the courts have been restricted and a variety of offenses are punishable without trial or appeal. Under many circumstances a person is guilty until proven innocent. To be a Communist is a crime and a Communist is defined as anyone "advocating, defending or encouraging . . . the achievement of any of the objects of communism or any act which is calculated to further the achievement of any such object." The crime of subversion is similarly all-embracing. But all of these measures pale before a catch-all act passed in 1963 under which, among other things, a person may be detained incommunicado for 90 days without charges or trial; and such imprisonment *may be renewed indefinitely* "this side of eternity," in the words of the Minister of Justice. The law was rushed through parliament with but one dissenting vote in time to detain indefinitely the leader of the most effective of the several African nationalist underground movements. (White South Africans who by word or deed displease the Government are granted the greater dignity of house arrest, but also incommunicado.)

Sarah Gertrude Millin was writing in a happier day before the more restrictive of these laws had been imposed. She is in the great tradition of South African writers with a conscience and an acute sensitivity to their country's dilemma. She tells not only how it is but how it feels. Implicit in what she says is an important point that is even more true today: There is no solution that can assure full justice to both black and white.

Mrs. Millin was born in Russia, and settled in the Cape as a small child. By the time she was 35 she had established herself as one of South Africa's leading novelists, with "God's Stepchildren," a moving but unsentimental evocation of the plight of the "coloreds." In addition to writing a score of novels, she was the biographer of Rhodes and Smuts in the thirties, and the author of a two-volume autobiography. In 1944 she wrote a series of radio plays for an American network. The widow of a Supreme Court justice, she lives in Johannesburg, still writes regularly. In 1962, at the age of 73, she published her latest novel, "The Wizard Bird."

Fear in Africa

by SARAH GERTRUDE MILLIN

The dark people who came to South Africa through Mono-potapa are the Basuto-Bechuana and the Zulu-Xosa. They all have Negro, Hamite and Semite blood. In America they would be described as Negro or colored. In South Africa they are called Kaffirs, Bantus, Natives, Africans.

They arrived with the name, given them by the Arabs, of Kaffirs—unbelievers. The Xosa wars were the Kaffir Wars; where the Xosas lived was Kaffirland; until a generation ago, officials and missionaries called them Kaffirs. Tiyo Soga, the first Christian Xosa minister, having married white, said in his testament to his children: "If you wish to gain credit for yourselves—if you do not wish to feel the taint of men which you sometimes may be made to feel—take your place in the world as colored, not white, as Kaffirs, not Englishmen."

The word Kaffir is, however, not liked today, and (though they no more originate in South Africa than the Europeans, and probably came after them) they are now officially and generally called Natives.

The term Bantu means simply people—that is, not dumb animals. The latest expression—used by dark intellectuals and their European friends—is African. This is correct on the analogy of Europeans. But it gives the colored folk no home or nationality: for the white people alone are South Africans. And it cannot be translated into the official language, Afrikaans, because the people, once known as Dutch or Boers, are now the sole Afrikaners.

The fact is that the inhabitants of the Union of South Africa need a national name as badly as do the inhabitants of the United States of America.

II

It was the Xosas the Boers first met as they were trekking east and the Xosas, having descended to the Cape southeast, were trekking west; and almost at once it was arranged that black and white should separate: the Great Fish River was made the inviolable (but of course violated) boundary between them.

This was the first manifestation of what Dr. Malan's followers today call *apartheid. Apartheid* (literally, aparthood) is not yet a dictionary word, but it won Dr. Malan the last election and it stands for separation of blacks from whites. Real, full, separation became impossible when the Voortrekkers, in the 1830's, abandoned, as they declared, "the fruitful land of their birth" to the English, and left the Cape "to enter a wild and dangerous territory" and find a life for themselves. It became impossible because this wild and dangerous territory they entered was the home of the Basutos and Bechuanas. In the end, the Basutos were left, under British protection, with 10,000 square miles, and the Bechuanas with a quarter million square miles.

In 1779 the Xosas began a fight that lasted 100 years; that ten years later dragged in the white people. It began because the one Xosa Paramount Chief insulted another by offering him a lobola (marriage settlement) of only 100 cattle for his daughter. During this hundred years, too, Chaka, the Napoleon of the Zulus, in a great passion for blood, killed 1,000,000—some say 2,000,000—Zulus.

On the other side of the Drakensbergen then, the Queen Mantatisi, scorned in love by a fugitive from Chaka, fell in rage upon the world until she had not only eliminated whole tribes of Basuto and Bechuana, but left their country so bare that even her own naked, blackened, black-plumed, satanic warriors became cannibals. Following upon Mantatisi's carnage came Moselikatze, escaping from Chaka with half his Zulus; and, through what was left of the devastated Basutos and Bechuanas, drove north on a pathway of blood—which is what his name means.

The Boers, the Voortrekkers, fought their way through Zulus; through Moselikatze's People with the Long Shields, henceforward Matabeles; through Basutos and Bechuanas.

After the white people had defeated the black people that had all but destroyed themselves, after they were in control and the black people had to give up fighting, the black people recovered so quickly that, in 1894, Rhodes told the Cape Parliament: "The natives are increasing at an enormous rate. The old diminutions of war and pestilence do not occur. . . . The natives devote their minds to a remarkable extent to the multiplication of children." . . . He asked what was now to be done about them.

He answered himself. He was responsible, he said—speaking as Rhodes of Rhodesia; Rhodes, Prime Minister of the Cape; Rhodes, the Chairman of de Beers and his Goldfields companies—for 2,000,000 human beings. He put before Parliament what he proudly called his "Bill for Africa"—not South Africa. Africa. "You are sitting in judgment," he told the Members, "on Africa." The Bill was passed almost unanimously.

In 1947 General Smuts said: "Today, if you discuss the native question . . . you cannot look at it merely from the South African point of view. If you touch this question, you touch Africa."

Africa is that continent which has 160,000,000 blacks and 4,000,000 whites, has overcome all previous civilizations below the Nile, is faced, as in times past, by Asiatic invasion, and is now confronted in its darkness by this group of 2,500,000 whites, crying, from its thinnest, lowest end: "Black shall not pass."

There were certain words, certain thoughts, Rhodes applied to the black races. For instance, the word "human." "They have human minds." "Help them use their human minds." He spoke the word human as though to combat the suggestion that they were not human. "I do not believe they are different from ourselves," he said boldly, challenging Darwin's thought that, even in God's eyes, they were not as white people. But yet he called them children, declaring them thus a people, retarded. Rhodes' Bill for Africa was a measure to separate these retarded people from the advanced white people. . . . He went on to say: "The natives in the past had an interesting employment for their minds in going to war and in consulting in their councils as to war. By our wise government, we have taken away all that employment from them. We have given them no share in the government— and I think rightly, too—and no interest in the local development of the land, which cannot continue to provide enough for all of them. . . . We do not teach them the dignity of labor, and they simply loaf about in sloth and laziness. . . . These are my premises."

This was his solution: To give the natives, under European direction, their own land, which no whites, except officials, approved traders and so on, might enter. To train them to govern, manage, tax and educate themselves; to take liquor from them; teach them to work; train them to build their own roads and bridges and grow their own food and forests. There would be individual holdings (Rhodes had no faith in the natives' communism, under the dictatorship of their chiefs). There would be primogeniture (he believed this system to be a source of England's strength). Property owners, as was the Cape law, would have a vote. The younger sons would labor three months in the year (a ten-shilling tax on "loafing" if they did not) on Europeans' farms and mines. The reserves were more than natives' reserves. They were South Africa's reservoirs of labor.

So was the Glen Grey Act of 1895 a success?

Rhodes considered Glen Grey "the best portion of South Africa." The Encyclopaedia Britannica of 1911 described it as "well-watered and fertile." A Government Commission of 1932 called it desert.

For this the Commission blamed both black and white. The Europeans, said the Commission, had changed the environment of the native, but had not taught him how to adjust himself to the new environment. The native still planted as his forefathers planted, he practised the animal husbandry of his forefathers, he believed religiously in a plenitude of cattle and then could not understand why "man begets, but land does not beget"—why, in short, land eroded by cattle eating its growth to the roots and worn out by continual planting of the same crops should become a desert.

And yet in Glen Grey, thought the Commission, lay a great idea. These very reserves, so depleted, might, with help and teaching, be rescued and restored; the native could still be taught to govern himself; the reserves alone offered a basis for the solution of the native problem—a practical method of natural segregation. Where Glen Grey had failed, Europeans had their difficult material, their limited experience and not their evil intentions, to blame. The policy of segregation, said the Commission, should continue.

Seven years later, a leader of liberal opinion in South Africa, the President of the Institute of Race Relations, put it like this: The liberal, he said, had, for the good of the native, to consider three policies—total assimilation, total separation, a native life among Europeans running parallel to theirs. "When liberals support or demand some measure for improving the Reserve, they are in principle working for Total Separation. When they approve the admission of Native, or other non-European students, into Universities which are predominantly white, they take a step on the road towards Total Assimilation.

When they encourage the Native to organize for, and among, themselves some service or institution similar to those available for whites, they are practising the policy of Parallelism." As things were in the world, he thought that "total separation should be the liberal's choice."

Today Dr. Malan's supporters, who condemn liberals as the enemies of the white race, say exactly the same: but for different reasons. Practical men—businessmen and economists—do not know how it can be done. Where is the land to come from? Where the money for the industries and developments in the native reserves? Where will they themselves get labor if the natives are too ardently devoted to their own affairs?

The farmers do not want "black spots" among their own lands. They say, "The natives should restore the land they have destroyed before new land is got for them."

The sort of young natives that call themselves African mostly hate the thought of the reserves. It is the white romantic, not the new young African, who sees a noble picture as the native, in his bright blanket, strides along eroded red paths on rock-crested mountains, with his wife behind him, on her head a load, and on her back a child.

What the educated young native sees is the misery of the crowded reserves where the land is so badly farmed and the yield so poor that a cow will give "not even a can of milk;" and the family has to be broken up by its men becoming migrant laborers. Often, too, these men don't want to come home again. For in the towns, so they say, one learns trades; gets better wages, work, food, education, medical help, a chance to play European games, see films, read news, meet men of other tribes, find out modern thoughts and ways.

Finally, there are the old men at home who so dislike European interference that they will not let boreholes be sunk in their lands, or use the Government ditches, or send their children to the preschool feeding centers. Often their children starve.

III

Yet the dream of separation does not fade, and always it is based on Rhodes' Bill for Africa. Three years after Union, General Botha, the first Prime Minister, decided to add 20,000,000 acres to the native reserves, which would have made, with their other holdings, 13 percent of the Union's land. Considering the natives' numbers, this figure does not look well; but, again, only 15 percent of the Union's land is arable, and the natives, like other people, prefer to live in towns. Today 60 percent of them live in towns.

Botha's plan naturally made the price of land go up. The German War of 1914 began and South Africa was in it and had a rebellion besides. A depression followed the war; 50 percent of the white population was on the bread line. After General Botha died and was succeeded by Smuts and Hertzog, there was no more talk of 20,000,000 acres: the best one could now do was 13,000,000 acres. But there was also another interesting idea: £500,000 would be spent on getting land and sinking boreholes in it.

What land? Every Union Prime Minister has bitterly demanded the three British territories, all dependent on the Union: Swaziland, Basutoland, Bechuanaland. Each, it seems, has had in his heart the thought to solve the Union's native problem with these—with one of these. Which one? Which has much space and needs boreholes?

Obviously not Swaziland, a small country whose Queen-Mother is the most prolific rain-maker in southern Africa. Not Basutoland, so eroded that almost every able-bodied man has to go and work in the Union. Well, naturally, Bechuanaland: 250,000,000 square miles big; a desert, reputed to have under its sands much water; the very land for boreholes.

Only the territories will not come into the Union: under Britain's mild protection, they like to rule themselves. Particularly will Bechuanaland not come into the Union. Bechuanaland has already a man to each square mile. It is enough. The Bechuanas want no millions of Union natives thrust upon them.

The educated young Africans who hate the reserves deride the thought that one can "change from a subsistence to a money economy; change the whole relationship between people and land; introduce tax-paying and wage-earning as necessities; introduce western material culture," and then expect the old social structure of Africans to remain as before. "The Africans," they say, "will not willingly go back to the ancient and fast-dying fields of primitive life. Whether we like it or not, we shall have to cope with what the rest of the world coped with—namely the adjustment of our life conditions to the demands of western culture."

The Africans say that the Europeans, too, once "lived like savages and constantly fought one another, and all the nations of the world have been through that stage of development." They recall that western culture itself came from the valleys of the Euphrates, the Tigris and the Nile, and that Peter the Great went west for the civilization he brought to Russia, and "What," they ask, "is the position of Russia today? Is Russia not one of the two World Powers today?"

They know about the French Revolution.

"Are not Africans," they say, "getting the treatment which caused the French Revolution?" And they too, they vow, would die for an African revolution. . . . Sometimes they wonder what, after a successful revolution, they should do with the whites of South Africa. Send them back to that devastated old Europe? The gentler souls think one could not do that. There is room enough in Africa for all. "As other peoples have done, and as other peoples of this land have already done for 300 years, black and white can develop together. Together we have made this land what it is today. We have made it our joint fatherland."

There are, however, cynics among these African intellectuals. Are the white people, they ask, afraid for their white women? "White women," they say, "are repulsive to us."

If only, they say again, the black peoples had, in the beginning, united to ward off the Europeans from South Africa, "we should not today have a white problem."

The quotations in these paragraphs are from private papers of Africans, 20 to 25 years old, educated in the Transvaal.

Most Europeans feel about such Africans as these that they are "intellectuals entirely sequestered from the thoughts of their people, quite incapable of independent thought, who merely repeat the precepts of their mentors." And it does seem likely that the native intellectual finds himself far away from the people in his kraal. He can no longer think like them, he can no longer feel like them. He has been trained to think and feel like a European. He is not merely—and crudely—a native. He is a particular kind of native: an African with a European standard.

What, failing the reserves, can South Africans offer the black man and yet stay white?

Always there is the white man's fear that to give the black man too much may mean his own submergence. At present, the native may become a teacher or preacher to other natives; he may become a doctor who runs a risk if he sees a white patient, but who is so desperately needed for his own people that the Government will give him a bursary to attend a medical school; he may become a lawyer, and then he treats his fellow-Bantu ruthlessly, and often dishonestly; he may become a craftsman, a trader, a pieceworker in industries or mines. But he cannot, as in other parts of Africa, get a position that will give him authority over whites. In the public services he is employed only as a menial or a low-grade clerk, except in the Native Affairs Department where he may become an agricultural demonstrator, an interpreter or a clerk. In the police or defense services he cannot get a commission. He can—he somehow does—run a business, a bus or a taxi.

IV

France's colonials are divided into three groups: the thousands of *citoyens*, representatives of French civilization; the lesser *notables evolués*; and the millions of *sujets* (many of whom do not want the obligations of a superior status) who fall under native law.

That they may be citizens, even on rigorous terms, is as much as friends of the South African natives ask for them. It is what members of the native parliament, the Bunga—a helpless affair, directed by white officials—mean when they say: "We think that peace will come about in this country only when all the positions are open to us and we can fill them. . . . If the native is sufficiently educated, he is fitted for work any other man can do. . . . Why has the native departed from his former primitive state and acquired education and trustworthiness if he is not allowed to go forward?"

This is just and reasonable, but can this going forward include the vote, direction of the country? Many friends of the natives say it should include the vote: they say no more is asked than the French give: that is, full equality—citizenship—according to a man's civilization. This, they say, would mean that only a few natives, and not dangerously many, would get the vote. But do they not also think every native ought to be educated? And should not every educated native then get the vote? And would this not be dangerously many for the white people that are a fourth of their number and, above all, want to maintain their white civilization?

What South Africans say is:

"Frenchmen have France to live in. We have only South Africa. We cannot afford to do what Frenchmen can do."

Yet even the French colonies had forced labor until 1946. The Portuguese in Africa, who do not mind blending their blood with that of the blacks and then giving them European status, also have forced labor. The Belgian Africans suffer a social, if not an economic, color bar; but they are not allowed to attend universities, unless they are to become Roman Catholic priests; and so shocking was the scandal of the treatment of natives by the Congo Free State, so alarming the reduction of native population from 15,000,000 to 10,000,000, that now there are a Charte Coloniale and a Protective Commission to guard their full rights as Belgian citizens.

The British hold before their black colonials the vision of self-government. But, in 1945, a government welfare report said of Kenya that "poverty of a massive and grinding nature, assessed by modern standards, is at present the outstanding feature of African society everywhere in the Colony." British Trusteeship in East Africa has had a bad report from a U.N. mission.

There is a thing in Africa stranger than any. The greatest oppressors of African natives are the descendants of the freed Negro slaves, now running the Negro Republic of Liberia. No one despises what they call the "bush" people as they do.

Who can deny that black men are exploited throughout Africa? Who can believe white men come to Africa out of simple love of black men? Of all African countries, South Africa, with most to fear, has done black man the least hurt. Her social services for Africans cost more than those in the rest of Africa put together. Her African population has doubled in the last 40 years. In other lands it has barely moved.

But what is the cause of it all? What makes decent people lose their humanity in Africa? Is it only the question of skin? Then where is the answer to Liberia?

There is a deeper cause than color. There is a terrible answer. It is that it lies in human beings to kick those that are down. What does the saying mean about not kicking those who are down? That the impulse is to do it. All commandments, laws, proverbs are testimonies against human nature. One need not be forbidden to do what one doesn't want to do. The Africans are kicked because they are down.

v

But the Africans have discovered the power of their numbers, and they will not stay down. In this year of 1949, there have been native riots in Kenya and Uganda. Over Kenya flew Lancaster bombers;

European and Asian members of the Kenya police reserve were mobilized. One saw that, if the Africans spread riot over Africa, the Asians would stand with the Europeans: as one saw, through the Durban native riots against the Indians in January 1949, if the Asians advanced down Africa, the Africans would stand with the Europeans—though who would eventually dominate one could not tell, except that it would not be Europeans.

There have been riots in the Sudan: again civilians mobilized. They guarded planes, halting for the night, on the journey north. There are fears in Tanganyika. Black talk down the East Coast is of driving Europeans into the Indian Ocean.

In 1948, a commission, inquiring into native disturbances on the Gold Coast, found a leading cause to be the Communism learnt by Africans in England. They had evidence of a secret society, the Circle, whose watchword was "service, sacrifice, suffering;" whose aim was a Union of African Socialist Republics; who had a shadow government ready to displace the white government and drive out the Europeans.

They say in Rhodesia and Nyasaland that the Russian consulate in Abyssinia is sending black Communists to excite their natives. Talk about Communists is sometimes exaggerated; but it is a fact that, in the 1920's, the Colonial Department of the Comintern, acting in Moscow, instructed Communists in South Africa to work for a Black Republic, with a guarantee of minority rights for Europeans. There is talk (black) of strikes in South Africa.

One can see what may happen in African territories by looking, not only at Asia, but, more appositely, at Trinidad. Here were Indians, despoiled in turn by the Spanish, British, Dutch and French, taken by the British in 1797 and kept by them after the Treaty of Amiens. Here came Negro slaves and indentured Indian laborers from the east. Today, one may enter a law court in Port-of-Spain and find only the judge—a British official—white. Lawyers, litigants, witnesses, spectators are all, from yellow to black, dark men. One may see a procession of school-children of whom only two are white. Englishmen of good class are happy to be invited to the homes of colored dignitaries who maybe have British titles. The white man is on his way out.

Now what, thinking of all these things, is the South African who, alone of white men in Africa, has no other home—what is he to do? He can withhold the vote, the essence of democracy, from the black man. He can give the educated black man the vote. If he also gives the black man education, then all educated black men will have the vote, and the white man will in time be enormously outvoted.

The South African can be utterly just and give the black man the same voting rights as the white man. The white man needs only to be 21 to have the vote. If the black man, too, at 21 gets the vote, then the white man will immediately be outvoted by people, four times as many as himself, and mostly barbaric. There is the fact of the 4,000,-000 whites in Africa and the 160,000,000 blacks. His position, under absolute justice, would be that of the American if America had, say, 500,000,000 Negroes, nearly all raw men. The South African smiles at the fuss Americans make about their tenth of Negroes.

Even Jan H. Hofmeyr, Deputy Prime Minister in General Smuts' last Government, South Africa's wonder-boy, as General Smuts called him on his death, the greatest brain (sheer genius apart) South Africa has known—even Jan Hofmeyr, who died fighting for the rights of the natives, could not think of giving them absolute equality, absolute justice.

Abraham Lincoln did not understand the Declaration of Independence to mean that all men are in all ways equal. "Certainly the Negro is not," he said, "our equal in color."

Judging by the preponderance of dark-skinned people in the world, one might think the Creator had different ideas and preferred the colored to the white people. Their preponderating representatives at the U.N. begin to think so too. South Africans look at the equal vote at the U.N. with almost the dread they have of an equal vote in South Africa. The U.N., indeed, points to their own dilemma. How, under it, they ask in despair, can they have justice? How can the *white* man have justice?

We are indeed past the stage where Lincoln may further be quoted on the Negro: "If God gave him little, that little let him enjoy." . . . They say at the U.N.: "Why little?"

The South African, in his fear, withholds this, withholds that, from the black man. The black man knows the deprivation of the day. His millennium is not yet here.

Against that time there are in South Africa negrophilists who offer the native what they call Christian Trusteeship. This is a smug and unpronounceable term and likely to be suspect by people who see how often in our world the name of Christ is attached to works directly against His teaching. All, however, that the apostles of this creed mean (Hofmeyr belonged to it) is that they wish, for those who need it, a measure of humanity. They stand with Dickens:

"Did you hear him say that he could have shed his blood for me?"

"Do you want any blood shed for you? . . . Does he shed anything for you that you do want? Does he shed employment for you, instruction for you, pocket money for you? Does he shed even legs of mutton for you?"

They ask for the native employment, instruction, pocket money and —something like legs of mutton.

Note

ALTERNATIVES TO APARTHEID IN SOUTH AFRICA
BY J. W. PATTEN

January 1952

About the time this article was written, the eminent South African historian, Arthur Keppel-Jones, declared that "It would be easier to drive the white man out of South Africa than the black man out of the society the white man has created." After a decade in which a determined South African Government has sought to drive the black man out of that society, and out of that economy which he made possible by his toil, there is no reason to doubt the truth of this observation.

In the following article, a leading South African journalist makes clear why the concept of complete separation could never be workable. He was writing in the early years of the Nationalist Party régime when the lines that apartheid would follow were not yet clear. Today it is still unclear how the races can be effectively separated even under the most determined and ruthless direction, but it is altogether clear that apartheid has subsequently been given the literal and purist interpretation which the author of this article feared.

J. W. Patten is South African-born and grew up in the Cape Province. He joined the Johannesburg *Star* in 1929 and, except for a three-year interlude when he was editor of the Pretoria *News*, he has been with it ever since—as assistant editor when he wrote this article, as editor today. The *Star*, one of the Argus group of newspapers, is the. largest daily in South Africa and, like most of the English-language press, has been relatively liberal in its view on racial questions.

Strangely, the press in South Africa has continued to enjoy a measure of freedom, partly because it agreed to self-censorship. Moderate criticism of the Government is still possible, but proscribed persons—which means virtually all the African leadership and scores of whites—cannot be quoted, and the "Incite-to-Riot" Act is a threat hanging over every editor's head. More than a dozen journalists have been gagged and several liberal papers have been banned; to avoid their reappearance under another name a 1962 law requires a new newspaper to post a £10,000 bond, which is forfeit if the paper runs into trouble again. Even so, most South African journalists feel that they have gotten off lightly thus far and that more stringent measures may be on the way. A stricter censorship is imposed on books and magazines, and many of the best known South African writers, such as Nadine Gordimer, Peter Abrahams and Ezekiel Mphahlele, are banned.

Alternatives to Apartheid in South Africa

by J. W. PATTEN

South Africa's policy of apartheid, or separation of the white from the colored races within its community, has been denounced abroad as repressive. Most South Africans are at a disadvantage in meeting this charge—with which a great many of them agree—because they still do not know, in spite of earnest questionings of themselves and others, exactly what the policy is. In theory there are two kinds of apartheid. South Africa has not yet made up its mind which kind it wants, and it stands in fretful indecision between them like an ass between two bales of hay.

Last year there were disturbances in the small Witzieshoek Native Reserve, an offshoot within the Union of South Africa of the British Protectorate of Basutoland. The natives there opposed orders to cull stock on their overgrazed lands, destroyed government-erected fences and ignored summonses to appear before the Native Commissioner. They contended that the remedy for overgrazing was more land, and that much of their traditional land had been taken away from them last century. The dispute eventually led to a clash with the police. Lives were lost on both sides.

A commission of inquiry investigated. It recommended additional land for the natives, but noted that the Reserve could not permanently hold the whole of its population and the natural increase. Many had already migrated to the towns of the Free State and Transvaal, and the commission proposed that they should be formed into communities there with some measure of local self-government. It recommended that natives who have been absent from the Reserve for many years should no longer regard it as their home to which they are entitled to return at any time; after two years they should be considered to have left permanently.

Apart from the clash with the police, the dispute and the report caused little stir. The Reserve is small and unimportant and few natives are involved. Yet there were two significant reactions to the report. The first came almost automatically from the neighboring white farmers, who instantly condemned the proposal to give the natives more land. The same thing has happened wherever an attempt has been made to extend the Native Reserves. That is one reason why the promise of some 15,000,000 more acres made in General Hertzog's "final solution" of 1936 remains only half fulfilled after 15 years.

The other reaction, which is more to our purpose here, came from the South African Bureau of Racial Affairs. SABRA is of fairly recent origin and provides a center for Afrikaner intellectuals devoted to the cause of apartheid. In general it stands in opposition to the long-established South African Institute of Race Relations, which makes a study of race relations on liberal lines. SABRA thus enjoys government patronage and is intended to rationalize government policies.

The Witzieshoek report, although signed by a prominent supporter of the government, was instantly condemned by SABRA as the negation of apartheid. The recommendation that the majority of the natives should be integrated into the European economy was described by the Bureau as "extremely dangerous." The commission, it said, had rejected the theory that the Reserves should be the national home of the natives and advocated their permanent residence in urban areas, with local self-government. To imagine that in such circumstances they would be content with local self-government was wishful thinking. The recommendations, in SABRA's view, gave the impression that the commission was indifferent to the implications of the rival policies of integration and separate development. It regarded the Reserves as undeveloped farming areas and ignored the need for their industrialization. This reaction from the purists of the apartheid theory exposed once again the controversy within the apartheid controversy.

II

To understand what this argument is about it is necessary to look at the over-all picture. When the expanding white settlement at the Cape of Good Hope met the slowly advancing Bantu tribes 400 miles

east of Cape Town at the beginning of the nineteenth century, repeated attempts were made by the governments of the time to set up
a boundary between the two and keep it intact. The attempts broke
down again and again, and for more than 50 years Cape history is the
history of the struggle for the border lands. By the time the last of
the long series of Kaffir Wars was fought the boundary had been
pushed nearly 200 miles eastward. In the process large numbers of the
Bantu had either been isolated in scattered groups on the white side
of the frontier or had become landless and had been absorbed into the
Colony as laborers on white farms and servants. The frontier was at
last fixed at the Kei River, and the Transkei became the first permanent Native Reserve, in which no white man might acquire land.

Long before this had happened, however, the head-on collision of
these two forces and the consequent pressure on land had burst the
Colony's seams and produced the Great Trek into the vacant lands
to the north. These plains were vacant for two reasons. The Bantu in
their slow progress down Africa had followed the fertile, well-watered
eastern seaboard. Less numerous offshoots had turned westward,
skirted the Kalahari Desert and reached the Atlantic in southwest
Africa, or settled on the eastern edge of the desert in what is now
Bechuanaland. They had spread thinly over the interior plateau of
what are now the Orange Free State and Transvaal; but the Great
Trek was preceded by a period of intense tribal warfare, and the
trekkers found the interior between Natal and Bechuanaland almost
cleared of inhabitants by the Zulu and Matabele impis which had
passed that way. They drove the Matabele across the Limpopo to
found the dynasty which Cecil Rhodes was to extinguish in his settlement of Rhodesia.

In Natal the trekkers from one side, and the British from their
settlement at Port Natal on the other, cut a broad corridor through
the long strip of Bantu land in the east, isolating the Transkei in the
south from Zululand and the great mass of black Africa in the north.
The patchwork pattern of black and white with which South Africa
entered the twentieth century derived from these movements and
conflicts.

But although boundaries are fixed, populations are fluid. The trekkers in their progress overran and absorbed many sub-tribes before
halting at the main tribal boundaries, just as they had done on the
Cape eastern frontier. They had been accustomed to Hottentot servants and imported slaves long before they came into contact with

the Bantu, and although slavery was never revived, the familiar pattern of colonial life with its ample colored labor on the farm and in the home remained unchanged, although it now came to include squatting by native groups on European farms, labor-tenancy and sharecropping.

This sudden fixing of boundaries had a profound effect on Bantu economy, which had from time immemorial been based on shifting agriculture and grazing. This way of life had carried the tribes down Africa; if white settlement had been delayed another 200 years Europeans landing at the Cape of Good Hope would undoubtedly have found the Bantu instead of the less powerful and more nomadic Hottentots in occupation there. This impetus continued and still continues to carry the Bantu forward; but they move across the boundaries now as hired laborers, leaving their cattle and often their families behind. The movement is inescapable. Their primitive methods of agriculture have not changed greatly, their cattle still serve a social rather than an economic purpose. The Reserves, devoid of towns or industries, are overstocked and overcrowded in terms of a peasant economy and are in danger of deteriorating into agricultural slums.

In these circumstances the able-bodied men move out of them at a steady rate, at first as migrant laborers in the mines, farms and industries, after a time as permanent emigrants. The great South African gold mining industry is almost entirely dependent on the first kind of migration; secondary industry is responsible for a great deal of the second type. The unsatisfied demands of the cities and farms for labor of all kinds, including domestic labor, with the consequent steady rise in cash wages offered, provide additional inducements. But in fact little inducement is needed, for the flight from the land is a result of hard necessity.

Various South African Governments have tried to do by legislation what the frontiersmen did by warfare. The "pass laws" and controlled entry to the towns were designed to check the exodus and place some sort of governor on the rate of flow. Natives were prevented from acquiring land outside their Reserves (which are likewise closed to white ownership) except in restricted areas in a few townships. The great mass of urban natives are municipal tenants. The Hertzog laws of 1936 were aimed at the abolition of squatting and tenant farming. Segregation, as apartheid was still called, seemed a realizable ideal. But the success of these measures was limited. South Africa was already in the midst of its industrial revolution, with growing demands for labor and a steady movement away from the land by both white and black.

That this was seen as a continuation of the old battle in a new form is shown by an address delivered by Dr. D. F. Malan, now Prime Minister, on the occasion of the centenary of the Great Trek in 1938. Speaking at Blood River in Natal, where the decisive battle between the trekkers and the Zulus was fought a hundred years before, he drew attention to the fact that whereas the European population of the towns had increased in the last 15 years by 460,000, the non-Europeans had increased by 812,000 in the same period.

"If you think that in this New Great Trek of the Afrikaans-speaking section to the towns the centers of our industrial and commercial life are becoming whiter you are indeed mistaken. They are becoming blacker. On this new Blood River battlefield our people and the non-Europeans meet one another and come into very close contact. And they are in much more stressful struggle than 100 years ago, when the white-tented waggons protected the laager and rifle and assegai clashed. . . . The Afrikaans-speaking men of the New Great Trek meet the non-European at the new Blood River half or completely unarmed, without the entrenchment between them and without the protection of the river. They meet him defenceless in the open plain of economic equality." The significance of this long-forgotten speech can now be seen. Ten years later Dr. Malan's party came to power on an apartheid program, and it at once set about disposing its forces for the new Blood River battle.

III

The situation with which it found itself faced was this: In round figures the total native population at that time was 8,000,000 (as against 2,400,000 Europeans). Of these natives some 3,000,000 lived in the Reserves. The rest were distributed throughout "white" South Africa, outnumbering the whites by more than two to one. Nearly 2,000,000 were in the towns, forming a growing industrial proletariat; the remaining 3,000,000 were on the farms or settled in "black spots" outside the Reserves.

The pure theory of apartheid was, and still is, that the Natives' Reserves are the "national home" of the Bantu. There they shall develop "on their own lines" apart from the Europeans, although under European tutelage. In this way conflict and competition, the clash of a higher with a lower civilization, are to be avoided and justice and harmony will prevail. The obstacle in the way of this ideal is the knotty figures just quoted. If 60 percent of the Bantu are now outside the Reserves, how are these to become their "national home?" And if they could in fact all be put back there, what would happen to the South African economy, based as it is on unskilled native labor, and the South African way of life with its almost unlimited supply of black servants?

The apartheid theorists have ridden uneasily over this problem. More than 25 years ago a commission of inquiry formulated the position to which "practical" apartheid has now returned: "If the Native is to be regarded as a permanent element in municipal areas and if he is to have equal opportunity of establishing himself there permanently, there can be no justification for basing his exclusion from the franchise on the simple ground of colour . . . [therefore] the Native should only be allowed to enter urban areas, which are essentially the white man's creation, when he is willing to enter and to minister to the needs of the white man, and should depart therefrom when he ceases so to minister."

This formula is still serviceable, not only for the urban areas but for the whole of "white" South Africa. It is, of course, completely unreal. The Fagan Report (the Native Laws Commission), the modern textbook of native policy published just before the change of government in 1948, quoted the passage with distaste, and remarked that "now, 25 years later, we cannot get away from the fact that there is indeed a considerable Native population permanently settled in the urban areas, and that an argument about the desirability or undesirability of that state of affairs is purely academic—it is a state of affairs that is going to remain and that simply cannot be altered."

Nevertheless the formula is fundamental to the apartheid policy for the very reason given by the earlier commission. It is realized that in the long run no permanent part of the population can be denied some form of political rights irrespective of the stage of development reached. As political rights for natives are in any circumstances inadmissible, it is necessary to maintain the fiction of impermanence indefinitely. Thus the 60 percent of the Bantu population outside the Reserves are officially regarded as expatriates from the Bantuland beyond the border, from which they are temporarily absent in search of employment. They have been compared with Italian laborers in France.

It is not, of course, only political rights that are involved. Dr.

Malan's picture of the white man meeting the impact "defenceless in the open plain of economic equality" is of crucial importance. The entrenchments must be dug, the laager must be drawn against the invasion of the skilled trades and professions which are the white man's preserve. This is being done; but it must be defended. In theory it is defensible only on the assumption that the native is a "foreign worker" holding a conditional passport.

There are, however, many earnest and honest believers in apartheid to whom these polite fictions are unacceptable. Early in the régime one of them, Dr. Eiselen, was taken out of an academic post and made Secretary for Native Affairs because, it was said, it was necessary to have in this position a man who supported the apartheid policy. When he was still Professor of Social Anthropolgy at Pretoria University in 1949, Dr. Eiselen published a paper in which he dismissed any inherent inferiority in the natives as unscientific and the "master and servant" relationship as unfair and unacceptable. In a mixed society, he said, the natives would never be given the opportunities to which they were entitled. A caste society was being produced, with an increasingly resentful black proletariat. His solution, therefore, was complete separation, the break-up of the present white-and-black society into two distinct and autonomous societies.

He therefore proposed the withdrawal of all native labor over a period of 20 years. White South Africa would have to pay the price in poverty and hard work. They would have to bend their backs, encourage immigration from Europe and maintain a high standard of quality to hold their own against the competitive industries in the native areas. They would also have to give up much land. The chief difficulty, he foresaw, would be to convince the whites that they were not a Herrenvolk entitled to cheap labor. But the only alternative would be for the white group to "cling frantically to its master-people complex, to become embroiled in progressively more inescapable economic, social and political entanglements, and ultimately to forfeit its cherished superiority and perhaps its racial identity."

His was not a voice crying in the wilderness. His views, already shared by many apartheid intellectuals, were soon to be powerfully reënforced. In April 1950 the Federated Dutch Reformed Churches, which claim the adherence of the great majority of Afrikaans-speaking people and therefore have very close affiliations with the government, held a congress in Bloemfontein to discuss native affairs. It agreed on a policy of complete racial and territorial segregation, for which it would be essential for all native labor to be systematically and gradually superseded by European labor in all European industry, including farming. The natives should be removed into an industrial system of their own to be established in the Reserves. This policy, said the congress, would mean the complete reorientation of European industry and economy, and would call for "great sacrifices."

In a document prepared by the "action committee" and privately circulated among the delegates, the arguments in favor of this policy were set out. The authors point out that "we cannot keep Natives in our service, educate and develop them, and keep them pegged to unskilled occupations. On the other hand we cannot expect that if we give them full opportunity for economic development and allow them to rise to the highest rungs they will be satisfied to leave their economic, political and social interests to the care of others. They will fight for a say in national affairs, and in this struggle they will seek support from various sides and even abroad."

The treatise goes on to discuss, although in no great detail, a transition period lasting possibly 50 or 100 years, and including "intensive" native development. Elsewhere it reiterates that "no people in the world worth their salt will be content indefinitely with no say, or only an indirect say, in the affairs of the State or in the socio-economic organisation of the country in which decisions are taken about their interests and future."

This formidable challenge was politely declined by the government. The Minister of Native Affairs said the government would treat the resolution with "great respect," but was in no way committed to it. He described it as an "idealistic extension of and not in conflict with the Government's stated policy."

The Prime Minister, Dr. Malan, was also somewhat equivocal when taxed in Parliament with the Church's views. He described total territorial separation as "an ideal" but not practical policy nor the policy of the Nationalist Party. Europeans and natives must continue to live together "for a time." The first aim would be to check the flow of natives from tribal areas without harming the demand for labor in European areas. This policy, he said, was not in conflict with that of the Church. The government would further the Church's aim but much would have to be done before it was achieved. Meanwhile, as many natives as possible would be returned to their tribal homes. A "great increase" in native areas would be necessary for this.

It is nevertheless legitimate to believe from these pronouncements that the government is fundamentally in agreement with the Church and that its appointment of Dr. Eiselen to a key post was not without significance. The new Minister of Native Affairs, Dr. H. F. Verwoerd, has indicated that present policies are the first step toward a distant goal. It would, however, be politically inexpedient, perhaps suicidal, to announce a program that would, even in the long run, deprive white South Africa of its native labor and so revolutionize the whole pattern of its life. It is seldom really wise to go to an electorate with talk of "great sacrifices."

The apartheid program, therefore, has taken the form almost exclusively of popular apartheid. When the Prime Minister was asked, not for the first time, what apartheid is, he pointed to the separation of Cape colored passengers on Cape Town's suburban railway trains and said: "You ask what apartheid is: this is it." Separate queues were instituted at Post Office counters. Large notices at Johannesburg railway stations and elsewhere indicated that certain entrances were for "Europeans only" and "non-Europeans only." Legislation began with the prohibition of marriage between white and colored and the extension of the Immorality Laws to make casual unions of this kind illegal. It proceeded to the Group Areas Act, which is intended to bring about social separation by defining areas of residence, ownership and trade, although only in the local sense as between one part of a town and another. The next move was on the economic front, where provision for training native builders was balanced by a ban on their employment outside the native townships and areas.

Finally the government turned to the difficult but vital political problem. The franchise is already confined to whites everywhere except in the Cape Province, which entered the Union with a liberal tradition not shared by the other provinces. General Hertzog segregated the native vote in the Cape in 1936 by removing the native voters from the common voters' roll and giving them three (white) representatives of their own in the Assembly and four in the Senate. Now the government proceeded to apply the same policy to the colored voters in the midst of a stormy constitutional controversy arising from the fact that the requirement of a two-thirds majority of both Houses sitting together for any such change was set aside. The effect of this is to confine the 1,000,000 colored people to four (white) representatives in the Assembly and one in the Senate, and to prevent them from influencing elections in the other Cape constituencies.

At the same time a move has been made toward modifying the

1936 settlement by abolishing the Natives' Representative Council, an advisory body designed to create an extra-parliamentary institution in which the natives of all provinces could discuss legislation affecting themselves. In practice this body was neglected and ignored and was in open revolt against its own impotence before the change of government. General Smuts had proposed to meet the situation by extending its functions and giving it some executive powers with a view to developing a kind of subordinate Native Parliament. The new policy, however, is to establish a number of tribal and regional councils with some return to native tribal institutions. A central assembly which could be a focal point of native nationalism is viewed with disfavor.

The apartheid pattern as it has so far evolved, therefore, is one of social, economic and political separation within the framework of a mixed society. The National Register about to be compiled will fix the race and with it the status of all the inhabitants of the country. Europeans, natives, colored and Indians will each be confined to their own residential areas (as the natives have long been by the Urban Areas Acts), many trades and occupations will be similarly divided by barriers which will in theory be vertical but in practice often horizontal, and all political power will be concentrated in European hands, with some local self-government for each ethnic group. This system, it is contended, will preserve racial purity, maintain white political supremacy, and minimize economic conflict.

It was set out recently by the Minister of Labor, Mr. Ben Schoeman, in Parliament: "We have never advocated total apartheid. We accept the position that there will be a permanent Native population resident in the urban areas." It was absolutely essential, he continued, that secondary industry should have non-European labor and there was no intention of withdrawing it from them. "We have no intention of disrupting the economy of this country by withdrawing non-European labour from secondary industry." Already many thousands of natives were doing semi-skilled jobs, and he agreed that the native must be allowed to advance and that, with some training, would be able to do operative jobs. "The whole crux of the policy of the Government is that we do not want to create a permanent stratum of European unskilled labour and then allow Native labour to advance beyond the European."

This somewhat confused policy might succeed for a time. It would be acceptable to most Europeans, who regard an adequate supply of non-European labor within easy distance as essential, yet combine a fear of economic competition with a strong distaste for any form of social contact except in a master-and-servant relationship. Above all, they dislike the possibility of miscegenation which economic and social equality might bring. Antagonisms, economic and racial, also exist between non-European groups. Separation so far as it is possible seems to be the answer. It is certainly not an entirely new policy.

IV

In the long term, however, it is clearly no solution. It is theoretically possible to create "separate but equal" social amenities. In practice the equality is usually lacking, and the separation is costly, as the duplication of transport and other services is already proving. It is not even theoretically possible to offer separate but equal economic opportunity in an integrated society. The whole range of industry and other economic activity cannot be duplicated in a single city, yet without such duplication the best jobs must remain permanently closed to those on the wrong side of the dividing line. And it is not even theoretically admitted that there should be equality of political opportunity. In order to justify this bar-in-perpetuity to political evolution it is necessary, in spite of Mr. Schoeman, to invoke the doctrine of impermanence previously referred to—the doctrine, that is, that "the Native should only be allowed to enter urban areas, which are essentially the white man's creation, when he is willing to enter and to minister to the needs of the white man, and should depart therefrom when he ceases so to minister." Yet this doctrine conflicts violently with the conception of parallel development that the kind of apartheid just described is designed to bring about.

There is, in fact, no escape from the moral and practical dilemma to which the Dutch Reformed Church, Dr. Eiselen and others have drawn attention. It remains true, as Dr. Eiselen said, that in a mixed society of this sort the natives would never be given the opportunities to which they are entitled. It remains true, as the Church pointed out, that "we cannot expect that if we give them full opportunity for economic development . . . they will be satisfied to leave their economic, political and social interests to the care of others."

Now the leaders of apartheid thought are by and large neither unintelligent nor lacking in moral sense. They believe firmly, it is true, in white supremacy because throughout the history of their people in Africa the white man has represented civilization, and it has always been true that any real dilution of his power or his blood would have threatened civilization itself in this continent. They see no reason to believe that this is not still true. But they are well aware of the political stirrings going on among the non-white races of the world, on the African continent and among their own subjects. They would like to believe, as many South Africans do, that these movements can be kept at arm's length, and they will do their best to control and discourage them; but they know that the line cannot be held indefinitely against the whole world. For these reasons the tidy pattern of local segregation and the Group Areas Act cannot be the final solution. The logical end of apartheid can be only the total apartheid which Dr. Malan recognized as "the ideal."

Thus while Dr. Malan has announced that the government has almost reached the end of its apartheid program, cautious steps are being taken toward a reversal of the trends of a century. Not much can be hoped for from the stricter control of native migration, although this is being tried. It is realized that the native can be drawn back into the (possibly enlarged) Reserves, if at all, only by powerful economic counterattraction. There is much talk of developing industries in these areas and thus diversifying and enlarging the peasant economy and opening up large new fields of opportunity. A government commission is at present investigating the industrial possibilities.

The prospects, however, are not encouraging, and the over-all task is so formidable that only the conviction that national survival is at stake would impel any people to undertake it. That conviction is present, but it is still necessary to disguise the full scope of the operation from those who would have to attempt it.

Many of the Reserves, it is true, lie in the most fertile and best-watered parts of the country. But their fertility has been greatly reduced by misuse and overcrowding. No minerals have been found in them and no industrialists have yet been tempted to transfer their enterprise from the big centers of population with their modern power and transport facilities and ready-made markets to these depressed agricultural areas. The Social and Economic Planning Council, whose reports are a modern textbook of South African society, surveyed the Reserves situation and disclosed possibilities of planned development which included some cautious industrial beginnings based on the processing of agricultural produce. It visualized, too, the creation of villages (now almost entirely lacking) in which landless natives would find occupation in providing local services. But the

Council emphasized that these steps are necessary if the Reserves are to retain their present populations and some of the increase, and if they are to be raised above a subsistence economy. There could be no question of making room for more from outside.

Whether the new commission will be able to report more hopefully may well be doubted. Even the improvement of native agriculture is a slow and thankless task in the face of immemorial African conservatism. It is certain that the transformation of the Reserves into modern industrial states—and nothing less would be required—would call for an enormous expenditure of capital, if indeed it could be done at all. There are no signs yet that this or any South African Government would be prepared or able to devote large capital sums to these purposes.

The effects on the European economy if such a policy is ever seriously attempted are incalculable. Not only would it create an acute and apparently insurmountable manpower shortage, while calling into being a whole new white laboring class which is now nonexistent, but it would set up a parallel Bantu economy which would be a formidable threat to South African standards of living. These standards are based on high wage levels made possible by the wide gap between white skilled and non-white unskilled labor. Given expert white direction, which would in any case be necessary for a long time to come, Bantu industry, mechanized and using operative labor, could become highly productive at low cost. Only the color bar has prevented this happening before on a larger scale, although a pilot textile industry on the borders of a Native Reserve is already proving that it is possible. Indeed, this form of industrial organization is being tried with success in some of the cities, for the color bar is still customary rather than statutory and can be overcome.

These difficulties in the way of real apartheid have not yet been squarely faced, and it is unlikely that they will be unless and until the policy is openly admitted and discussed. Meanwhile the attempts to achieve it by stealth, as it were, are so puny as to be insignificant. The stream is flowing so powerfully the other way that something much more heroic will be needed to turn it back. The preliminary census figures for 1951 recently released show that whereas the European population of Johannesburg has remained almost stationary during the last five years, the Bantu population has increased by nearly 100,-000. Johannesburg, the Union's largest city and preëminently the "white man's creation," has a European population of some 330,000 and a native population of 480,000. And the process goes on apace. The National Resources Development Council estimates that the new Orange Free State gold areas will by 1966 have a European population of 146,000 and a native population of 277,000. This was until a few years ago virgin soil. The same pattern is repeated wherever a new project comes into being. Thus a large power station is being built on a Free State coalfield to supply the new mining area; 200 Europeans and 3,000 natives will be required to operate it.

All this is happening while the theorists discuss apartheid, and timid measures are being taken to sweep back the sea with a mop. It is plain that the frontiers so tenaciously defended 100 years ago have been crossed, and the onward march of the Bantu goes on irresistibly.

v

Dr. Malan's apartheid government can therefore be seen (as it sees itself in moments of emotion) as the last gallant stand of the white man in Africa; or merely as an anachronism. A new kind of society is being created in South Africa, and for better or worse it is a multiracial society. Its pattern has not yet been worked out. Residential separation on Group Areas lines will undoubtedly remain its social design for many years to come, but solutions have yet to be found for the economic and political problems such a society presents. Economic opportunity cannot be indefinitely withheld from any section of a community; political representation in some form cannot indefinitely be denied. In other words, if total apartheid cannot be applied, then the alternatives, not unfairly stated by the Church and other apartheid theorists, must be faced. Similar problems are being faced elsewhere in Africa and tentative solutions are being tried. The Union of South Africa has the problem in a much more advanced stage than any of these territories and can also draw upon a much longer experience.

The real misfortune of the apartheid policy is that it postpones, but only postpones, the day when a real attempt will be made to solve the problems of a multi-racial society composed of layers at several different stages of development and civilization. Valuable time is being wasted on impracticable and wishful policies when time is the one thing South Africa cannot afford. No South African can, however, afford to be self-righteous in dismissing the apartheid solution as illusory, for few of those who condemn it are prepared to come to grips with the real problems South African society presents. No political party has yet ventured to produce a formula and stand by it.

It is, of course, not difficult to put such a formula on paper. The Native Reserves are to a great extent self-contained units with a way of life of their own not yet too greatly influenced by direct European contact. They are, in fact, South Africa's "colonial" territories, and it is still possible to apply to them a "colonial" policy of indirect rule. As with other colonial territories in Africa, they are in urgent need of economic aid and development, and the need is the more urgent in South Africa if their populations are to be stabilized and prevented from erupting into South African society. Indeed, all the energy apartheid can muster in its treatment of the Reserves will not to be too much for the task in hand there. Politically, tribal institutions are capable of adaptation to modern conditions, and would stand in the same relationship to the Union Government as other colonial institutions stand to their colonial powers. Their ultimate destiny, however, would be a federal relationship rather than complete independence; in the meantime Senate representation would be appropriate.

This policy differs from that of the apartheid policy in only one important respect: it is complementary to and not a substitute for a native policy. The Planning Council's report on the Reserves commented that "no Reserve policy, not even the policy advocated in this report, will make it possible for South Africa to evade the issues raised by the presence of Natives in European farming and urban areas."

Outside the Reserves, therefore, the large Bantu population might be divided into two classes—those capable of exercising a direct franchise, and those for whom some less direct method is more suitable. The first class, to whom educational and other "civilization" tests would apply, might be entitled to enrolment on a special roll for the election of a specified number of native representatives to the Assembly, which is the main legislative chamber of the South African Parliament. These voters would be the equivalent of the *évolués* of French and Portuguese colonies, but would nevertheless be confined to communal and therefore relatively inelastic representation. This is necessary to prevent the voters' rolls being overwhelmed in a short time by "advanced" natives, who would thus replace the Europeans as the dominant political group. Faced with this possibility there would be every inducement to Europeans to check rapid Bantu progress.

The less advanced Bantu, who still form the great mass outside as well as inside the Reserves, might have local and regional councils on the lines now proposed as part of the apartheid policy, with suitable representation in the Senate. It should be noted that the South African Senate is a house of review with powers that are more apparent than real. It is, however, already an outlet to a limited extent for native opinion through representatives chosen for the purpose, and Senate representation in some form is conceded by apartheid. It might be necessary to make some more far-reaching change in the character and functions of this House, if it is to serve a real purpose in a system of multi-racial representative government.

An alternative solution, put forward by the South African writer and historian Dr. A. Keppel-Jones, is the federalization of South Africa, with a number of states in each of which one of the races (European, Bantu, colored and Indian) would predominate and rule. This is an extension of the apartheid idea without the need for physical separation, except in so far as racial groups chose to migrate to neighboring states in search of a more congenial régime.

Important as political arrangements are in a country in which racial security is regarded as of paramount importance, the economic problem is the more immediate. Color apart, a low wage group is always a threat to an artisan class with high living standards. The obvious defense—a minimum wage for all in skilled trades—is nevertheless regarded with misgiving by many of the white trade unions and most of the political parties. The color bar is more effective and avoids the complication of social equality at the workbench. Yet it is difficult to see how economic injustice is to be avoided in any other way than through a standard wage divorced from color; and, more urgently, how the country's economic problem of poverty and underproduction is to be solved if the straitjacket of the color bar is not removed.

Such solutions as these are vague and unformed chiefly because South Africans refuse to discuss them, and policies that have not withstood the test of public controversy necessarily have an academic unreality. The reason why they are neglected is that most white South Africans have an instinctive belief that once they have set such a course they will be caught irresistibly in the current that will sweep them and their particular values into oblivion.

For the argument hitherto has been entirely between Europeans about the Bantu. The Bantu themselves have remained silent; or when they have spoken their views have been dismissed as the voice of agitators and extremists. Most of them, it is true, are inarticulate and politically indifferent. Yet events in other African territories and the subtle change in the South African atmosphere itself are a warning that the argument may soon be with the Bantu, not merely about them. The effective opposition to apartheid will eventually come not from an opposing political party but from the non-Europeans themselves. And that opposition may extend beyond apartheid to any policy that falls short of complete equality. The president of the African National Congress, the main Bantu political movement, Dr. Moroka, remarked recently, with the kind of tolerant understanding that Europeans find more frightening than threats, that the Afrikaner had not been satisfied in the past with anything less than equality; he could see no logical difference between the nature and purpose of the Afrikaner struggle and the nature and purpose of the African struggle. Each was a struggle of a nation to ensure for itself those conditions that make life possible. Dr. Moroka added that the outcome of apartheid would be the death knell of civilization in South Africa and the complete collapse of the edifice of white *baasskap* (boss-ship) which apartheid sought to construct.

The question has still to be answered whether the civilization, if not the boss-ship, can be preserved undamaged either with apartheid or without it. Mere repression is bound to fail, and any apartheid other than the unattainable total kind (and perhaps even that) will inevitably be repressive. But will concession fail too? To put the question in another way, will the education of the Bantu in Western culture and Western democracy keep pace with his political demands? If it does not, the well-meant alternatives to apartheid may not avert the conflict. The best that can be said is that in the one case the conflict is certain, in the other the way is left open for peaceful solutions in the future.

Note

TOWARD A WORLD POLICY FOR SOUTH AFRICA
BY PATRICK DUNCAN

October 1963

The four contributors to this section have much in common; they are all white South Africans, well informed and of some prominence in their own society; all are deeply disturbed by their country's racial problem and in varying degrees critical of official policy. The three preceding articles have further been characterized by their lack of dogmatism, a sense of groping toward solutions rather than offering final answers. Only the fourth, written after an interval of ten years, is uncompromisingly committed to a point of view.

The author of the following article is the son of the former Governor General of South Africa whose article, written 37 years earlier, appears on page 201. The events of those intervening years, both in South Africa and in the world at large, have left little room for the moderate, humane, middle-of-the-road view that the elder Duncan expressed. Today, positions are rigidly drawn, and Patrick Duncan, the younger, is among that handful of white South Africans who have taken the side of the African. Having struggled unsuccessfully for moderation and compromise, he is now wholly identified with the cause of those who are fighting for the end of apartheid, equality for all without qualification, hence a state in which the black majority will gain control.

He is one of the few white members of the Pan-Africanist Congress, which has emerged in recent years as the most effective of the African nationalist organizations—though it must work underground and its leadership has repeatedly been decimated by arrests. Duncan himself is now a political refugee. Previously, he was editor of the liberal fortnightly, *Contact*.

Patrick Duncan, the younger, is no more a wild-eyed radical than his basically conservative father, but a man of conscience who has been forced by circumstances and the uncompromising attitudes of the South African Government to adopt what he feels is the only alternative to the present system—namely, constitutional government by the majority. In the following article, he describes conditions in South Africa and answers some of the arguments of apologists for apartheid. He then goes on to argue that only the world community—with the United States exerting the lead—can save South Africa from certain violence and destruction, with incalculable consequences for the peace of the world.

Toward a World Policy
for South Africa

by PATRICK DUNCAN

yeah
Duncan!

In the Security Council on August 7 the United States voted for a ban on the shipment of arms to the South African Government, and in the course of the debate the American representative announced that the United States would suspend all arms shipments at the end of the year. Since South Africa has in the past found it difficult to obtain licenses for the purchase of American arms, this decision represented only a small shift in policy. But as the vote was taken under African pressure, and as it separated the United States from Britain and France (which abstained), the shift was significant; for it showed that when faced with a choice, the United States is more prepared than before to take a stand against apartheid.

The supporting speech defined American policies toward the South African Government with some precision: though hostile to apartheid, the United States is not yet convinced that force is a necessary ingredient in the solution of the problem, for "we cannot accept the conclusion that there is no way out, no direction to go except the present collision course toward ultimate disaster in South Africa." Rather, steps are envisaged "to induce that government to remove the evil business of apartheid . . . from the continent of Africa."

The American view that a clash is avoidable is not shared by most observers. It is certainly not shared by the Government of South Africa, nor the majority of its white citizens. Never has so much been spent on arms in South Africa; the figure is now running at a published rate of $219,000,000 a year. Military service is bulking ever more prominently in the lives of the white people. And, apart from national armaments, the three million white people privately own two million firearms.

250

An ever-tightening code of security laws buttresses this armed oligarchy. There is, for example, a recent law which permits any police officer to detain anyone for successive periods of 90 days without limit and without warrant; such persons can be held incommunicado and the courts are prohibited from intervening. This is only the latest in a 15-year series of increasingly repressive laws which show a growing fear and hostility toward the Africans.

The Bantu Laws Amendment Act of 1963 took away the legal right of all black South Africans (68 percent of the population) to live anywhere outside the "Native Reserves" (13 percent of the land). Continued residence in the 87 percent of the land reserved for whites is a matter of privilege, and requires permits that can be administratively cancelled at any time. Freedom of movement for Africans has already dwindled until the majority of the population are not able to move from their places of work. One-third of the Africans live on white men's farms; they may not leave to look for work in the cities without the permission of their masters and of the government. The one-third who live in the cities generally dare not have a dispute with their employers for fear of being forced by the government to go to live in the decaying reserves. And for the remaining third who live in the reserves, it is illegal to move out unless they have work waiting for them. For most, this is an impossibility, unless they contract to work in the mines.

Strikes by Africans have been made illegal, and almost every act of their lives, including often the right to live with their spouses, and even the right to go to the church of their choice, has been made subject to official permits. Another law prohibits the courts, in certain matters, from issuing injunctions in favor of Africans. In mid-1963 over 5,000 persons were held as convicted political prisoners, and at least 2,800 members of one movement, the Pan-Africanist Congress, had been arrested and were awaiting trial.

Education for white children up to the eighth grade is compulsory and free, and the schools provide free meals. The government spends about $170 on each white child in school, while the comparable figure for African children is $17. But for African children education is not compulsory and most children of school age are not in school. The Bantu Education Act specifically designs education for Africans which shall fit them for an inferior place in life. One of the first acts of the Afrikaner Nationalists when they came to power was to cancel the existing schemes for free food for African school children—the very children who need it most.

These and other facts do not bear out the contention of apologists for apartheid that the African in the Union enjoys a standard of living unequaled in Africa. Despite the fact that South Africa is the richest country of the continent and has been enjoying great prosperity, an official study shows that the real wages of Africans in the main urban centers generally declined in the 1950s. Moreover, the incidence of malnutrition and related diseases in parts of South Africa is the highest recorded in the world. The infant mortality rate in the Port Elizabeth divisional area in 1961 was 480 per thousand live births. African children die at 25 times the rate of white children. According to a survey carried out by the reputable *Rand Daily Mail*, 57 percent of African children die before they reach the age of five years. A University of Natal survey found signs of malnutrition in every one of 240 African workers visited: they were earning $28 a month. A bus company gave out free meals and found that absenteeism among African workers dropped by half.[1]

This low standard of living is a reflection of the African's votelessness and his inability to influence political movements. Political rights, long enjoyed, have been reduced or abolished. In 1853 Britain gave the Cape a parliament, and gave the vote to all men earning $140 a year. Many black and colored men qualified, and for most of the nineteenth century the Cape parliament was responsible to the aspirations of all races. But the white minority never accepted this situation, and in the hundred years after 1853—but most drastically in the last 15— managed to abolish all political and civic rights which the African people had enjoyed. (Vestigial rights are still enjoyed by some colored people.)

At the same time that the white minority has been reducing the political power of the non-whites, the Africans' ambitions and aspirations have been rising. In this fact lies the refutation both of those who plead for more time and of those who believe that a conflict is avoidable. The all-pervasive ideas of democracy have found ready acceptance among the non-white people of South Africa. Despite rigid censorship of books and films, and despite an ideological decision not

[1] I am indebted for the above facts on malnutrition to "The Coming Struggle for South Africa," by Sandor (Fabian Society, London, 1963). "Sandor" is the pen name of a well known South African publicist specializing in research on labor conditions. For the wage study see the article by Professor W. R. J. Steenkamp, Chairman of the Wage Board, in the *South African Journal of Economics*, June 1962.

to have television, there has never been so great a flood of modern ideas into the minds of the voteless South Africans. Another gauge of the situation is that some 100,000 non-whites own cars, and a rising class of business and professional men is inching its way upward against almost insuperable obstacles.

The Africans are determined to win full status and dignity and power. Their determination is reflected in a remarkable growth recently in militancy and political courage. Two principal organizations have emerged: the Pan-Africanist Congress (of which I am a member) and an earlier protest movement, the African National Congress. PAC was founded in 1959 by a university lecturer named Mangaliso Robert Sobukwe, who completed a three-year prison sentence on May 5 but is still detained. It was born out of the impatience of the younger and more ardent Africans with the A.N.C., which for some 40 years had voiced the protests of the Africans. Sobukwe and his followers claimed that the A.N.C. had failed too often in its ambitious protests and strikes, that it was dominated by Communists and whites, and that it paid too little regard to the African personality. He rapidly won the confidence of the masses and in March 1960 he launched the non-violent campaign of positive action that led to Sharpeville. Thereafter, both movements were outlawed, and the leaders of PAC were given heavy sentences. Both movements went underground, the PAC more effectively. Its committee functions in Basutoland, in the center of South Africa. There are about 100 cells, and at least one cell has 1,000 members. According to a recent public opinion survey conducted by the South African Institute of Race Relations, the Pan-Africanist Congress is the leading African party and has particular support among the more militant and the students.

Growing African militancy has bred and will continue to breed growing government oppression. The extremes are nourishing each other at the expense of the middle. It is this that makes the coming clash inevitable unless the white South Africans can be affected by external pressures. The first of these is already being mounted. In May of this year at the Addis Ababa Conference, free Africa declared war on apartheid. It was this issue that made it possible for the 32 independent states meeting there to overcome every other divisive factor. All agreed that the emancipation of Africa and of Negroes everywhere could not be regarded as complete while there subsisted in Africa's most wealthy state a constitution based on the proposition that men are incurably unequal, and that whites alone deserve the vote.

Subventions have already begun to flow into the Liberation Fund, a war chest for the extirpation of apartheid. Africa intends and is able to fight apartheid. Let those who doubt it, or who may underestimate the dimensions of such a war, bear in mind that apartheid treats as inferior not only South Africans of African origin, but also those of Indian and Chinese origin, and that the theory of apartheid has already stirred to anger the representatives of nearly three billion people.

The danger of a world split on the basis of color has been feared for many years; it is a division that could destroy civilization and a great part of the human race. Already, if we are to attach weight to the July letter of the Russians to the Chinese Communists, the Chinese have used the racist argument to secure the expulsion of the Soviet Union from some organizations in the Afro-Asian world. As a result, some observers are predicting that the Chinese will attempt to build a Fifth International based on color. Such an attempt would be greatly assisted by the existence of a régime in South Africa which professes to be leading a crusade against Communism, but which, in the name of "Western civilization," oppresses the colored races. It is, moreover, a government that displays most of the weaknesses which Marx and Engels predicted for capitalism: increasing poverty for the workers, increasing wealth for the capitalists, and aggressiveness against the outside world.

II

Hitherto American policy in Africa has tried to avoid making choices. Only in the Congo were choices made and strong policies executed. Elsewhere the Government of the United States has tried, and largely succeeded, in remaining friend to both the departing metropole powers and the emerging African nations. Wise though this may be when there is a continuing dialogue between contending parties, or when political movement is generally in the desired direction, or when either side is subject to persuasion, such a policy merely ensures the hostility of both sides when, as in the case of South Africa, none of these conditions applies.

Two facts are generally overlooked by those who hold that time should be afforded to the South African authorities to solve the problem themselves, and that interference from outside merely aggravates the situation by making the supporters of apartheid more militant and unified. The first is that developments in South Africa are going the wrong way: where there were rights, these have been taken away; where there was a little integration, it has been abolished; where there was some hope in the minds of the ruled, it has given way to despair. The second is that there is no longer any effective opposition to apartheid within the South African electorate. Any legislation presented by the Nationalist Party can be passed in Parliament with almost no debate and but one or two dissenting votes. Indeed, it is probably no longer within the power of the government to reverse the trend toward increased oppression, for a fearful electorate would remove even Dr. Verwoerd's government if it showed a disposition to make concessions. Thus the initiative has already passed irrevocably away from the whites to the voteless, and to their friends and allies. For all these reasons, it is difficult to see how intervention can make matters worse than they are.

If this analysis is correct, what can America—if it so wills—do about it? The question is often asked in a tone of despair that is unjustified. There are two main kinds of action that can be taken: small-scale measures that can be taken quietly and immediately, and that require no major policy decisions; and more telling actions that require major decisions of state.

Having voted in favor of the arms embargo, the United States might use its influence to discourage its NATO allies from supplying arms of any kind to the South African Government. Under pressure from Africa, the British and French have announced that they will no longer supply arms that could be used to enforce apartheid. The United States tried this policy from 1961 to 1963, and could point out to the British and French that the distinction is unreal, as it found when it refused licenses to the South Africans for supersonic jet combat planes in 1961, yet allowed the export of Lockheed Hercules C-130 military transport planes in 1963. In any event, it is to be hoped that the recent undertakings by the British and French will be observed. The temptation to waver will be especially strong for the French, who have been the principal suppliers of helicopters and armored cars— weapons of particular value in the kind of war that is likely to occur in South Africa.

Mr. Stevenson told the U.N. that "we have utilized our diplomatic and consular establishments in South Africa to demonstrate by words and by deeds our official disapproval of apartheid." With a nation that has taken the bit between its teeth, words have limited value; of deeds, only one has been made public. Although individual Africans have previously been entertained at the American Embassy, only this year, for the first time, were non-whites invited to the Independence Day celebrations—a secondary party to which South African Government representatives were not invited. While this partial desegregation of an official reception must be welcomed and applauded, one wonders why all entertainment at the embassy could not be integrated. To be sure, the last Soviet representative to South Africa was expelled from the country because he refused to accept apartheid in his consulate-general; but is this an argument for or against the proposition? Or again, might not a Negro foreign service officer be posted to the embassy? Is it necessary for American naval vessels visiting South Africa to have none but white officers? Might "awkward" social situations be reduced if the American Ambassador were replaced by a consul-general who might find it easier to establish contacts with all elements in the population?

Similarly, it might be appropriate to end grants, student exchanges and links of all kinds which involve the acceptance of segregation. Of the various schemes, both governmental and private, for the exchange of students and leaders, all involving South Africa are under the close control of the South African Government, for it exercises strict passport and visa control. It permits these schemes to continue, and uses them as propaganda to demonstrate its respectability in the eyes of the world. Strong opponents of the government are not allowed passports to travel, so the exchanges are limited to supporters of the government, to apolitical persons and sometimes to people who have become instruments of apartheid. In general, non-whites do not get passports for these exchanges unless they are regarded as politically safe. These schemes thus have value to the government, for they are regarded as plums to which supporters can aspire, as well as some innocuous opponents whose opposition is not embarrassing to the government. In the circumstances, it would not appear that the American dollars which so often finance these schemes are working in American interests.

As links with the white supremacist minority are attenuated, so links with the majority might be extended and strengthened. At this stage what is required is an increase in scholarship schemes for young people who manage to smuggle themselves out of the country. America's record in this field is good, but needs are growing fast. Such schemes could play an important part in strengthening democracy now and in assisting reconstruction later.

Another useful move would be to discourage American investment in South Africa. It is true that investors have a concern for the country in which they have substantial economic interests, but understandably this concern is primarily to maintain the status quo, to avoid change which may adversely affect the climate for doing business. Moreover, each dollar that moves into the South African currency control area is, in effect, a vote of confidence in the system, and builds currency reserves which are being built up for military expenditure against the coming storm. Thus investment strengthens apartheid today and imperils the whole private-enterprise system tomorrow—for the African majority, when it votes, will vote against all who did business with apartheid.

In any case, since the Addis Conference it has become apparent that foreign businessmen will probably have to choose between South Africa and the rest of the continent. By trading and investing in South Africa businessmen stand to win a substantial (but brief) return at the cost of losing their whole position in a rapidly developing market of 250,000,000 people. American investment in all of southern Africa, from the Congo to the Cape, amounts to only $413,000,000, compared with a British stake in South Africa alone of over $2,800,000,-000. The withdrawal of $413 million would not hurt the United States, but would be likely to make a considerable impact on the South African Government.

III

None of these recommendations could be called radical. It would be unreal, however, to expect that more far-reaching decisions leading to a world policy for South Africa can long be postponed. One of the first big questions which will come before the U.N. is that of South West Africa, on which the World Court is expected to render a judgment some time in 1964.

To summarize the case very briefly, the South West African question had its origin in the First World War, when the territory was taken from the defeated Germans and entrusted by the League of Nations as a mandate to the South African Government. The South Africans were permitted to administer the territory "as an integral portion of the Union of South Africa," but must "promote to the utmost the material and moral well-being and the social progress of the inhabitants of the territory." Despite this injunction the South

African Government has ruled the non-whites of South West Africa as they have ruled the non-whites in South Africa.

The basis of this rule was defined by Mr. J. G. Strijdom, the South African Prime Minister who preceded Dr. Verwoerd, as follows: "The European is the master in South Africa, quite apart from his economic hold on the country, and quite apart from his culture and civilization, because he is the ruler of the country. . . . The entire position of the European is based on discriminatory legislation in so far as the races in South Africa are concerned." [2] Since then Dr. Verwoerd has introduced apartheid more definitely into the mandate by placing the non-whites of the territory under the South African Department of Bantu Administration and Development, and by creating segregated townships.

The South West African question has been debated at the United Nations annually since 1948 without any material results. Now the matter has been taken to the International Court of Justice at The Hague. The plaintiff countries are Ethiopia and Liberia, which, having been members of the League of Nations as well as of the U.N., were felt to be the most suited for the role. They have asked the Court for a declaration that the introduction of the apartheid policy is inconsistent with the terms of the mandate. The Court has not been asked to issue any order, merely a declaration.

The judgment, when it is handed down, is expected to favor the plaintiffs, in which case an interesting and unprecedented situation will exist. One possibility is that the South African Government will then make a virtue of necessity by abandoning its mandate and transferring it to the Trusteeship Council. This may depend very much on whether the South African Government believes the United States is prepared—if the mandate is *not* surrendered—to support collective U.N. action against South Africa, with economic sanctions or force if necessary.

If South Africa does not respond favorably to the Court's judgment, the matter is almost certain to go the Security Council where a resolution will probably be introduced to detach the mandate from South Africa. Then the position of the United States and the Council's other permanent members will be crucial. A veto in the Security Council would not necessarily affect the outcome, because action by the General Assembly would still be possible and probable. But it would remove American and European influence from the action;

[2] Hansard, 1952, v. 77, col. 252.

even to abstain would greatly reduce the capacity of the United States to influence events.

It seems evident that the Soviet Union will strongly support a U.N. resolution on South West Africa. But the experience of the Congo should discourage both of the major powers from trying to frustrate United Nations action on this issue. In the Congo the United States supported, though with great difficulty, the majority of member states, and paid a large part of the costs. The Soviet Union tried to boycott the operation and has refused to pay its share of the costs. It is no coincidence that Russian policy in central Africa lies in ruins, whereas the United States attained its major objectives.

If sanctions are likely to be used, or threatened, over the South West African question, are they likely to be used or threatened over the question of apartheid? In the Security Council in August the United States opposed sanctions against South Africa, and Mr. Stevenson called for the examination of peaceful alternatives to the use of force. But Chapter VII of the Charter identifies sanctions as the principal alternative to the use of force. The continued call for sanctions by free Africa is not mere trouble-making, but is on the contrary a sincere attempt to handle—in a manner provided for by the U.N. Charter—a situation which the United States itself acknowledges is a threat to peace and security. In any case there is a ground swell running for sanctions, and spontaneous trade-union boycotts are growing in Britain and Scandinavia. It is thus reasonable to expect that, even apart from South West Africa, the world will shortly be seeking effective methods of penning up and weakening the apartheid system.

Of all possible trade embargoes, only one has any chance of being truly effective: a blockade of oil imports. South Africa is more than self-sufficient in foodstuffs and clothing, and can even make automobiles. But it has no petroleum, though an oil-from-coal industry supplies about 10 percent of its gasoline needs. Cutting off oil imports would have unpredictable results, but it may be said that it would make the continued administration of the country either extremely difficult or impossible.

There are of course many arguments against the use of sanctions. One of the most frequently heard is that "they will hurt the very people they are designed to help." But there is not one African leader in South Africa who would not welcome effective action of this sort, and there are few non-whites who would not accept great inconvenience and suffering if apartheid could thereby be ended.

Another argument heard in America is that the United Nations should not call for sanctions against apartheid, because the resolution would be ignored. This prophecy is in some degree self-fulfilling. But if the United States were willing to adhere to an oil embargo, and assuming that the Communist countries followed suit, the pressures that could be mounted on the remaining oil producers would be overwhelming. What would particularly distinguish this effort to impose sanctions from earlier, unsuccessful efforts is the unusual degree of unanimity that exists throughout the world on the apartheid issue. And it is because intervention of some kind is almost inevitable—whether or not the West wills it—that controlled intervention under the aegis of the United Nations offers the best hope of the human race of escaping from the worst consequences of apartheid.

As the crisis grows one hears voices increasingly being raised in America in favor of a "just" partition. But there is no just partition, for any scheme would remove some innocent individuals from their homes and employment. In particular, there is no just partition that could leave the white territory with any sizable infrastructure. For it was the whites who unified a naturally partitioned South Africa in the nineteenth century, and who forced the non-whites to coöperate in building the industries, farms and mines. If now it is the whites who wish to destroy the partnership and undo the union, they could not reasonably expect to keep what was built in partnership. In any event, partition has no hope of being accepted by either side.

Mr. Stevenson ended his August 2 speech with a comparison between the South African question and the nuclear test-ban treaty. The comparison is just, for South Africa like the atom contains potentialities for great good or for great evil. A democratic and non-racial South Africa could do much to conquer the backwardness of the entire continent, and could ease the relationships between black and white everywhere. But if apartheid were to continue much longer, or if the world were to stand aside from South Africa while the races mutilated each other and ruined the land's productive capacity, race relationships everywhere could be poisoned.

Between the possibility of great good and the possibility of great evil lies a field awaiting the exercise of creative world statesmanship. Here, as in so many other areas of world tension, nothing is possible without an American lead.

Part VI

The New Leaders

Note

BLACK AFRICA AND THE FRENCH UNION
BY FÉLIX HOUPHOUET-BOIGNY

July 1957

In the postwar period the most influential politician in French West Africa has been Félix Houphouet-Boigny, President of the Ivory Coast. His is the most prosperous of the former French territories in Africa; his has been the strongest African voice in Paris, where he served as minister in a succession of French governments; his has been the most powerful political organization in West Africa—the *Rassemblement Démocratique Africain*—which before independence extended into every French African territory. Whether swimming with or against the tide of African politics—and he has done both without breaking stroke—he has been a force to reckon with.

In the following article Houphouet-Boigny acknowledges his long love affair with France, asks not for independence but for close association. Today he has both. Independence came almost irresistibly in 1960, but the close cultural and economic relations with France remain. Abidjan is alive with Frenchmen—businessmen, teachers, civil servants—and the Ivory Coast is booming. Hence, though the present political relationship with France is not what President Houphouet-Boigny foresaw, his assertion of interdependence and of the need for close ties with the former colonial power has in fact been accepted by the French-speaking independent states of Africa. Even Guinea, which alone opted for independence when it was first offered—thereby earning the uncompromising hostility of de Gaulle—is moving back into closer relationship with France.

The more nationalistic African leaders like Nkrumah—and even some Western observers—say that the new French-speaking nations are compromising their political independence by their heavy economic reliance on France. Houphouet-Boigny is unruffled by such charges; for him more than most politicians, support of France in the United Nations and the suppression of protest when France conducts atomic testing in the Sahara are a small price to pay for rapid economic and social development of his country.

The President of the Ivory Coast did not always have the unqualified confidence of the French. He was once considered a dangerous radical whose R.D.A. (with Sékou Touré as vice-president) openly coöperated with the Communists. But in 1950 he broke with them and reversed many of his former positions as a nationalist leader. Thereafter he became a Deputy to the French National Assembly, a member of the French delegation to the U.N. in 1956–57, and a confidant of Prime Ministers of several French governments. He is the son of a chief, and before entering politics in 1940 he practiced medicine with a qualified license obtained 15 years earlier.

Black Africa and the French Union

by FÉLIX HOUPHOUET-BOIGNY

In this second half of the twentieth century, a newcomer has made its appearance on the international scene: Black Africa. Strategists, politicians, economists are no longer indifferent to what happens in Dakar, in Abidjan, in Accra, in Lomé. Never has our old continent been honored by so many visitors of such high rank nor been the object of so much study. But since the era of colonialism is over, it is first of all the Africans themselves who must be consulted on the future evolution of Africa and on the relations between the former subject peoples and the former colonizers.

I am a man of the African soil, having lived constantly in the midst of our rural Negro masses, sharing their joys and their sorrows, and making their great hope of liberty my own. For ten consecutive years, they have elected me to represent them in the French Parliament. I am the leader of the most powerful African political movement—a movement which continues to this very day to denounce the abuses and errors of colonialism, and to call untiringly for justice and equality. For these reasons, I think I have the right to consider myself the authentic spokesman of the millions of African men and women who have chosen, in preference to the type of independence just acquired by the neighboring state of Ghana, a Franco-African community founded on liberty, equality and fraternity.

In considering where the real interests of the colored peoples of the French territories in Africa lie, we do not begin with a blank slate. The relations which prevail between Frenchmen of the mother country and Frenchmen of Africa already exist in an historical complex of events lived in common, in which good and bad memories mingle. I forget neither the good nor the bad, but I think that the bonds thus forged are, like childhood memories, understandable and emotionally significant only for the initiated, for those near to the events, for those whose lives these bonds have cast in the same mold. I will therefore examine only the present state of relations within the French Union, as they have evolved during the past ten years.

As a preliminary, we must remove the aura which the concept of independence holds in our imaginations. Why do we not demand independence? To answer this question, I can only ask another: What is independence? Industrial and technical revolutions are making peoples more and more dependent on one another. I asked my friend Mr. Nkrumah whether he was ready to leave the sterling zone now that Ghana was independent. "Not only will we remain in the sterling zone, but also in the Commonwealth," he answered immediately.

Indeed, who doubts that close and sustained economic relations are essential to a country which wants to raise its standard of living? What countries are self-sufficient? Not even the United States. Indeed, the countries of Europe in the Coal and Steel Community, in Euratom and in the Common Market are prepared to relinquish a part of their sovereignty, that is to say, a part of their national independence. Why, if not to bring about, by association and mutual aid, a more fully elaborated form of civilization which is more advantageous for their peoples and which transcends a nationalism that is too cramped, too dogmatic and by now out of date?

This is also our goal, because it is in our interest. We want to cooperate within this great aggregate which is the French Union, because it is there that we can safeguard the advantages and the interests of the black people of Africa.

I am a native of a territory whose development has scarcely begun. Between 1939 and 1955 the tonnage handled by the port of Abidjan in the Ivory Coast went from 231,250 tons to 930,000 tons. The population has increased tenfold in the space of a few years and this rate shows no sign of diminishing. The Ivory Coast could not, by itself, find the means of providing the investment monies needed to cope with this heavy and continuing expansion. For many more years—10? 20? 50?—it will require enough capital aid to allow its inhabitants to make up for the heavy handicaps which nature imposes on tropical countries.

This outside capital assistance is needed by all countries undergoing rapid expansion, whether they are nominally independent or not. We wish to remain in the French Union because it furnishes us this assistance and does it by an arrangement which seems to us the surest and best adapted to further the social and technical progress of our peoples.

The Investment Fund for the Economic and Social Development of the Overseas Territories (F.I.D.E.S.) was created in 1946 to centralize and coördinate, with the coöperation of the Central Fund for France Overseas, a major program of internal development. In the space of ten years, more than 600 billion francs of government funds have been devoted to territories whose area is 9,000,000 square kilometers but whose population does not exceed 30,000,000.

The Administrative Council of the Central Fund, which manages the F.I.D.E.S., is composed of representatives of the important bureaus of the government, and also of members appointed by Parliament and by the labor unions. Several of its members are Africans, who can thus keep a check on the use and apportionment of these government funds and make sure that the interests of the people are effectively safeguarded. It should be understood that we are speaking here of government funds provided by the mother country, leaving aside private investments on the one hand and local budgets on the other.

It has often been said that France has devoted more money to underdeveloped territories than any other country. I would add that France's accomplishments are even more praiseworthy if it is remembered that she has borne the impact of two wars and that in 1945 she had to reconstruct her own territory, ravaged by military campaigns and pillaged by four years of occupation. Nevertheless, the sums which France puts at the disposal of the overseas territories are not so extraordinary that they could not be duplicated. Why attach oneself to this single source?

The fact is that the manner in which money is given can be a guarantee of continuity and stability. Perhaps we will on occasion find some creditor, public or private, capable of loaning, if not of giving, the billions necessary for the industrial, technical and social development of the African territories. But what guarantee would we have that this aid would be forthcoming year after year? How could we control the allocation of the loans offered? For what would we be asked in exchange?

We know what France asks of us—to share in her institutions and to share in them as equals. The right of citizenship has been granted without restriction to all the inhabitants of the French Union, and all the electors, whatever their origin, are gathered in a single college. At one stroke universal suffrage has been instituted everywhere—a privilege that not even the state of Ghana nor British Nigeria has yet dared extend to the tribal regions of the interior. No racial or religious discrimination prohibits any activity, public or private. Opportunities are legally the same for all, and if inequalities exist they arise from circumstances or local conditions which the authorities are making every effort to eliminate.

Thus the democratic institutions of republican France have little by little been established in the overseas territories. During the past several months, free elections throughout French Africa have enabled the people to choose those who would direct communal, urban, rural or territorial institutions. As a result, Africans are now in a position to exercise their responsibilities and to assert their political personality. Municipal councils exercise sovereign power over local affairs. Territorial assemblies are endowed with broad deliberative powers allowing them to adopt autonomous laws distinct from legislation which applies to the mother country. They have an executive responsible to them, to whom is entrusted the direction of territorial affairs with the exception of foreign relations, defense and security, which remain in the hands of the central power. It is in some degree self-government, but it maintains essential links with the Republic, and is not without analogy to the federal structure of the United States of America.

What makes it certainly unique, however, among various relationships that have existed in modern times between a mother country and its dependencies is the participation of overseas populations in the central government of the Republic. There are, in the National Assembly and in the Council of the Republic, Negro deputies and senators, elected in the same way as their colleagues of the mother country. The fusion has succeeded so well, mutual courtesy and comprehension have developed so naturally, that no one in France finds it remarkable any longer that the third-ranking dignitary of the Republic, the President of the Senate, is a Negro—Mr. Monnerville. It will seem then just as unremarkable that other colored people have for several years played a part in the Government, and that I myself was able to represent France in the United Nations at the time of the debates on Togo.

It is not vanity which makes me emphasize the importance of the positions occupied by colored people in the highest functions of a great nation. It is simply to explain our attachment to the French

Union as it is conceived. We feel at home in it. We participate in family discussions. Nothing is hidden from us—neither hopes nor dangers. How could we better preserve the interests of the Negro people who for so many years have put their confidence in us again and again? It is this awareness of a comprehensive interdependence of mutual interests which has permitted the creation of a Franco-African community based on equality. It is expressed by autonomy in the management of local affairs and intimate association in the management of the general interests of the Republic.

Since the French Union is dynamic, our evolution continues on the national level, and other ties are contemplated in a constitutional reform now being prepared and soon to be debated in the French Parliament. We took part in the preparations for this debate, maintaining as our guiding principle the idea of a federal community, freely joining the peoples of French language and culture. The specific terms by which the principle will be expressed must now be decided by French legislators—black and white.

Naturally, we cannot help but compare our own evolution with the experiment which Great Britain has just undertaken in granting independence to the state of Ghana. Actually, the terms of agreement do not differ greatly, although we have not asked for the type of independence which Mr. Nkrumah has just obtained. After much reflection, bearing in mind the highest interest of this Africa which we dearly love, the human relations existing between French and African, and the imperative of this century—the interdependence of nations—from which no power can claim to escape, we have preferred to try a different experiment, more difficult perhaps, but unique of its kind and unknown until now in the long history of nations—that of a community of peoples, equal and fraternal.

Should we turn away from this community, made possible by recent political, economic and social reforms? Should we demand our total independence, as so many other countries have? No major African political party has thought so, and none has put independence into its platform.

Today, no nation, however powerful, can pretend to impose its absolute will on another for long. By doing so, it would irremediably compromise its own future as a great nation. France knows this. Its own best interests no less than its sensitivity to human values and the absence of any racist feelings among its people have led it voluntarily to renounce force as an instrument of policy in Black Africa and to seek new political arrangements with us, actively and sincerely.

Those arrangements which we have chosen, and which are going into effect now, offer assurance of stability and security—conditions that are indispensable to the creation of an economic and social environment in which the African people can attain a standard of living comparable to that of the peoples of the great modern nations. These institutional arrangements are such as to attract investments in all forms—imports of capital, technicians and methods—which are indispensable to our territories. They allow us to prove our maturity, within the forms and modes of thought to which our culture has accustomed us.

As our evolution continues simultaneously at the international level, other bonds are to be created through the reorganization of the franc zone. Moreover, in recent international negotiations, the French Government has proposed that the overseas territories be included in the European Common Market. This proposal has now been incorporated into the treaty which has just been signed by the representatives of the six member states.

At the request of Premier Mollet, I took part in the Brussels discussions and in the negotiations which preceded the writing of the definitive text of this treaty. Since my colleagues from metropolitan France were no less eager than myself to defend the interests of the African territories, we succeeded together in overcoming a number of reservations which no territory acting individually could have dispelled. Thanks to the Franco-African community, our territories will enter the Common Market with more guarantees for their future than they could possibly have achieved if they were independent. We can continue to enjoy our liberties without fear that some economic enterprise will interfere in our political life, causing us to degenerate into neo-feudalism, as in the Middle East, or into dictatorship, as in Egypt.

Some of us, of course, have had to fight so that France would not impose on us certain abusive forms of its sovereignty which are associated with the term colonialism. Many well remember the battle waged for emancipation. But I can say, as a member of this group, that despite the violence of some of the encounters, very few of us still feel bitterness.

The presence of the French in Africa is the result of military conquests or of peaceful penetrations which go back to the end of the last century. France has suppressed slavery wherever it existed and has put an end to the quarrels which set different ethnic groups against one another; it has given its education to the African masses and its culture to an élite; it has instituted sanitary and medical improvements without precedent. In French ranks, in turn, we have poured out our blood on the battlefields for the defense of liberty, and we have won a place in the history of France and of the free world. We do not want to abandon this recent heritage by trying to go back to our origins.

Moreover, we have, in common with the French, qualities which have facilitated our relations with them: good sense, realism, discrimination, which are as widespread among the black peasants of Africa as in the rural sections of France. In difficult times these qualities have enabled us to establish distinctions between colonization and the abuses of colonization. They enable us to understand today that in a world where interdependence has become the supreme rule, outbreaks of fanaticism and nationalism accomplish nothing and run the risk of merely increasing misery.

The example of the young state of Ghana is very tempting. The seizure of power has something exciting about it, we know. But the exercise of this power in a fashion consonant with national and human dignity is difficult. There doubtless are powerful nations which would provide us with the means to overcome our material difficulties. But which of them would allow us to join them in equality and fraternity? The modern world offers so many examples of barriers to race or class which pen in human beings that we cannot help but want to respond to France's loyalty and humane conduct in like fashion. It is important that the Franco-African community—egalitarian, humane and fraternal—appear to all nations not only as an example to be emulated but also as an element of international stability on which a sure future can be built.

In our view, that community is an act of faith in this future and also an act of human solidarity. It enables us to bring our stone to the world edifice without losing either our national identity or the French citizenship which we have earned and acquired worthily. And it constitutes a home we wish to keep, as in the definition which Robert Frost gave of it:

> Home is the place where
> When you have to go there,
> They have to take you in.

Note

AFRICAN PROSPECT
BY KWAME NKRUMAH

October 1958

It is sad but true that British colonialism excited no such warmth
as the foregoing article conveys. Much as some Africans respected the
British—especially for their integrity and sense of justice—genuine
affection was rare, and there is no record of a leading African politician
referring to his people as "Englishmen of Africa," as Houphouet-
Boigny speaks above of "Frenchmen of Africa."

President Kwame Nkrumah of Ghana disagrees with the author
of the preceding article on almost every point. While Houphouet-
Boigny believes close economic ties with the former colonial power
are essential, Nkrumah holds that real political independence cannot
be achieved without economic independence and that the Ivory Coast,
as well as other former French territories, has hopelessly compromised
its position. While Houphouet-Boigny glories in the influence of
French culture, Nkrumah accepts Western technology, but rejects
much of the rest, seeking instead a purely "African personality."
While the President of the Ivory Coast strongly opposes federation,
much less union, with other states, the President of Ghana is in the
vanguard of the Pan-African movement and is perhaps the only
African national leader who seems genuinely willing to surrender
sovereignty in the interest of some larger unity. "Africa Must Unite,"
he says in the title of his latest book, or perish.

For several years after the following article was written, it was
widely considered the most eloquent argument that had yet appeared
for non-alignment and for foreign economic aid without strings. It is
still of interest in this regard, but since October 1958, when Ghana
was the only newly independent nation south of the Sahara, the states-
manlike tone reflected here has given way to something more strident
and palpably anti-Western. For him colonialism has been an unmiti-
gated evil on which all African problems and shortcomings can be

blamed. For him neo-colonialism—the effort to keep Africa economically dependent and politically subservient—is a menacing reality. He nevertheless relies heavily on Western aid and Western technicians while following a brand of neutralism that has often seemed weighted in favor of the Soviet Union. Ambitious to lead all Africa, his name is still one to reckon with throughout the continent, but his influence in Afro-Asian councils appears to be on the wane.

Within Ghana, the last vestiges of a legal opposition have been obliterated, but though serious threats have been made on his life, he remains popular. A rich country by African standards, Ghana has made considerable economic progress despite a weakness for extravagant, eye-catching projects.

Nkrumah was educated in the United States at Lincoln and Pennsylvania Universities and at the London School of Economics. After several years of political activity among African nationalist groups in London, he formed the Convention Peoples Party in 1949 and demanded immediate self-government. After a tour in prison which served to heighten his popularity, he achieved his goal in 1952 and became Prime Minister of the Gold Coast. In March 1957 it emerged as the independent state of Ghana.

African Prospect

by KWAME NKRUMAH

The twelve years since the war have brought a staggering change in the tempo of African development. Vast new economic resources have been opened up, export incomes have soared. The whole area has been spanned with new links and communications; where else, I wonder, has the airplane drawn together so much that formerly was isolated? Education has advanced, new African universities have been founded. Above all, political ideas are on the march. In 1939, apart from the special case of the Union of South Africa, only one African state—Liberia—was completely independent. Today eight are independent, while many others stand on the threshold. And everywhere men and women are beginning to search consciously for political means to solve their problems and advance their hopes.

This is a general situation which I feel we in Ghana can, without presumption, help to interpret. As a country we have shared intimately in all the major developments of postwar Africa. New prosperity has flowed into Ghana due to high postwar commodity prices. In Ghana, too, this wealth has been used for sustained development and, with special emphasis, for education. Ghana is the site of one of Africa's great new universities. And Ghana has been a spearhead of African political advance. The agitation for full self-government goes back many decades in our history; but the last decisive phase of the struggle opened as late as 1948. After that, it took only a little more than eight years to bring Ghana to complete independence.

Our sense of sharing in the profound, creative movements of change in Africa has been enhanced by our experiences at the recent meeting of independent African states held in Accra—the first such conference ever to be convened on African soil. I had the honor to preside at this meeting of statesmen from Ethiopia, Ghana, Liberia, Libya, Morocco, Sudan, Tunisia and the United Arab Republic, and after it I visited each of the capitals of the participating Powers in order to consolidate my impressions of our common problems and purposes. Thus it is on the basis both of Ghana's own development and of my own very recent contacts outside Ghana that I feel I can advance a genuine interpretation of some aspects of what we called at our conference the "African personality," and also of the African approach to world problems.

There are, above all, three traits that should be stressed. In a continent of the scale and diversity of Africa, it is only natural that there should be divergences and differences and varying points of emphasis. But these three points I believe to be common to all emergent Africa and they must decisively affect its relations with the rest of the world.

The first is our desire to see Africa free and independent. The second is our determination to pursue foreign policies based upon nonalignment. The third is our urgent need for economic development. There is no area in Africa today where these three points are not on the agenda of politics.

There is no need to underline for American readers the reason for Africa's rejection of colonial status. We believe, as do Americans, that to be self-governing is one of the inalienable rights of man. In Africa, if peoples are to be truly independent, their governments must reflect the fact that in all parts of the continent the overwhelming majority of the population are native-born Africans. Even in countries of considerable European settlement, such as Southern Rhodesia, nine-tenths of the people are African. When, therefore, at our recent conference, we called for an end to colonialism, we were doing no more than stating our belief that the fact of a vast African majority should be accepted as the basis of government in Africa.

It is important to underline this point of majority rights. We are often accused of black nationalism, of racialism in reverse. I think I can honestly speak for my own government when I say that we are more concerned with a fundamental human right than with any particular color of skin. Of course, we feel a special sympathy with those who are kin to us in race. But equally we have special relations with other African states, such as Tunisia, which are not bound to us by any racial ties. And we feel ourselves part of a general human community in which man as such, not his pigmentation, is the decisive fact.

We can claim, I think, that in Ghana there is ease and naturalness of contact and genuine mutual respect between people of different races. It is not a forced thing. Visitors coming from other parts of Africa have been impressed by the atmosphere they find of good will and confidence. We certainly do not intend to project into our foreign policy a racialism we do not practise at home. But we cannot accept racialism in reverse and reconcile ourselves to the prolonged rule in Africa of minute minorities of alien stock.

Now I am not unmindful of the difficulties. As I see them, they are twofold. There is the general problem that in this century groups drawn from a different race, speech, color or religion find it very difficult to settle down and form a community. The deep division of religion which tore India apart and the recurrent disturbances between Tamil and Sinhalese in Ceylon remind us that the difficulty is certainly not confined to black and white groups in Africa. Since minorities tend to fear majority rule, safeguards and guarantees are needed in Africa just as they are in Asia or elsewhere. These safeguards should be part of the country's constitution, or created by legislation.

The second difficulty lies in the fact that in such areas as Kenya or the Rhodesias the European minority still has something of a monopoly of education, skill and resources, and European activity sustains to a very great degree the whole economic life of the community. Disrupt it and everyone suffers.

For these reasons we at our African conference proposed a *phased* political transfer of power. We asked for the fixing of definite dates for early independence and called upon the administering Powers to take rapid steps to implement the provisions of the United Nations Charter and the political aspirations of the people, namely, self-determination and independence. These steps should, in my view, include a greatly accelerated and enlarged program of education and technical training, the opening up systematically of new opportunities for Africans in agriculture and industry and a rapid growth of African participation in the country's political life. They would restore what we believe is most lacking in Africa's plural societies—and that is the element of confidence and hope on the part of the African majority.

How can Africans believe in talk of partnership if they see so little evidence of the efforts in education and development which are needed to make them effective and responsible partners? They suspect that the talk is double talk, a device to keep them quiet while the rule of the minority is endlessly prolonged. No independent African government can accept this situation. Our conference called in fact for reasonable evidence that the metropolitan Powers genuinely intend to make progress in Africa. Take away that evidence and it may well be impossible to achieve Africa's aspirations in the atmosphere of good will and order which have so happily pervaded the process of gaining independence in Ghana.

Does this determination of ours place us in opposition to the West? It is, after all, the old colonial Powers of Western Europe that still exercise control in Africa and it is migrants from Western Europe who make up Africa's dominant European minorities. Perhaps after Africa's concentrated experience of total colonial control you might expect the pendulum to swing back towards a total rejection of the colonial Powers and all their works. Statements have been made in Europe and America that "the whole African continent will be lost to freedom." It is, therefore, important to clear up some of these misunderstandings which give a totally false picture of the mood of emergent Africa. At this point, inevitably, we come to the question of what is really meant by Africa's claim to base its foreign policy upon the principle of "non-alignment."

First of all, non-alignment can be understood only in the context of the present atomic arms race and the atmosphere of the cold war. When we in Africa survey the industrial and military power concentrated behind the two great Powers in the cold war we know that no military or strategic act of ours could make one jot of difference to this balance of power, while our involvement might draw us into areas of conflict which so far have not spread below the Sahara. Our attitude, I imagine, is very much that of America looking at the disputes of Europe in the nineteenth century. We do not wish to be involved. In addition, we know we cannot affect the outcome. Above all, we believe the peace of the world in general is served, not harmed, by keeping one great continent free from the strife and rivalry of military blocs and cold wars.

But this attitude of non-alignment does not imply indifference to the great issues of our day. It does not imply isolationism. It is in no way anti-Western; nor is it anti-Eastern. The greatest issue of our day is surely to see that there is a tomorrow. For Africans especially there is a particular tragedy in the risk of thermonuclear destruction. Our continent has come but lately to the threshold of the modern world. The opportunities for health and education and a wider vision which other nations take for granted are barely within the reach of our people. And now they see the risk that all this richness of opportunity may be snatched away by destructive war. In any war, the strategic areas of the world would be destroyed or occupied by some great

Power. It is simply a question of who gets there first; the Suez Canal, Afghanistan and the Gulf of Aqaba are examples.

On this great issue of war and peace, therefore, the people and government of Ghana put all their weight behind the peaceful settlement of disputes and seek conditions in which disputes do not become embittered to the point of violence. We are willing to accept every provision of the United Nations Charter. We go further and favor every extension of an international police force as an alternative to war. One of the most important rôles of the smaller nations today is surely to use their influence in season and out of season to substitute the peaceful settlement of disputes and international policing of disturbed areas for the present disastrous dependence upon arms and force. For this reason, at our African conference we underlined our demands for controlled disarmament, we deplored the use of the sale of arms as a means of influencing other nations' diplomacy and we urged that African states should be represented on all international bodies concerned with disarmament.

Thus it is not indifference that leads us to a policy of non-alignment. It is our belief that international blocs and rivalries exacerbate and do not solve disputes and that we must be free to judge issues on their merits and to look for solutions that are just and peaceful, irrespective of the Powers involved. We do not wish to be in the position of condoning imperialism or aggression from any quarter. Powers which pursue policies of good will, coöperation and constructive international action will always find us at their side. In fact, perhaps "non-alignment" is a misstatement of our attitude. We are firmly aligned with all the forces in the world that genuinely make for peace.

This is not empty rhetoric, as two concrete examples can help to illustrate—one in the field of policy, another in our international relationships. When the coup d'état in Iraq suddenly heightened the sense of crisis throughout the Middle East and led to the dispatch of American troops to Lebanon, my government at once issued a statement of policy which said that all attempts to pass judgment on what had happened would simply heighten tension and that the task now was to secure a workable solution for the future. This, we suggested, would be based on three principles: the substitution of a United Nations force for the American troops, the holding of free elections in Lebanon under United Nations supervision and the subsequent establishment of Lebanon as a free and independent state with a status of neutrality internationally guaranteed on the analogy of Austria.

Subsequently I went further and proposed that the entire Middle Eastern area should be quarantined, that the sovereignty of every state should be guaranteed by the great Powers and that the oil resources of the region should be brought under international arrangements similar to those now operating successfully at Abadan.

My second illustration concerns Ghana's continued association with the Commonwealth. Some Americans have expressed surprise that Ghana, after emerging from colonial status, should choose of its own free will to remain within the Commonwealth and thus— amongst others—in partnership with the United Kingdom, which the day before yesterday was still our colonial overlord. But we believe that the evolving form of the Commonwealth is an institution which can work for peace and international coöperation. It is the only organic world-wide association of peoples in which race, religion, nationality and culture are all transcended by a common sense of fellowship. No policies are imposed on it from above. It does not even seek unity of policy. But it provides a unique forum in which men of different culture and different approach can sit down together and see what can be done to lessen tensions and to increase the economic and social well-being of themselves and their neighbors. This is not a bloc. It is not a power grouping. It is a club or family of friends who see their continuing friendship as a strand of peace in a troubled world. It is because the Commonwealth is this kind of association that Ghana was happy to become its first independent African member, on the basis of free association and unfettered sovereignty.

But, as a result of the old colonial link, many of our ties are with Europe. We welcome them. Links with schools and universities, the mutual benefits of trade, the capital invested in our roads and utilities, the service and help of European men and women in many fields— these contribute a web of common interests which we can freely acknowledge, once we are free ourselves. You cannot cancel 100 years of history, and history has brought Africa and Europe into close community. This historical experience can lead to continued coöperation provided independence and equality are recognized in time. It turns to bitterness and enmity only when foreign rule is maintained. Hope deferred, they say, maketh the heart sick. But where hope is realized, sane and healthy friendship is the result.

And there is yet another reason why friendship between the peoples of Africa and the West could, under certain conditions, be close and lasting. No responsible African leader would make much secret of the extent to which he needs outside economic assistance in the decades to come. One may sometimes wonder if the Western Powers fully understand the dilemma facing political leaders in the emergent lands. They have gained independence for their peoples. The hazards and excitements of the struggle lie behind. Ahead lies the workaday world in which people must live and eat and hope to prosper. Independence of itself does not change this world. It simply creates the right political atmosphere for a real effort of national regeneration. But it does not supply all the economic and social tools. The leaders are now expected, simply as a result of having acquired independence, to work miracles. The people look for the new schools, new towns, new factories. They expect political equality to bring economic equality. They do not realize what it may cost. In this situation, however poor the country, the new government cannot sit and do nothing. Construction must begin. There must be something to show for independence. And if there is nothing to show, popular discontent may split the country apart.

This is the dilemma of recently-won independence. If independence is the first aim, development comes straight on its heels, and no leader—in Asia or Africa—can escape the pressure. We in Ghana can, I think, approach this vital issue of economic development with a measure of objectivity. Ghana, in part by good fortune and in part, I hope, by good management, is not in the dire straits of some other newly-independent lands. There is as yet no extreme pressure of population on our resources. We have been fortunate in that our export crop, cocoa, has commanded a very high world price since the war and has not fluctuated as violently as some other primary products. And we have pursued a policy which, I believe, has enabled us to gain a maximum benefit from the high postwar prices. We have held the internal price fairly stable at a level about eight times that of prewar and the balance over and above that level has been put aside for general economic development. On the one hand, we have avoided internal inflation. On the other, we have been able to set aside some $700,-000,000 for development which, in a country of only 5,000,000 people, gives us some elbowroom for the future.

Yet we are short of much that we need for a really rapid economic advance, the kind of advance our people expect and want. We need technicians. We need experts of all kinds. We have hardly enough teachers for our expanded program of education. We need—and welcome—foreign private investment from all countries to help our people to learn the new industrial skills. This fits in with our determination to diversify our economy, to increase agricultural production, and to industrialize. It is perhaps necessary to emphasize that Ghana does not seek direct financial grants; we want investment, both public and private, only in sound projects which can ultimately repay the original investment. Above all, we need to end our dangerous dependence upon a single export crop, cocoa. Yet to do so and to develop our chief alternative—the export of aluminum—we need outside capital and technical assistance to launch our great Volta River scheme. At present this scheme, which would bring into play our large bauxite reserves and our important hydroelectrical potential, is unhappily stalled by the decline in Western economic activity over the last 18 months.

Yet if Ghana with its real measure of stability and prosperity needs this outside support and stimulus, how much more urgent is the need in other less fortunate communities? On my recent tour of African states, the impressions I gathered were again and again of the direst pressure and necessity. I remember with respect the industrial and agricultural efforts being made in some of the countries I visited, but I remember even more vividly the endless crowds of children we encountered wherever we went. I wonder how even the most active and determined leaders can achieve even a measure of economic stability while the inexorable birth rate presses each year more heavily against the limited agricultural resources. It is surely not surprising that such leaders look outside for economic help. They have no alternative. The pressure of population mounts all the time. They must have help or founder. It is as simple as that.

I believe, therefore, that the Western Powers have the opportunity to play a new and vital rôle in Africa. The colonial phase is dead or dying. But a new phase is opening in which the whole of this continent will struggle to achieve the institutions and opportunities of modern life. Leaders are fully aware of how much is lacking. Education is limited in spite of heroic efforts since the war. Since so many areas are only now emerging from a subsistence economy, local capital is often absent. Vital needs in agriculture are not met for lack of basic research or of trained technicians. The endless list is a measure of Africa's need and the Western Powers' opportunity.

Nor is the advantage one-sided. Under the impact of postwar prosperity, Ghana's imports have nearly doubled in little more than five years. A growing African market based upon a steady increase in African productivity is of vital interest to all the great trading Powers of the West and quite especially to Western Europe, which already conducts nearly a quarter of its extra-European trade with the African continent. Although not on so great a scale, American trade and American interests have also steadily increased in Africa since the war. Exports, for instance, have quintupled, and all responsible African leaders wish to extend this trend on the basis of reciprocity and equality. It is the surest guarantee of permanent friendship between Africa and the West.

But Africa's desperate need is not only the West's opportunity. There is a risk here as well. As I have said before and must emphasize again, the leaders of the new Africa have no alternative but to look for outside assistance. The hopes and ambitions of their peoples have been planted and brought to maturity by the impact of Western civilization. The West has set the pattern of our hopes, and by entering Africa in strength it has forced the pattern upon us. Now comes our response. We cannot tell our peoples that material benefits and growth and modern progress are not for them. If we do, they will throw us out and seek other leaders who promise more. And they will abandon us, too, if we do not in reasonable measure respond to their hopes. Therefore we have no choice. Africa has no choice. We have to modernize. Either we shall do so with the interest and support of the West or we shall be compelled to turn elsewhere. This is not a warning or a threat, but a straight statement of political reality.

And I also affirm, for myself and I believe for most of my fellow leaders in Africa, that we want close coöperation with our friends. We know you. History has brought us together. We still have the opportunity to build up a future on the basis of free and equal coöperation. This is our aim. This is our hope.

Note

WEST AFRICA IN EVOLUTION
BY LÉOPOLD SÉDAR SENGHOR

January 1961

Poets are not supposed to be politicians, but Léopold Sédar Senghor has shown himself to be a master in both fields. As a teacher, writer and poet with an international reputation he stands in the first rank of African intellectuals; as politican and statesman he served for many years as Deputy from Senegal in the French National Assembly and in the Consultative Assembly of the Council of Europe; and as the leading political figure in his country, he has, since independence, survived two threatened coups d'état by moving with greater speed and resolution than his opponents.

The first was at the time of the break-up of the Mali Federation (shortly before this article was written), when Modibo Keita of the Soudan (now Mali) made a rather heavy-handed attempt to impose his will on his Senegalese partners. The result was a complete rupture and the failure after only a few weeks of one of the most substantial and promising efforts to achieve African unity. More recently, as President of Senegal, Senghor came to a parting of the ways with his able Prime Minister, Mamadou Dia. But it was Dia who departed from office and Senghor who consolidated almost limitless power in his own hands, ramming through a new Gaullist-type constitution with a 99.4 percent majority.

Senghor is remarkable in other ways; he is a Roman Catholic who has never lost an election in his predominantly Muslim Country; he is an intellectual whose appeal is to the peasants and whose opposition comes from other intellectuals who find him too conservative; he is a reflective man who respects action and urges his fellow African leaders to avoid "flights of oratory, of fiery eloquence and poetry."

What is perhaps most interesting in the following article is Senghor's sense that a synthesis of Western and African cultures and institutions can emerge into something that is both distinctive and authentic. Though few men are more imbued with French culture, Senghor has kept his African roots and more than any man, perhaps, has given substance to the concept of *négritude*. He speaks for a large number of educated Africans who are conscientiously seeking their way between two worlds.

The moderate socialism which Senghor espouses here is probably the least that can be expected in most of the independent African states. It is not merely that capitalism is associated in the Africans' mind with colonialism and exploitation, or that a large measure of state enterprise and direction seems to them necessary for the rapid economic development they seek. It is also that traditional African society was communal rather than individualistic, so that most aspects of socialism seem to them merely a modern extension of the kind of organization of the community that they have known.

West Africa in Evolution

by LÉOPOLD SÉDAR SENGHOR

The French Community, created by General de Gaulle in full agreement with Africa's true representatives, is one of the greatest achievements of our time. Besides being a masterly concept to which I and with me the majority of the leaders of Senegal are deeply committed, it also is one of those ideas capable of catching the imagination of the masses. Sweeping away the contradictions of the colonial system, it enables the former mother country and its erstwhile colonies to form a friendly cultural and economic union and thus forge a lasting link between Western Europe and Africa.

But if the Community was to evolve properly it could not remain frozen in juridical forms. Therefore paragraph XII of the French Constitution which defined the framework of the Community made the necessary provisions for a smooth and harmonious evolution.

Let me say right away that in my opinion the Community could not have been federal. History has many examples—among them the United States, the Soviet Union and Germany—to prove that a federation is really possible only between states that are at equal economic levels and have equal political maturity. A federation has a natural tendency to build up federal power at the expense of the member states. If one state dominates the others the federation becomes simply a screen to hide that domination. This is the view which I upheld in 1958 in the Consultative Constitutional Committee created by General de Gaulle.

The Constitution of the Community stressed the principle of equality among the member states; in legal terms this means that equality between France and the other states will be achieved as the Community evolves. Had this equality been incorporated in a federal framework, France obviously would have had to relinquish some of her prerogatives of sovereignty. Can one conceive of this being possible

285

in view of the fact that France is economically 20 times as strong as all other members of the Community combined? However, this situation did not point necessarily to the extreme solutions advocated by some people who were more concerned with verbiage than with people's happiness. If federation was impossible, the alternative was not the breakup of the Community but its evolution in conformity with the spirit and letter of the Constitution.

In spirit, the Constitution is liberal and egalitarian; in letter, it allows for a legal evolution to keep pace with political reality. Thus under special agreements between the French Republic and the states which have become independent, various functions have been transferred to the latter, notably diplomatic representation, a function vital to the development of relations between the states of the Community and the rest of the world. These transfers within the constitutional framework have given the new states—de facto and de jure—all the prerogatives of sovereignty. In other words they have achieved independence, with all its mystical value—yesterday rejected and now ardently demanded by so many.

As the peoples of French cultural background and language evolve in this manner, the Community will become the same fruitful means of coöperation that the Commonwealth became among the states which are the descendants of the British Empire. The new bridges between Africa and Europe will be built without mental reservations on one side about colonial domination and without fears in Europe that she is about to be colonized in turn by her former colonies. Thus the economic and social development of Africa and Western economic expansion will both be advanced.

Two years after the foundation of the Community by the referendum of September 28, 1958, the Mali Federation, on April 4, 1960, deliberately chose independence within the Community, thus stating its desire to attain independence without a rupture with France and the other member states.

However, the Mali Federation was not able to resist the separatist tendencies which endanger any federation of states not of equal weight. Many centrifugal tendencies existed. The Soudan is much more heavily populated and much less rich than Senegal; the proportion of children in school there is much smaller; and its political leaders though not themselves Communists have been indoctrinated in the schools of the French Communist Party. For these reasons the Soudanese developed a sort of revengeful complex against the Senegalese. They schemed month by month to gain an upper hand over the Senegalese section of the African Federation Party, to put functionaries of their way of thinking into key positions and, in contradiction with the Federal constitution, to make Mali over into a unitary state dominated by them. Faced with Senegalese resistance, Modibo Keita, head of the Federal Government, resorted at last to the desperate expedient of a coup d'état. The reply was instantaneous. On the initiative of the Senegal Government the Legislative Assembly voted that Senegal should quit the Federation and proclaim its independence as a sovereign state. Since August 20, 1960, then, the Republic of Senegal has been an independent state. In its new role it will exemplify not so much a pan-African as an inter-African policy.

Senegal with its European (60,000), Berber, Arab and Negro populations, stands on the frontier of the white and black races. We are a true example of coexistence among several races and I would say also among several religions; for even though the majority of our population is Moslem, there are also Catholics, Protestants and Animists.

Senegal occupies a privileged geographical position since the city of Dakar is the gate to the South Atlantic. Its political position is also special. Unfortunately, the majority of the independent African states have not yet recovered from the effects of colonialism. Now that they have obtained their own independence, most of them start exuding the imperialism of their former colonizers and want in turn to colonize other African nations. So it was that the Soudan tried to use methods borrowed from the totalitarian régimes to "colonize" Senegal—and thus blew up the Mali Federation. In comparison, Senegal's attitude toward such matters is constructive. Several peoples belonging to the same races as we and speaking the same languages find themselves outside our borders. There are Senegalese living on the right bank of the Senegal River. The Gambians are racially the same as ourselves and speak the same languages. Despite this, we accept the frontiers of African states the way they are; and in any case we refuse to use violence to change them.

This is an extremely important fact today in view of the way in which the concept of African unity is being worked out. I am confident that the independent Republic of Senegal will be an example not only of peaceful coexistence but also of peaceful coöperation with the other African states and with other countries of the world. Guinea serves as an instance. In all my statements I have shown myself friendly towards Guinea. We Senegalese were the first ones to fight for Guinea to be recognized by France. Recently I repeated my offer to normalize our relations with Guinea and that offer has been accepted. As a result, Senegal and Guinea will exchange diplomatic representatives and negotiate commercial and cultural treaties.

We are glad that the member states of the Council of the Entente have changed their course recently. Like the countries of what used to be French Equatorial Africa, they have decided to follow the road of independence if not of socialism. They want to build an African Community—so as not to call it a federation—with us.

Senegal believes firmly in the renovated Community, the contractual Community. We are maintaining, with some changes, the vertical solidarity which throughout our history has tied us to France. At the same time, we shall maintain, with some changes, the horizontal solidarity which ties us to the French-speaking African states and, so far as possible, to the other states of Africa as well. In a word, there must be a new extension of our relationships vertically to Europe and to America, the child of Europe, and horizontally to the whole of Africa, even to Asia. This will be our positive contribution to the building of a universal civilization.

But let us turn first to Africa where our lot has been cast and where the population is mainly African-Negro and Arab-Berber. Here we come face to face with the problem of a United States of Africa. I shall not dodge it any more than the other problems, but examine it objectively, which means without succumbing to the lure of empty words. Like President Bourguiba, I believe that a United States of Africa is not something to be achieved overnight. I feel free to say this since I was one of the first to talk about it. Some ten years ago when Ousmane Socé and I were at the Consultative Assembly of the European Council we signed a draft of a resolution envisaging the creation of a United States of Africa. But let me emphasize again, it is not something to be brought into being overnight.

There are several reasons against it. The first is that continentalism is actually a form of autarchy. Like all autarchies, it denies the interdependence of peoples and in consequence collaboration between them; thus it makes for impoverishment. Africa cannot do without the other continents, especially Europe and America, except at the price of increasing its relative backwardness. At the last Pan-African Conference at Tunis there was talk about an African Common Market. Have the difficulties in the way of such an undertaking been adequately weighed? Actually, the African economies are more competitive than complementary. We spend our time appealing to the idea of solidarity between the developed and the underdeveloped countries, between the rich and the poor. Are not such appeals in contradiction to the tendency toward autarchy? The second difficulty in the way of achieving Pan-Africanism is our lack of realism, our wordiness. Resolutions are voted which are not followed by actions. If the resolutions were more realistic we could perhaps begin to apply them. The third reason is that the actual deeds of the independent African governments contradict their Pan-African statements.

In fact, it is paradoxical that at the very time some of the newly independent African states pretend to champion African unity they quarrel about their frontiers and claim pieces of neighboring territories, support émigrés and phantom governments at great expense, see Fifth Columns everywhere. Of course, there is no law against hoping that certain frontier rectifications may become possible before long with the consent of the people concerned. But in the moment of achieving independence this is hardly an essential problem.

What we must do first of all is analyze our situation as it presents itself at this point in time. We shall have to evaluate the various components which make up our mixed civilization and disentangle the skein of the component parts as we go along. Each element, be it European or African-Negro, will be historically analyzed, traced back to its exact place of birth, given the time and circumstances of its development. Only in this way shall we be able, if it is a European element, to adapt it to our African personality, or, if it is African-Negro, to adapt it to the twentieth century. For let us not forget that what we are aiming at here in Senegal, outpost of West Africa, is to create a modern nation: an African-Negro civilization, certainly, but one that meets the requirements of the present day.

The responsible government and party politicians of Senegal have recognized this for more than ten years. They have begun to trace out the African road to socialism based on the seminal cultural values of both Africa and Europe. I emphasize cultural values for they are the leaven of all civilization. Our recognition of this has determined the social and economic evaluations on which we are basing our development plans for Senegal; and when various choices have to be made as we go along, we shall make our decisions on the same humanistic grounds.

To build a nation, to erect a new civilization which can lay claim to existence because it is humane, we shall try to employ not only enlightened reason but also dynamic imagination. In the first place, we shall go back to the sources of African-Negro and European civilization in order to grasp what is essential in both—their spirit, their ferment. Thus inspired, we shall seek to create new forms and institutions—cultural, political, social and economic—suited to our present situation. Once we have put forth our full effort of heart and spirit and intellect, once we have achieved this inner revolution, the rest will be given to us in addition—that is to say, the capital, the technicians and the techniques. France has already offered to supply them.

Above anything else, however, the future of our nation depends on our own efforts—on our collective and individual efforts and the sacrifices we are willing to make. As I have often warned, independence in its first stage is solitude. It is a people's coming of age. As the African-Negro proverb says: "It is no good calling on God for help before you have tilled your field." The Senegalese nation will be our own handiwork or it will not exist at all.

Senegal's independence will cost two billion C.F.A. francs [1] extra at the start, and this sum will increase from year to year. Our first task is to find an equivalent amount from new resources. There can be no question of increasing the burden of taxes, nor of cutting salaries and wages as some of the independent African states have done, and there also will be no question of slowing the rate of investment to any important extent. Thus in order to increase the national revenue we shall be obliged to reduce the country's standard of living. There are limitations to what we can do, however, if the public services are to function properly. Civil servants will therefore have to change their habits in the direction of greater precision, greater discipline and a rationalization of their working methods. They will do so because they are aware of the revolutionary fact that they are no longer working for somebody else, for a colonial administration, but for themselves, for a national state in which they are, after all, privileged members.

But thrift and greater efficiency in the public services will still not be enough. The whole national economy must be restudied. The market economy will have to be abolished and replaced by a rationally

---

[1] About $8,000,000. The franc of the Communauté Française d'Atlantique is equivalent to the old West African franc. Hence one new French franc equals 50 C.F.A. francs.—ED.

planned economy. Hence, an inventory is being made of resources, deficiencies and potentialities. Already the guide lines of local and national planning are becoming clear. Without waiting for the plans to be put in final form, our government, at the initiative and under the supervision of the African Federation Party, is starting to construct the new national economy. It must press forward without yielding to either the blackmailing power of money or the demagoguery of self-seeking individuals or opponents. It is not our plan to set up a so-called "popular" democracy or a liberal laissez-faire régime. We aim to hold firmly to a middle-of-the-road socialism which is liberal and undoctrinaire—one which socializes all that should be socialized, beginning with the rural economy, but no more than that.

As I said at the Youth Seminar of the African Federation Party, Senegal must stand as an exemplary African state in the concert of nations. In spite of destroying our traditional institutions and most of our works of art, France has left us with a positive asset: a cultural, political, social and economic infra-structure. And with ideas. So far, these are but means to an end. Luckily, although African-Negro values are emaciated they are not uprooted. As we accumulate what means exist, as we adapt them to our needs rather than trying to create them whole, as we give them life and set them in proper order, and all this in a spirit of humanity and mutual tolerance, we shall reëstablish our civilization, or rather—as is my hope—create a new one. Senegal ought to be a research laboratory, a vast workshop, where new creations take form, the product of a new spirit, a new effort of heart, mind, will and imagination. Thus, along with real independence we shall have acquired the right to speak as a sovereign nation; thus, and only thus, shall we make a positive contribution to peace, to world civilization.

Note

AFRICAN PROBLEMS AND THE COLD WAR
BY SYLVANUS E. OLYMPIO

October 1961

If large standing armies are a threat to political stability and legality, apparently there are also domestic dangers in having an army that is too small. In the early morning hours of January 13, 1963, President Sylvanus E. Olympio of Togo was cut down by gunfire a few yards from American Embassy grounds in Lomé, the victim of a coup d'état by what was probably the smallest national army in the world. Although mystery still surrounds the death of Togo's able and independent president, it seems clear that the revolution was sparked by the dissatisfaction of soldiers who were either unemployed or felt ill-rewarded for their services to the 250-man army, and that the revolution had little or no ideological content. But the assassination sent shivers through Africa, and the event has shaken the alignment of political forces in West Africa in surprising ways.

Sylvanus Olympio was unique among African leaders. When he professed neutrality, he meant it, and not only was he unaligned in the cold war but he refused to take sides in African disputes and groupings. He tended to the business of his own country and believed African leaders meddled too much in each others' affairs. His outspoken opposition to Pan-Africanism won him many enemies, especially President Nkrumah, who thought that Togo ought to become part of Ghana. (The border between the two countries was sealed for months before Olympio's death.) He was a realist who did not permit himself or his people those grand illusions on which African policies and practices are so often based. His penchant for economy and a balanced budget may have been his undoing.

Olympio was part Portuguese and spoke German, French and English fluently. A wealthy businessman before he turned to full-time politics, he rose in the United Africa Company to the highest post then reached by an African in an expatriate firm—that of district manager for Togoland. He was married to the sister of former Prime Minister Nicholas Grunitsky, whom he soundly defeated in a U.N.-supervised election just before independence and who returned from exile to head the Togo Government after Olympio's death.

Opposition to Olympio was known to exist in Togo, but no one supposed that his position was threatened. He ruled with a benevolent but authoritarian paternalism, had little regard for such public opinion as existed, and was remiss in failing to draw into government the ablest of the young educated Togolese. Yet he was a man of good will and good sense—a leader perhaps too big for his little country.

African Problems
and the Cold War

by SYLVANUS E. OLYMPIO

Since we achieved our independence, several distinguished foreigners have visited our young Republic, and among the many questions they have asked have been those concerning our approach to Pan Africanism, our views on policies intended to keep Africa free of the restrictive forces of the cold war, and the measures we would suggest to implement our policy of neutrality. In the lines which follow we will endeavor to answer these significant questions.

There can be little doubt that there is a present need for coöperation among the newly independent African states, that a working arrangement, at least on a regional basis, is overdue. Unfortunately the situation inherited from the colonial powers, while making plain the necessity for such agreement, has tended to hinder it. Within each nation there are serious discontinuities arising from the existence of different ethnic groups, language differences, disparities in ideological orientation and basic economic conceptions. At the same time national boundaries were artificially drawn to meet external political requirements. Today we find that tribes are split in two, cities are divided and people of the same language and cultural traditions are separated into two and sometimes three different nations.

To resolve this last issue, so prominent in the minds of many African leaders, Pan Africanism has been put forward as an all-embracing remedy. (Some people call the same idea African Unity.) Apart from the proposition that few real-life problems are so simple that they possess only one solution, no two African states can agree on a single interpretation of the terms. To discuss the common heritage and institutions of Ghana, the Belgian Congo and Ethiopia is clearly unrealistic. More important, however, are the character and complexity of the problems facing us at home. To speak of African Unity in the face of existing economic and social disunity is to avoid the central task to which we are committed—the earliest possible economic and social betterment of our people. This task has as one important aspect the unification of disparate socio-economic groups toward common economic goals. Accomplishment of this objective in turn requires much honest work on the part of African leaders and their people. It requires also collective leadership, for through collective leadership the multiple interests of the African people can best be expressed.

In their struggle against the colonial powers the new African states, arbitrary and unrealistic as their original boundaries may have been, managed at last to mobilize the will of their citizens toward the attainment of national independence. Achieved at great sacrifice, such a reward is not to be cast away lightly; nor should the national will, once unified, be diluted by the formation of nebulous political units. Even if tribal, ethnic and linguistic loyalties begin to reassert themselves— and this is less likely to be true with the present trends of development in Africa—there is little to support the theory that intranational groupings would be more effectively represented by a supranational political organization than by a national one. In fact, the reverse seems quite evident. Furthermore, few serious governments would be willing to relinquish their hard-won seats in international councils, seats which permit them to be heard and which grant them the moral security provided by access to world opinion.

It should be added that existing governmental units are in an administrative sense workable and that it would be a grave mistake to undercut at this early date the frail but growing roots which sustain them. In our present stage of development it is necessary for us to build both workable administrative organizations and responsive political mechanisms to transmit the interests and needs of our people to their leaders. Thus we must retain the principle of national sovereignty already enshrined in the struggle of African states for their independence.

This alone, however, is not enough to strengthen the ties between us. We suggest as an alternative to Pan Africanism the homely word coöperation, knowing that in building a house one starts with a foundation, not a roof. It is our opinion that an active policy of coöperation in good faith will bring the African people the most beneficial results. Such a policy does not begin in over-all political amalgamation but rather in freely given agreement concerning matters of economics and commerce. In this realm urgent action is required, and in this realm coöperation will be most acceptable to the parties concerned.

By breaking up Africa into economic and commercial compartments the colonial powers did their greatest harm. The effect of their policy has been the economic isolation of peoples who live side by side, in some flagrant instances within a few miles of each other, while directing the flow of resources to the metropolitan countries. For example, although I can call Paris from my office telephone here in Lomé, I cannot place a call to Lagos in West Africa only 250 miles away. Again, while it takes a short time to send an airmail letter to Paris, it takes several days for the same letter to reach Accra, a mere 120 miles away. Other problems are more serious. Trade is the most effective method of creating good will among nations, but in Africa trade barriers are legion. Railroads rarely connect at international boundaries, and where they do, differences in gauges necessitate transloading. Highways have been constructed from the coast inland, but very few connect at economic centers of trade. The productive central regions of Togo, Dahomey and Ghana are as remote from each other as if they were on separate continents. These are the problems which we must tackle first. Then we will be on the way to true African Unity.

Fortunately some concrete action has already been taken which leads in the desired direction. The Monrovia Conference last spring opened the way to international coöperation while preserving the national sovereignty of African states. It was laid down at this conference that all the countries of Africa should work together irrespective of their size, ideology, system of government or economic structure. No state, however powerful or large, should interfere in the internal affairs of others; territorial boundaries must be respected. These are wise rules of conduct and if pursued should strengthen our will to coöperate.

In the economic sphere, the 20 states pledged that coöperation should take the form of reductions in trade and monetary restrictions and the development of international transportation and communication networks. It was further proposed that a study be made of problems relating to the creation of a customs union among the African states. Finally, the conference pledged its members to further cultural, scientific and technical coöperation through the exchange of experts and the establishment of permanent committees. To these principles and to the method of agreement which occasioned their approval the Republic of Togo has heartily subscribed.

Before turning from the subject of Pan Africanism, American readers might well consider the struggle of their own country's founding fathers in deciding between the principles of state sovereignty, confederation or federation, and the strong economic, cultural and geographic forces which eventually caused federation to prevail. In the case of African governments, political leaders emerged from within indigenous cultures, and many of their constituents maintain even today diverse and separate traditions, tracing their customs to ancestors who lived at the dawn of history. To these people their land is their fathers' land and their country the country of their forebears. To them even the national government is but an arbitrary and incomprehensible authority. It will be many years before a higher power will be able to maintain a really acceptable authority over these traditional peoples. In the meantime their lawful governments must tackle the problems at hand—education, the introduction of better health and living conditions, an increased productivity in agriculture and industry.

II

The newly independent African states are now beginning to have an impact on world affairs. Their presence in the great councils of the United Nations is bringing international publicity to their views and preoccupations. Because of this new-found status, the two world blocs generally referred to as East and West are making efforts to attract or keep the African states in their spheres of influence. This struggle of the power blocs is leading to the introduction of the cold war into Africa, which until recently has succeeded in keeping out of it.

Our duty in this matter is clear. We cannot afford to be involved in the cold war with all its consequences. The African states are at the lowest stage of economic growth and should wisely devote all their energies and resources to the development of their peoples. To make a success of this task we are largely dependent upon the capital and technicians which only more advanced nations can supply. It is understandable that some of these nations wish to be assured that the African states will employ their assistance to the best advantage, but this must be resolved through practical planning, not political domination.

Our dependence upon external assistance carries with it certain dangers which the African states must recognize if they are to prevent further cold-war intrusions. It is by now a commonplace to refer to Africa as the land of rising expectations. The danger of which I speak is that certain African leaders will encourage these expectations too far, that they will overestimate their capacity to transform our traditional economies into modern industrial states. Let there be no mistake in my meaning. This is a job which can and will be done, but it must be done with careful attention to our needs and a realistic appraisal of the capital that will be available to meet them. The African leader who seriously overestimates his country's capacity for growth will soon find that he is forced to rely on foreign aid to maintain his political position, and it will be then that the temptation to turn to one or the other power bloc will be greatest. The political leader who promises his people a new highway network or a hundred new schools may find that he has promised too much, that he will at best be voted, and at worst forced, out of office unless he can fulfill his promises. At that moment he may well revert to the dangerous policy of making external political commitments, and this policy may be multiplied by its effects upon neighboring states; for these, anxious to preserve their sovereignty, may turn to the other power bloc.

African leaders must also beware of pushing their peoples too far. The mechanism of national government is new, and our people must be taught its meaning before they will accept its dictums. Those leaders who propose to finance their projects by broad and heavy taxation should consider whether their people are yet ready to accept it, whether preliminary programs of education with moderate increases in living standards are not more meaningful at this stage than vast programs of public works. The leader who rules with a heavy hand, assuming that his desires are the desires of his people, will eventually be forced to take drastic measures of repression to safeguard his power. Then again stability will be endangered and peaceful government threatened.

To counter these difficulties we must first assess the resources of our countries, then estimate the capital which will be made available to us from abroad. In this manner African leaders will not find themselves forced to make the choice between unwanted foreign commitment and domestic instability. For their part, the developed nations must never forget that until very recently the African states were subjected to colonial rule, a rule which did severe harm to their institutions. We have struggled for many years to attain the privilege of self-government and are wary of any association which may suggest a new bondage.

Thus we have chosen to be neutral in all issues concerning world blocs. As a practical matter Togo's size and geographic location also dictate a policy of neutrality. This policy has implications which extend beyond East-West differences. For one thing it signifies plainly that in her relations with former colonial powers Togo shall negotiate as an independent, sovereign nation, that ties of the past are not to be construed as ties for the present or future, that choice of preferences will be made by Togolese representatives on the basis of agreements which will most benefit our people's development. For another, it signifies our desire to remain clear of all groups which seem designed to perpetuate divisions on racial, linguistic or ideological grounds. In Africa today there are signs that some states are regrouping to form African blocs. In this connection there has been much talk about the Yaounde Group, the Brazzaville Group and the Casablanca Group. This is to be regretted because these new moves can only make much-needed coöperation more difficult if not impossible. We think, as noted above, that agreement among freely associated sovereign states can do much to halt this deplorable segmentation.

Concerning bilateral and multilateral aid, I believe that specific types of assistance are more effectively suited to specific sources of aid and that it is our responsibility to match our needs with the external agency or government most capable of meeting them. This policy requires that development projects in our country be evaluated on the basis of their expected social and economic impact and not on the political position of the donor or creditor nation. If the wealthy nations of the world are sincere in their desire to develop the natural and human resources of the African states, they must approach this task pragmatically and be willing to do the job at hand rather than digress into political manoeuvring. In the long run there is little doubt that effective developmental policy will help the cause of peace and stable democratic government. The European and American powers who promise to see progress in Africa should thus accept the desires of African states to remain neutral. Their offers of help should be without strings. Otherwise the African continent will soon be divided into the familiar East and West groupings with a resulting intensification in the cold war.

The wealthy nations of the world must also regard our determined efforts with respect. We know that we can improve the living conditions and productivity of our countries, and we are certain that with help we can do it more rapidly than was done in the past. The gains made in method and knowledge over recent decades in the social and productive sciences are not to be wasted. Modern technology and planning techniques must be applied flexibly and with the conviction that obstacles can and will be overcome. Experts arriving in our countries should not expect that plans will be as neatly executed as they have been in their home countries, that the last refinement in information will be available. Too many foreign experts forget this; too many fear what seems to them to be impossible. The technical expert assigned to work in an African state is rightly an agent of change. He must be willing to innovate, and he must bring with him the will to work.

III

We should consider, finally, the United Nations organization and the role we are to play in it. I may say that from our viewpoint this has been a cornerstone of foreign policy since independence. The United Nations has much to offer the newly independent countries, and they in turn can accomplish a great deal through active and responsible participation in the organization. The Republic of Togo is particularly aware of the advantages to be gained from such participation because of our history of association with the United Nations through the Trusteeship Council.

Today the United Nations can be of particular assistance in the administration of foreign aid. We are not opposed to bilateral agreements, but in our opinion more aid should be channeled through the international organization. This would solve the problem of how to grant technical and financial aid without strings and would demonstrate to the African states the good faith of donor and creditor nations. It would also reduce the very real temptation of the African states to play off the big powers one against the other, a temptation which can easily develop from unrealistic planning or irresponsible leadership. Lastly, it might help to solve a problem which is increasing in magnitude with the growth in new foreign aid programs and the revision of old ones—that is, the coördination by the donor nations of the destinations, kinds and amounts of assistance to be offered. Presently there is needless and costly duplication in the administration of these programs, and the multiplicity of agencies, restrictions and delays makes it difficult for recipient nations to allocate rationally the assistance granted.

In spite of its shortcomings, the United Nations can and should play an important role in this period of transition while the economies of the African states are progressing from colonial dependence to self-sufficiency. It can be used as an effective instrument to prevent wars between states and in some instances civil wars within them. The United Nations should strive to instill in these young countries the ideals of its Charter, then guarantee their territorial integrity. If this guarantee is forthcoming, the new nations will be free to devote a major part of their resources to economic and social development and will tend in time to reduce their dependence on external aid. In this respect I feel certain that most new African states would welcome a strong and effective United Nations. Such strength can endure only as long as member states respect the principles of the Charter and refrain from using the organization as an instrument for securing political power. The machinery of the United Nations is essentially democratic, and herein lies its value to the less powerful nations of the world: the assurance that their expectations, desires and fears can be brought to the attention of world opinion.

The Congo operation should be regarded as a useful experience which, far from weakening the United Nations, has made it more mature. It should also indicate to any leaders striving for the political unity of Africa the difficulties lying in their path. Indeed, no African leader can afford to neglect the lessons which have been taught by this chapter in the history of our continent.

Note

NIGERIA LOOKS AHEAD

BY SIR ABUBAKAR TAFAWA BALEWA

October 1962

Governing Nigeria has been a little like riding a tricycle with elliptical wheels. Federal in structure and multi-party in politics, the three (now four) regions represent different tribes, different religions, different traditions and different rates of development. Yet Nigeria remains perhaps the last best hope for the preservation of Western-type democracy in Africa. If its fragile institutions are preserved, if real stability is achieved, it will be thanks in no small part to its Federal Prime Minister, Sir Abubakar Tafawa Balewa.

In a continent where politicians are often flamboyant and self-serving, Sir Abubakar is calm and dedicated. Though by no means the leading political figure at the time of independence in 1960, he is today widely respected for his strong and sensible leadership and for an integrity that is above question.

In a land where political parties are divided along regional and tribal lines rather than upon issues, Sir Abubakar became Prime Minister not because he was the most active and articulate anti-colonialist, but by virtue of being the parliamentary leader of the largest party in the largest region with the largest tribes. A Muslim from the populous and conservative North, he was a school teacher and education officer before he entered politics after World War II. He was one of the founders of the Northern People's Congress which governs Nigeria today in coalition with the more radical party of the Eastern Region. The opposition has centered in the Western Region, the most advanced of the three in terms of education, economic development and political experience, but also the source of the most serious instability that the new nation has experienced.

Plagued by corruption and threatened with a thousand ills, Nigeria threads its uneasy but democratic way. With more than 40,000,000 people and relatively high human and material resources, it is destined

302

to be the leading power in black Africa if it can avoid flying apart. Even today Nigeria is looked to for leadership in the councils of the African nations. But as the following article demonstrates, the moderation and good sense which Sir Abubakar exercises at home is reflected in Nigeria's foreign policies. Unlike several other West African politicians, Sir Abubakar does not aspire to lead all Africa. Yet by his office and his person he has become a spokesman for the more moderate African states.

Nigeria Looks Ahead

by SIR ABUBAKAR TAFAWA BALEWA

The Federation of Nigeria became a sovereign independent state and ninety-ninth member of the United Nations less than two years ago. Our entrance into the arena of international politics marked an epoch in our history, made even more memorable by the good will and affection with which we were received from all sides. Everyone hailed the appearance of Africa's largest state. To the leaders and people of Nigeria, however, this event was also a grim reminder of the fact that, for the first time in our history as a single unified state, we now have to fend for ourselves, and to sustain and consolidate our unity and freedom. We have to give real meaning to this freedom by making it an instrument for a better and more prosperous life for our people.

But determined as we were to shoulder our internal responsibilities, it was our added task to demonstrate that democracy could work not only in our own country, but in the other parts of the continent, if there were a will and determination to do so. We have not shrunk from the belief that our greatest contribution to Africa and the world at large would be in the example we show of good sense and reasonableness in our approach to problems, and the projection of those qualities into our conduct of external relations.

National unity is, naturally, uppermost in our minds, as it is self-evident that planning and prosperity can thrive only in conditions of peace and orderliness. It is less than 50 years since Lord Lugard amalgamated into one country what were then the northern and southern protectorates of Nigeria, and it was not until 15 years ago that a constitution was introduced which for the first time brought Nigerians from every part of the country into a common legislature. National unity has made remarkable progress since then; a feeling of common citizenship has developed and has been increasingly sustained by the challenge of independence. However, we have not trusted merely to chance and have ensured that there is an instrument—that is, a written constitution—by which this unity can be supported.

A federal system of government is always full of problems and difficulties, but so is democracy, because the art of persuasion is much more difficult than a dictatorship though in the long run more rewarding and satisfying.

We are also fortunate in having a system of government with freedom of expression to provide a check on executive authority. Above all, we believe in the rule of law, and in an independent judiciary as an arbiter in disputes. The ready acceptance of both our governments and peoples of the decisions of courts of law even when against them is perhaps our greatest claim to maturity and confidence in our institutions and unity.

II

With a population of at least 40,000,000, growing at a rate of 2 percent a year and living in conditions considerably below those obtaining in the more advanced countries, our greatest task has been to make life more satisfying for our people. Even before independence, we had realized that this was the challenge before us, and at its tenth meeting held in 1959 the National Economic Council laid down that a National Development Plan should be prepared. The objective was to be the "achievement and maintenance of the highest possible rate of increase in the standard of living and the creation of the necessary conditions to this end, including public support and awareness of both the potential that exists and the sacrifices that will be required." It was to satisfy this aspiration that the first National Development Plan, 1962–68, was drawn up. The Plan was geared for growth—growth not in the sense of achieving spectacular, immediate or even short-term results, but rather in the sense of laying a solid and enduring foundation for future expansion—an essential prerequisite in Nigeria's evolution toward a self-sustaining economy.

The Development Plan, however, is not only an instrument for improved social conditions, but is also a forceful expression of the nation's faith in its future and unity. First, the conception and execution of a national plan is such that the program of the Federal Government or any one of the regional governments cannot be judged in isolation or be regarded as complete in itself. In other words, the development program of each of the four governments is an essential

part of a composite and coherent whole. Nigeria has a federal constitution in which the Federal Government has exclusive constitutional responsibilities for certain major fields of governmental activities which, apart from the conduct of external relations, include: the
defense of the nation and internal security; the development of communications of nationwide significance; the expansion of electric
power; certain major aspects of higher education; pure research in the
fields of primary production and mineralogy; and, above all, the creation of financial institutions appropriate to a sovereign state and the
maintenance of confidence in these institutions. It is, therefore, evident that the Federal Government not only can provide a lead to the
regional governments in the achievement of the major objectives of
the Plan—it has, for instance, voted £25,000,000 toward the expansion
of activities in the field of primary production—but can use its constitutional powers in making the program a means of fostering national unity.

Our Plan has been very carefully prepared; it has been scrutinized by
foreign experts and advisers, discussed and agreed to by all the governments of the Federation, widely discussed over the public media
of expression, approved by freely elected parliaments, and given general approbation by the people as a means of securing a more abundant and prosperous life for them and future generations in conditions
of freedom and unity.

Nigeria attaches the greatest importance to this Six Year Plan.
The Federal Government has not, however, allowed itself to be carried away by the temptation to use the Plan to achieve power, and
has not lost sight of the major objective, which is to maintain and, if
possible, surpass the average annual rate of growth of 4 percent. We
are, therefore, thinking of the benefits in real terms—the material
prosperity of our people. To achieve our desired rate of growth, it will
be necessary to invest approximately 15 percent of the Gross National
Product each year and to ensure that as much as possible of this gross
investment, whether undertaken by the Government or by private
business, is channeled into the directly productive sectors of the economy. Only the achievement of a substantial rate of growth will make
it possible to raise the standard of living and to provide the Nigerian
people with the means for increased employment and improved education and health. The National Plan, therefore, accords highest
priority to agriculture, industry and technical education.

In a country where over four-fifths of the population depend on agriculture, forestry, livestock and fisheries, and more than half of the Gross National Product is derived from these sources, expansion and modernization of agriculture and related production are of crucial importance to the development of the economy. For instance, the proceeds from export products will determine to a large extent the volume of imports which can be made available for economic development in other sectors; the efficient expansion of domestic food production will determine not only whether the people will eat better, but also whether they can effectively reduce their dependence on imported foodstuffs; the increased productivity in these sectors will determine whether the income of the great majority of the people can be effectively raised, and this will in turn determine the size of the domestic market for the new industries which are expected to spring up. Agricultural production, therefore, occupies the prime place in our Plan.

III

In order to implement our development program and sustain our independence, Nigeria requires the help, sympathy and understanding of other nations. The National Plan we have proposed will cost about £676,500,000, of which we expect to finance about 50 percent from domestic resources, leaving a gap of about £338,800,000. The governments of Nigeria, therefore, recognize the importance of contributions which the private sector of the economy and foreign capital can make toward the nation's economic growth. Nigerians will themselves make every sacrifice so as to be able to contribute themselves to the program, but it is evident that, with all the will in the world, our effort will be inadequate and have to be supported by help from foreign countries. Hence we welcome aid whether in the form of foreign investment, loan or grant. So long as this assistance is given in a spirit of genuine desire to make life happier for the people, we would gladly accept and welcome it.

We know that there is no assistance without some strings attached, and that those who invest in our country have a right to expect that their investment is secure, or that grants made to us are used in the over-all interest of the people rather than for the benefit of a few privileged persons. This, in fact, accords with our own national policy, and we cannot see a conflict of views or interests in this. We seek assistance, not only because we need it, but also because we think we deserve it. This is a challenge to those advanced nations which really desire to see the new African states stand on their own feet and make their own particular contribution to the peace of the world and the happiness of mankind. They should realize that many of the new African states are indeed potentially rich and could contribute to improving the world but for the fact that they lack the technical knowledge and the financial capital necessary to develop their resources. The best way to assist the underdeveloped countries to reach maturity is by genuinely assisting them to develop their resources, and to educate their human material up to the standards which are necessary for proper development, without fomenting trouble by using aid as an instrument of ideological propaganda.

This leads me to the question as to whether foreign aid or even trade with Western countries can compromise national independence. The answer is, of course, yes and no. Having stated before that it is virtually impossible for the underdeveloped territories to exploit their resources fully without the help of foreign capital and technical knowledge, it goes without saying that aid can be a useful instrument for reaching their goal of development. In our own particular circumstances, we believe that aid fits into its proper place in the national scheme and could never compromise sovereignty. If, however, owing to a lack of planning or through the machinations of self-seeking people, aid is used to bolster up selfish interests, it becomes injurious not only to the body politic but to the national integrity. Also, if those who are in a position to render this assistance use it only as an opportunity to project their own narrow national interest or to propagate their ideologies, rather than seek a normal, fair return on their investment or the satisfaction of being of service to humanity, national independence is bound to be compromised.

However, some countries are not in the fortunate position of possessing the leadership and the resources necessary to ensure that the national will is not perverted by external aid and influences. In their interest, therefore, and in order to resist the temptation of partisans to introduce the cold war into their territories, we consider that aid should normally be channeled through the United Nations organization and its agencies, in preference to bilateral arrangements. This will not only eliminate the possibility of unhealthy competition among the emergent nations, but also reduce the risks of promoting conflicts.

Trade, like private investment, is in a slightly different category from aid since it is largely a transaction between buyers and sellers where the profit motive dominates. Consequently primary producers in the newly emergent countries have found that, whereas their prices are subject to sharp fluctuations determined by consumer demand and other factors, the prices of the manufactured goods of the wealthier industrialized nations continue to rise at rates determined by the producer countries. This is not all. It is now clear that there is a long-term downward trend in the prices of most primary commodities on which the primary producing countries depend for their very existence. The gap in real income between the consumers and the producers is, therefore, ever widening at the expense of the primary producers. Our view, therefore, is that long-term trade arrangements should be considered at governmental and international levels, in order to ensure some price stability without which many underdeveloped countries cannot even plan in advance.

We appreciate the necessity for some countries to form themselves into the European Economic Community, and we understand Britain's desire to join this Community. But we are also interested in ensuring that the European Common Market does not impair traditional trade patterns to the great disadvantage of the primary producers, or create conditions of rivalry and unhealthy competition amongst them. As an African country, we consider that the Common Market is essentially a European affair and has political overtones which cannot appeal to Africans. We are, therefore, naturally distrustful of any institutions which may cause our future industrial goods to be discriminated against either outside or within the Continent, and which operate in a way to keep Africans perpetually as primary producers. This sense of dependence is itself an unstable basis for relations between the former metropolitan countries and the newly independent countries. We are also anxious to expand our trade outside traditional markets, for so long as the trade and industry of Africa are conducted with only one area of the world, so long will a feeling of dependency persist. In other words, having secured political independence, we are determined to see that this is also expressed in economic terms.

IV

We belong to Africa and Africa must claim first attention in our external affairs. Our policy has always been a pragmatic one, and even though we have been attracted by plausible expressions of Pan Africanism, we have thought it sensible to distinguish between ideals and reality. We appreciate the advantages which the size of our country and its population will give us even in an intercontinental organization, but we are determined to treat every African country—big or small—as our equal, because we sincerely believe that only on a basis of equality can peace be maintained in our continent.

The colonizing powers of the last century partitioned Africa in a haphazard and artificial manner, and drew boundaries which often cut right across former ethnic groupings. Yet, however artificial those boundaries were at first, the countries they have created have come to regard themselves as units independent of one another, seeking admission to the United Nations as separate states. Therefore, we shall discourage any attempt to influence such communities by force or through undue pressure to change, since such interference can only result in unrest and harm to us all.

In an atmosphere free of distrust and suspicion, African states can find ways to coöperate in those matters in which common interests compel them to do so. By this coöperation and willing pooling of resources, the smaller African states especially will find their guarantee of freedom and independence.

At present, I cannot speak by telephone with my brother Prime Ministers in most African capitals without going through London or Paris. Whereas I can talk directly with someone in New York, it is quite often impossible to call someone in a neighboring country 200 miles away. And even if telephone communications were adequate, it would probably be impossible for us to conduct a conversation except through an interpreter. The first task of true statesmanship appears to us to remove the practical barriers, and to create the conditions for coöperation and a climate of understanding without which no effective political organization can be established.

Fortunately, most African statesmen now realize that we must proceed from the known to the unknown. In this way the differences between the various African groupings are being narrowed down. It is a matter of historical interest, however, that when Nigeria attained her independence in 1960, there were then the so-called "Brazzaville" and "Casablanca" groups of states. It was in order to bridge the gulf between them that it was agreed that unaligned countries like Nigeria and Liberia and two members of the Brazzaville and Casablanca states respectively should summon a conference in Monrovia to resolve the differences. Unfortunately, some African states who were co-sponsors of this conference withdrew at the last moment, leading to a process by which the mediating group has now been labelled as partisan under the appellation of the "Monrovia-Lagos" group. We in Nigeria, however, still thought that it was possible to bring all Africans together, and issued invitations to all to attend a conference in Lagos this year. But unfortunately the rift continues. There are signs, however, that African leaders are beginning to realize the futility of this artificial division and are now doing all in their power to close ranks.

The unity of Africa presupposes the independence of all African states. Those that are now independent have a responsibility, therefore, to aid their fellows to freedom. We abhor violence because its memories persist and haunt the country long after independence has been won. Also, Nigeria's position, born of her experience, has been that peaceful and constitutional methods must first be exhausted in the struggle for freedom. In accordance with this belief, we have given, and will continue to give, moral and material support to dependent African states fighting for freedom.

We reject the view that any part of Africa is a province of a metropolitan country in Europe. We have consistently and vigorously condemned the attitude of those countries which persist in this outrageous and anachronistic belief. We are also equally opposed to a system which gives political power and authority to a minority community solely on account of an assumed racial superiority. We shall, therefore, continue to use all the means at our disposal, especially at the United Nations, to ensure that the last vestiges of racialism and colonialism are wiped off the face of Africa.

Our belief in the fundamental rights of all African states to freedom and independence does not imply that independence should be granted without regard to economic, sociological and political factors affecting the state concerned. There are obvious cases in which there is the need for a rapid build-up of administrative machinery and economic institutions to sustain the burden of self-rule. The European communities still have a contribution to make to the *over-all* development of Africa, and it will be a tragedy if by holding tenaciously to their present privileges they should compromise their future coöperation with the African. So far as Nigeria is concerned, we are committed to assuring independence for the whole of Africa.

v

In international affairs our position has been that with proper objectivity the policy for each occasion should be selected in Nigeria's national interest and in that of world peace. Our policy is to follow the path of truth as we conceive it, and we consequently consider it wrong for us to associate ourselves as a matter of routine with any of the power blocs. This freedom of action has been an essential feature of our policies and has been founded on the moral and democratic principle on which our constitution is based. We do not, however, deceive ourselves into thinking that, provided we ourselves are honest and well-intentioned, it will be easy to follow a successful foreign policy. We have therefore not been rigid or inflexible in our diplomacy; whatever foreign policy we have adopted since independence has had to be adapted to the changing circumstances of the world.

We know our true friends and cherish our traditional associations especially with the Commonwealth, but we have refused to inherit the prejudices of anyone and have opened our hands of friendship to all those who respect our sovereignty. Our foreign policy has never been one of neutrality, but rather nonalignment. We have never, for instance, been neutral in African affairs, nor can we be neutral in matters pertaining to world peace. We have demonstrated both in the Congo and at the United Nations that we have the courage of our convictions in supporting what we consider to be in the interest of peace and harmony. And if this has meant supporting the policies of one bloc or the other at the particular time, we have not shrunk from it.

We believe in the United Nations as the only effective machinery for world peace. That is why we are naturally distressed when we see this organization being perverted for purely selfish and national ends. I do not think that it was ever the intention of any of those countries which were responsible for the creation of the United Nations organization to turn it into an arena where party politics would be played at the highest level, and where ideological differences would obscure the main objective of securing peace among the nations and stability in the world at large. Rather, the purpose was to enable all countries together to work out solutions to problems in a friendly atmosphere and to procure the peace and progress of mankind without discrimination as to race, color or country. We therefore hope that the United

Nations will not only purify itself of these tendencies, but will also be reconstituted to reflect its present membership.

The history of the organization since the last war shows that the structure was based on a wrong conception—namely, that only the great powers should have the last say in world affairs. But the general movement since the war has been toward a close association of nations from all over the world. What we now want is to reduce the differences between the nations and bring the world together. The United Nations organization appears to me to be the best instrument for this purpose, and it is my hope that African countries will be given effective voice in it.

For these reasons, I would like to see the disappearance of the veto power and a review of the structure and position of the Security Council. It is also unreasonable to disallow the People's Republic of China and some other countries with great resources from participating fully in the work of the United Nations at all levels. To all independent countries, especially the new and less powerful ones, the United Nations is the one sure guarantee of their freedom, and that is why all true lovers of peace have a stake in ensuring that the United Nations grows from strength to strength in the furtherance of international peace and discipline.

Note

AFRICA'S FUTURE AND THE WORLD
BY SÉKOU TOURÉ

October 1962

When General de Gaulle in 1958 offered France's African territories the choice of entering a "Community" with France or becoming independent, only Guinea chose to go it alone. The man who gave
the order to vote "No" to continued association with France was a
trade-union leader and former deputy to the French National Assembly, Sékou Touré, the unquestioned leader and (since 1958) President
of the Republic of Guinea. For this rash act Sékou Touré and his impoverished country paid a fearful price. Almost overnight the French
pulled out, taking virtually everything movable with them. The
United States and other Western powers, unwilling to offend France,
stood aside while the Communist powers rushed in to seize their first
bridgehead in black Africa.

For several years Guinea was thought to be "lost." Except for the
presence of one Western mining consortium, its dependence on the
Communist bloc seemed complete; and besides, Sékou Touré was
known to be an old Marxist whose dictatorial, one-party system was
patterned on the cellular structure typical of Communist organization.
But African nationalism proved more resilient than many had thought;
Guineans became disillusioned by the Soviets' heavy-handed pressure
and inefficiency, while the economy went from bad to worse. A Soviet
Ambassador was asked to leave. Guinean students were recalled from
Moscow. Gradually, Sékou Touré turned back toward the West—
toward the United States and even to France which had recovered
from its blind fury.

Guinea is still Marxist, totalitarian, radical and critical of the West,
but it is independent. Moreover, Sékou Touré has set about to heal
the sores that had been opened in 1958 with his West African neighbors—with Houphouet-Boigny, whose lieutenant he had been in the
R.D.A. (see p. 263), with Léopold Senghor, whom he had offended by
his "union" with Mali (see p. 283), and with Sir Abubakar Tafawa

Balewa, around whom those countries which opposed the Casablanca Group had rallied. An ardent Pan-Africanist, Sékou Touré seems to have realized that the methods used by Nkrumah (with whom he was closely but uncomfortably linked) to forge unity in Africa were divisive and self-defeating.

The preceding article by the Nigerian Prime Minister and the one which follows by Sékou Touré appeared in the same issue of *Foreign Affairs* and afford a fascinating contrast in African leadership. The author of one is aristocratic, conservative, British-educated, temperate in language and manner; the other is radical, resentful, given to left-bank philosophy and Marxist dialectic. Both are authentic African leaders of the first (post-independence) generation.

Africa's Future
and the World

by SÉKOU TOURÉ

Subjective interpretations are at the root of one of the profound misconceptions that prevent a true understanding of Africa's problems and the concerns and activities of her peoples. For the interpretations made by foreign "specialists" in African affairs are as a rule based on the conditions of their own social milieu, and thus take little account of the specific conditions of the various African societies. If the problems of Africa are to be understood, analyzed and solved, we must take into consideration the historical, economic, social, moral and cultural conditions which shape Africa's particular identity in the world—elements of the African evolution, in which total emancipation of the African peoples remains the main objective.

An attempt to solve specific African problems out of context, according to some half-understood universal concept, neglects the especially important social factors. Such an approach assumes that science has reached its limits, that mankind's present knowledge is absolute and immutable, and that in these matters there is nothing further to be expected, attempted or desired. It implies that human society, having reached maturity, begins to decline. On the contrary, everything indicates that it is still full of contradictions and imperfections and that these are the causes of its difficulties, its crises and its disequilibrium. Thus the course of progress, far from being limited, is infinite in time and space.

It is absurd to suppose that an American laborer can think and act in the same manner as the president of a great New York bank. It is just as absurd to conceive of the African or the African nations acting in terms that are supposed to be universal but actually are only relative, depending on particular historical or social conditions.

There are no simple solutions to human problems, nor will there be while vast differences in living conditions keep peoples apart, while agricultural and industrial overproduction constitutes a permanent problem in the most highly developed nations, and while a tragic lack of consumer goods and equipment remains a serious peril for the peoples of the underdeveloped or undeveloped nations. Poor peoples, underdeveloped nations, have needs and demands which are essential to the fulfillment of their hopes and which have nothing in common with those of the highly developed nations and their rich populations. It is not strange that all peoples want security and seek to improve their standards of life, for man's universal aspiration is for progress, social justice, freedom, prosperity and peace. But each of these aspirations has a particular order of urgency for each people, and draws on infinitely varied potentialities and capacities.

Because of their historical past and their present state of underdevelopment, Asians and Africans obviously have more in common with one another than with Europeans. However, it is not from this point of view and with these given facts that we must study the problems posed by the relationships between peoples if we wish to avoid emphasizing the rift in the world and increasing the imbalance which already exists in society. These problems, it need hardly be emphasized, concern all peoples, nations and individuals, powerful or weak, rich or poor.

Hence it is pointless to expect the African farmer, with his rudimentary tools, his pathetically inadequate productive capacity, and his miserable living conditions (all of which may be interesting from an exotic point of view, but in human terms are tragic) to think and act like a factory owner. And it is pointless to expect the Guinean wage-earner, whether white-collar or factory worker, to think and act like a General Motors employee or like a worker in a metallurgical combine in a socialist country. In different social conditions, the same words refer to different realities, and these differences sometimes are very great. But to infer thereby that nations cannot understand each other does not advance the solution of the problem one inch. The fact that African crows are black with a white collar does not keep them from being crows, any more than the green plumage of Africa's pigeons keeps them from being pigeons. To understand both the language of Africa and its true content we must seek to find in its words, expressions, formulations, not the abstract character of a dialectic, but the substance and reality of the life they express. This life is made up of human imperatives, social demands and vital material needs; and these become increasingly explicit and urgent as the awareness of the African peoples develops and is able to measure the social injustice that characterizes their human condition.

II

The extent of the movement for national liberation, which has suddenly brought rebirth to a whole continent and made it part of international life, bears witness to the volume and strength of this collective awareness. It is not by putting Angolan heads on bamboo stakes that the Portuguese colonists—or for that matter colonialism in general—will stem the tide of this growing awareness. There would be too many heads to cut off for that. Actually, an important evolution in history is taking place, and its consequences, direct and indirect, will increasingly influence the evolution of world society as a whole. Indeed, the liberation movement will modify the international structure more profoundly than did the two terrible world wars.

The colonial and semi-colonial countries, although containing the majority of the world's population, had only geographical existence. They appeared on the map, of course, but their straitjacketed peoples were regarded as unimportant because they were dominated and enslaved by others. In appearance they remained mute and motionless, but in fact the conviction that a struggle for freedom was necessary was stirring within them. Today, most of these peoples have won back their right to a free and worthy existence. The shameful racial segregation rampant in South Africa will change nothing; on the contrary, it sharpens the awareness of the African peoples and strengthens their character. It will harden them still more when the inevitable showdown with the Afrikaaners, with their racist and reactionary views, forces the African peoples to face up to this problem. Steel is tempered by heat. Will not the same prove true of peoples? The more they are restrained and oppressed, the more able they become to fulfill their historic destiny. The more they are threatened in their liberty, their personality, their dignity, their hopes—in their very lives—the more powerfully they arm themselves for the battle to regain and keep their freedom and use their sovereignty in order to satisfy their needs and assure their survival and development.

Thus the struggle for independence, whatever the form, whatever the means, had just one meaning for the African peoples: to acquire the first tool to open the way for them to solve their problems as human beings fully conscious of their responsibilities. For anyone to imagine that everything is accomplished and that efforts can cease with independence (which in any case still remains to be consolidated in most of the African countries) is to close one's eyes to the human evidence, to contradict the evolution of history, and ignore the existence of poor nations which realize what injustices they have suffered and burn to exploit their hidden potentialities. The equilibrium to be thus attained is not one between antagonistic forces so much as a harmonization of the world-wide levels of development.

For us, the element of need prevails over more philosophical and even ideological factors; for the human needs of which man is consciously aware and which are part of his very being constitute the true motive force of history. The intensity of this force is a function of the forces which hamper and combat it.

It is vain, then, to hope that Africa will evolve according to any specific form which might be imposed upon her contrary to her own wishes or understanding. She will evolve within her own authentic framework and in accordance with her own personality until her economic conditions lose their particular characteristics and become normal. It is futile to talk of "protecting" Africa, or to give her alms which will salve the conscience of some, blunt temporarily the awareness of others, and perpetuate inequalities between peoples by maintaining differences in their living conditions. And it is futile also to try to trace any one path that Africa must follow. Africa must be left free to follow her own historical path, starting from the imperatives of her destiny and taking into account the requirements of a fraternal and united world.

In other words, it is a question of affirming our "Africanity," that is to say our personality, without attempting to dress it up in Western or Eastern costume. What must be constructed harmoniously and rapidly is an Africa that is authentically African. Africa has her own needs, concepts and customs. She does not seek to deck herself out in borrowed clothing that does not fit.

This destiny, while presupposing the total disappearance of colonialism, the liquidation of imperialism and the establishment of a society free from privileges, also opens new and inspiring perspectives of justice, progress and universal peace. Need we recall that by holding onto their present privileges and technical superiority the highly developed nations are depriving themselves of the creative talent and productive capacities of hundreds of millions of people in the under-developed nations? Already the modern world's scientific capacities can no longer be measured country by country. More and more, the utilization of recently discovered scientific methods calls for the co-operation of several countries, indeed of all countries together.

In view of this, it seems bitterly ironical that progress, upon which mankind's greater happiness depends, is hampered less by lack of knowledge than by the sealing off by certain selfish peoples of informa-tion about their scientific discoveries, experiments and achievements. As a result of their substituting the will to power for the will to prog-ress, human happiness and the interests of nations are deliberately and irrevocably sacrificed. Paradoxically, it is in the name of safeguard-ing human happiness and the interests of peoples that men choose the perilous path of military power, leading perhaps to the end of humanity.

So far as Africa is concerned, this situation leads to something that is tangible and easily grasped.

Compared to other continents, Africa is relatively retarded. But to what is this backwardness attributable? To some natural inequality between black man and white? No, for there are black men who by their culture have an intrinsic value superior to that of certain white men. Hence in so far as individual capacities are concerned, there is no such thing as intellectual inequality among men whatever their color or race. Inequality exists solely in living conditions, in the acci-dents of history, that is to say in the political, economic and social conditions that have dictated, and still dictate, the levels of develop-ment in different parts of the world. This is true of the political situa-tion within a nation in which political considerations have hampered national development (as in European countries like Spain, Portugal and Greece). It is true of the economic and social situation where foreign intervention has resulted in exploitation and social oppression (as in any country subjected to direct or indirect foreign rule).

But does the inequality exist in the realm of intelligence? We say categorically, No! Does it exist, then, in the ethics or social theory of the two groups facing each other? Again we say, No! Africa is not backward in the moral and spiritual domain. In truth, the African is keenly aware of the difference between good and evil, of justice, of liberty, of solidarity, of the virtues of work and human charity, as well as of universal peace; he has the same sense of his responsibilities as do the inhabitants of Europe, America, Asia or Oceania. He has, with some slight variations, the same scale of values; hence we cannot consider that he is, even provisionally, backward either morally or spiritually. If there is inequality, then, it can result only from economic conditions. Far from being an inherent defect, it is the consequence of the low level of scientific, technological and financial development of our countries. And although in these respects Africa is backward compared to other continents, she must not on that account underestimate her human personality, her economic, moral and cultural values, her spiritual force or the contribution she can make to world civilization.

In the past decade, Africa has become well aware of her lag in material things, and is eagerly seeking to attain the level of development of the highly industrialized countries.

When we analyze the ills that have beset the African, indeed the whole black race, we are obliged to admit at once that economic factors are what have favored slavery, the deportation of our populations, racial discrimination, colonization and, today, neo-colonialism. Africa has been exploited and oppressed for economic motives; her legitimate desire for rehabilitation—social, moral, cultural—must be fulfilled by her economic development.

III

We of course know that the world today is interdependent, and Africa, which cannot live in isolation, does not intend to remain at the margin of this modern world. She thinks she is entitled to benefit from the experience of other nations as well as from the fruits of her own efforts. In turn, she must contribute actively to the creation of a world society in which each nation, while retaining its own personality, will be considered on an equal footing with the others and will, like them, take on its proper share of international responsibilities.

Africa has been carved up and divided. The evil of colonialism has not consisted just of exploitation and discrimination but of loss of liberty and seizure of sovereignty. Only when a people proclaims its independence, therefore, and exercises its sovereignty, can it put an end to every form of exploitation by establishing democratic institutions, freeing creative initiatives and assuring individual freedom by social progress.

Colonialism's greatest misdeed was to have tried to strip us of our responsibility in conducting our own affairs and convince us that our civilization was nothing less than savagery, thus giving us complexes which led to our being branded as irresponsible and lacking in self-confidence. Our greatest victory, then, will not be the one we are winning over colonialism by securing independence but the victory over ourselves by freeing ourselves from the complexes of colonialism, proudly expressing Africa's authentic values and thoroughly identifying ourselves with them. Thus the African peoples will become fully conscious of their equality with other peoples.

The colonial powers had assimilated each of their colonies into their own economy. The French colonies were an economic branch of the French economy, the British colonies were an extension of the economy of Great Britain. Between Guinea and Sierra Leone, between "French Guinea" and "Portuguese Guinea," there exist common traditional bonds of custom, history and economy. Yet no economic relations existed between them, for each was a tributary of the colonial power's market exclusively.

We know that we must rebuild Africa. To win and proclaim a nation's independence but keep its old structures is to plow a field but not sow it with grain for a harvest. Africa's political independence is a means which must be used to create and develop the new African economy. Our continent possesses tremendous reserves of raw materials and they, together with its potential sources of power, give it excellent conditions for industrialization. This is why, though it would be unrealistic and irrational to think of associating the African nations with the European Common Market, or any other form of economic monopoly, it is to be hoped that an African common market will be organized which eventually can coöperate on a basis of equality and solidarity with other economic zones.

African unity is no more a goal in itself than was independence. It simply is a means of development, a force of inter-African coöperation. It is indispensable because of the unjust nature of the relationship between the underdeveloped African nations and the economically strong nations. The equality of this relationship must be improved in order to overcome the social inequalities and differentiations in the present levels of development throughout the world. The highly developed nations have economic relations among themselves either of coöperation or of competition. But their relations with the undeveloped nations are those of exploitation, of economic domination. The direct colonial exploitation of former days is being succeeded by exploitation by international monopolies, and this has a tendency to become permanent. Paradoxically, it is the underdeveloped nations, exporting raw materials and crude products, which contribute an important share of the costs and the social improvements from which workers in the fully developed countries benefit.

The nature of our economic relations on the world market can be easily illustrated. In the matter of customs tariffs, for instance, let us glance at a few figures. In the period 1957 to 1961, the exchange value of raw materials and crude products in relation to industrial products fell 34 percent, although from 1955 to 1957 this rate had already fallen 50 percent in relation to the 1948 market. The extent of the decline on the international market is shown by the following statistics: [1]

1. Immediately after the war the average per capita income in the U.S.A. was 1,000 dollars per annum, while in the underdeveloped countries of Asia, Africa and Latin America it was 100 dollars. Fifteen years later the average annual per capita income in the United States was 2,500 dollars, and in the underdeveloped countries barely 150 dollars. Thus while in the most developed part of the world the average income was ten times larger than that of the underdeveloped countries, which represent the vast majority of the world territory and population, this difference has now risen to seventeen times.

2. Since the war, the world average per capita production of food has increased by 13 percent. But in Africa the production per capita has fallen by 2 percent, in Latin America it has increased by 2 percent, in Asia by 12 percent, and in developed Western Europe by 21 percent.

3. Immediately after the second world war the underdeveloped countries' participation in world trade exchange was 38 percent. However, by 1953 its share was reduced to 36 percent, in 1959 to 31 percent, and in 1961 to 29 percent.

4. In the course of the last ten years alone the prices of industrial goods in international trade have increased by 24 percent, while the prices of raw materials have fallen by 5 percent. In other words, the underdeveloped countries exporting raw materials were, towards the end of the fifties, purchasing one third less industrial goods for a determined quantity of raw materials, as compared with ten years earlier.

In the light of these circumstances it is easy to understand that the economic unity and monetary independence of Africa do not signify, as has been naïvely suggested, that Guinea will be permitted to sell its coffee to the Ivory Coast, its palm-kernel to Dahomey and its bauxite to Ghana. It signifies that, as Africa enters the international market as a producer, all steps must be taken to establish a fair relationship in the active forces which dominate international trade, re-

---

[1] Janes Stanovnik, "Simple Mathematics of the Cairo Conference," *Review of International Affairs* (Belgrade), June 5, 1962, p. 3.

placing the position of dependence to which the underdeveloped nations are subjected now.

The mere fact that there are cries of alarm about the production of coffee, cacao or peanuts, while there is silence about the products for which the demand is increasingly active but whose prices remain stable, such as diamonds, gold, oil, radioactive ores, zinc and copper, illustrates the mercantile nature of the economic relations between the highly developed nations and the nations producing raw materials. In 1957, the total tax on coffee imported into France was 71 percent of its import value; it was 72 percent in Germany and 73 percent in Italy. Was it really a question of protectionist measures in the case of coffee, or of discriminatory taxation? It is a fact that in this same period the price of gold was lower on the French market than it was, for instance, at Siguiri, in Guinea, as a result of surtaxes designed to prevent its sale locally.

Actually, the difficulties appearing within the European Common Market with regard to the renewal of Association Agreements made by certain African nations prove that it is not the form of the economic relations that must be changed but their very nature.

Here, as in other realms, the interests of the African peoples are one, and the awareness of this unity is rapidly becoming more and more explicit. The African nations are realizing that in order to solve their urgent social problems they must speed up the transformation of their trade economy; and if this is to be done through industrialization, it cannot be done within the limits of our national micro-economies. But unconditional integration into a multi-national market consisting of highly developed and underdeveloped nations negates the possibility of industrial development in advance; it could only be the association of horse and rider. If they are to complement each other economically, the development of all associated nations must be carried out according to their united needs and common interests. Any concept which imposes implicitly and *a priori* a particular orientation and framework on the development of the various nations cannot work, for it does not bring a radical solution to the nature of the economic relationships involved or to the general problems facing integrated human communities. The leaders of the European Economic Community seem not to be aware of all this, at least as far as Africa is concerned, and make no secret of their desire to achieve a political community of Europe which cannot be reconciled with Africa's desire for political independence; Africa remains as grimly hostile as ever to the division of Africa which began with the Congress of Berlin in 1885.

IV

The unity so much desired by all Africans will not be achieved around any one man or any one nation, but around a concrete program, however minimal. The rules of the union must favor and reinforce generally accepted concepts: equality of all nations, large or small; fraternal solidarity in their relationships; the common use of certain resources; and respect for the character and institutions of each state. Not only must there be no interference in the internal affairs of any state by another, but each must help to solve the other's problems. If we do not rapidly achieve such a framework of solidarity, permitting the peaceful evolution of our countries, we risk seeing the cold war enter Africa and divide the African states into antagonistic forces and blocs, jeopardizing their whole future in common.

The evolution of our countries in peace and harmony requires a high degree of coöperation. We have always thought that Africa should be considered like the human body: when a finger is cut off, the whole body suffers. The growing awareness that we all share the same future must make us increase our efforts for this coöperation, for solidarity and active and conscious African participation in world progress.

When we speak, furthermore, of rehabilitating the African Man, we do not indulge in a racist doctrine but act in accord with a historical and moral imperative. We have suffered too much from the malice and scorn of others. We must act so that they will respect us in future and this we shall do by respecting ourselves and honestly and competently exercising our responsibilities. It is a problem of human dignity and of conscience.

Some have claimed to see political antagonisms in the formation of various African groupings. Actually these were the first concrete manifestations of unity, and were inspired by human and historical necessity. Skepticism notwithstanding, this tendency toward unity will increase. Political choices which do not correspond to the needs and aspirations of our peoples—and it is important that this be understood—will inevitably fail.

As for what face a united Africa will wear, whatever the choices she makes in her orientation, it will not be turned either against the

East or against the West. It will be above all and essentially directed toward the emancipation and progress of Africa and her peoples. In our struggle for freedom there is no room for negative choices, but only for positive thought and constructive action. What will be destroyed or defeated in this struggle are those things that historical necessities, human needs and the forces of progress consign to destruction and oblivion.

v

To attempt to interpret Africa's behavior in capitalist or Communist terms is to neglect the fundamental fact that Africa's present condition corresponds neither to the given facts of capitalism nor to those in the building of Communism.

Africa's way is the way of peaceful revolution, in which the morality of an action counts much more than its form and conditions. That some believe socialism corresponds best to the aims of the African revolution, while others suppose it is preferable, despite the lack of national capital, to espouse capitalist principles—these considerations will not in the last analysis prevent our peoples from deciding their own fate. It is they who are called on to make the sacrifices and the creative efforts necessary to ensure Africa's development. Their awareness is sufficiently keen to enable them to choose the way they want to go.

In deciding these matters our peoples will take account of the realities of the twentieth century: the tremendous possibilities of future human achievement as well as the knowledge, experience and discoveries accumulated in the course of past centuries. Their commitment will correspond to their hope of future benefits. It will be one which makes a real contribution to general progress in peace and human happiness.

African neutralism, then, is not shameful indifference, a sort of political demobilization. On the contrary, it is the expression of a lively faith in a happy future for mankind. It is something active, a participating force, an active agent in the struggle for the achievement of a world society—emancipated, fraternal and united. Let us hope that the highly developed nations and peoples can understand this historical movement in its universal significance, and that they will take full part in it, in the conscious desire to help build a free and prosperous Africa in a world of peace and brotherhood.

Note

THE PARTY SYSTEM AND DEMOCRACY IN AFRICA
BY TOM J. MBOYA

July 1963

In trying to see Africa whole—as it is and may become—one of the hardest things for a Westerner is to avoid parochialism on the one hand and, on the other other, a kind of easygoing tolerance of the African which is in fact patronizing. Yet we cannot avoid forming estimates and expectations of the Africans' capacity to govern, and for us who believe deeply in the political philosophy and institutions that have evolved in the West, it is not easy to see them trammeled or ignored. For us they have become part of the natural order to which all right-thinking men must aspire. On the other hand we know that even the very imperfect democracy we have achieved depends on education and the long cultivation of restraint and countervailing powers within the society—elements largely missing in Africa. We know, too, that Africa had and has a culture of its own and that whatever it adopts from the West will be sifted and shaped in ways that are not yet clear. How, then, are we to judge an African leader who infringes rights which we deem to be fundamental to democracy? That he is to that extent an autocrat and would-be dictator? That he correctly comprehends that his people are incapable of making democracy work? Or that he is intelligently adapting Western institutions to the environment and traditions of Africa?

The following article is addressed to one aspect of this problem—the prevalence in Africa of one-party systems, which Westerners tend to believe are incompatible with democracy. Most Africans—though by no means all—think otherwise and they can make a tolerable case, as is demonstrated here. Moreover anyone who has compared the one-party system of, say, Tanganyika to the two-party system of Kenya (at least as each has worked so far) must concede great advantages to the former in terms of free political expression as well as stability. A multi-party system in an unsophisticated society places a frightful

327

premium on political irresponsibility, with each party trying to outdo the other in proposing heaven on earth to the voters. In Kenya as in most of Africa where more than one party exists, political division is between groups of tribes with ancient fears and animosities, not between those with differing concepts of the national interest.

Tom Mboya is quite possibly the most capable politician in all of Africa. Intelligent, self-confident and poised, he has made a deeper impression on Americans than any other visiting African leader—beginning with his first visit to the United States at the age of 29. Similarly he has commanded the respect even of the white settlers in Kenya who hated him, and his effectiveness in London made him the architect of Kenya self-government more truly than any other African. With his own people he is among the most popular leaders, but he is less well liked by his peers, who often find him arrogant and impatient. Moreover, he suffers the liability of not being of the dominant Kikuyu tribe. He is nevertheless, next to Jomo Kenyatta, the Prime Minister, the most influential politician in Kenya.

Born of uneducated Luo parents, he was unable, for lack of money, to complete his own secondary school education at a Catholic mission, but received training as a sanitation inspector and moved to Nairobi in 1951, the year of his majority. There he began to build a trade-union movement which is still the basis of his political power. By 1953, and for nearly a decade thereafter, he was Secretary General of the Kenya Federation of Labor, a post that gave him the opportunity to travel and to gain an international reputation. Increasingly active in politics, he was one of eight African Elected Members of the Legislative Council in 1957 and has won every election since then in his Nairobi constituency. When the Kenya African National Union (KANU) was formed in 1960, he became its Secretary General, a post he still held when KANU won an absolute majority of seats in the crucial May 1963 election which led to self-government and independence. Minister of Labor in an earlier coalition government, he was Minister of Justice and Constitutional Affairs when this article was written. If an East African Federation is formed with Tanganyika and Uganda, he is quite likely to be its Foreign Minister. His book, "Freedom and After," published in late 1963, is among the most constructive and explicit works by an African leader.

The Party System and Democracy in Africa

by TOM J. MBOYA

Practically nobody in these islands understands the Party System. Britons do not know its history. They believe that it is founded in human nature and therefore indestructible and eternal . . . by the immutable law of political human nature.
—BERNARD SHAW, in "Everybody's Political What's What?"

. . . if you were to ask . . . an American concerning the two great parties of his own country . . . , a bewildered look would probably cross his face; he would scratch his head and murmur something about tariffs. You would be puzzled. If you asked five Americans you would be five times as puzzled.
—VIRGINIA COWLES, in "How America Is Governed"

Many people believe there is some special connection between the democratic form of government and the party system, so that one cannot exist without the other. This belief is strengthened by the fact that the freedom to form as many parties as people want is seen to be incompatible with a totalitarian régime. An ideal Communist government is run by a single party composed of the working class; a Fascist government is similarly run by one party in the interests of the capitalist class.

This type of thinking is based on a misconception of the true nature of democracy. It confuses cause and effect. There were parties before the advent of democracy. The first political parties in Britain, for example, are believed to have come into being in the reign of Charles II. This was long before the Reform Act of 1832, which was the bare beginning of change in the direction of democracy.

At present there are political parties in countries which do not even admit the correctness of the thinking behind democracy. Has not the U.N.'s 17-nation committee on colonialism ruled that there is no self-government—let alone full democracy—in Southern Rhodesia because of the denial of equal voting rights to Africans? And yet Southern Rhodesia has political parties which fight and win elections and form governments. South Africa also has parties which have been governing the country for over 50 years against the will of the majority of the people. No one can suggest South Africa enjoys anything like democracy.

The same conclusion is reached if we look at the circumstances which bring parties into being. In Britain there was an attempt to exclude James, Duke of York, from the succession to the throne because he was a Roman Catholic. Some people sympathized with him and started agitating in his favor. Their opponents called them Tories (which was the name popularly given to Irish pirates). Tories returned the compliment by calling their opponents Whigs (which was the name given to highwaymen in Scotland).

In giving such names to each other, the parties seem to have suggested that there was not much to choose between them. In my own country, Africans were united in a single political organization which put up a united front at the 1960 Constitutional Conference. Then, independence came into sight and politicians started dreaming of loaves and fishes. The Kenya African National Union (KANU) was created as soon as Africans were permitted to form national political organizations. The Kenya African Democratic Union (KADU) followed three months later, but it had no separate program and found it difficult to justify its existence until somebody's brain wave came up with the platform of "Regionalism." This fitted in with the traditional regard shown by British politicians and the press for the interests of the so-called downtrodden minority tribes or communities.

A great deal of political confusion and weakness in dependent countries has resulted from this sort of practice. A national movement starts sooner or later in every country seeking independence. It has a universal appeal and quickly gathers strength. This alarms the ruling race which tries to find forces to counteract nationalism. Agencies of propaganda (the press, the radio) are fully used, but they alone are hardly equal to the task of convincing world opinion that nationalism is wrong. What is really needed is an indigenous opposition to the nationalist movement. Because no foreign government could possibly succeed in setting up a completely artificial opposition party, the policy is adopted of giving every encouragement to disgruntled politicians, especially if they belong to a different religious denomination, tribe, race or area from that of the main body of leaders of the nationalist movement. Such disgruntled elements are sought out and supported.

India, for example, had one nationalist party at the beginning of its political struggle for independence. Later, props were offered to the leaders of a minority group. This induced other minority groups to demand special representation, and in every case the demand was acceded to. This process continued until the whole population was divided into warring sections. The same sort of thing has been seen recently in Kenya, where KANU originally represented the national front. Then KADU was formed and received the fullest support from the local press, which is largely European-owned. The European population generally, and also certain sections of the Asian community, joined it. In the first general election KANU received 67 percent of the African votes cast; KADU received 17 percent. But the constituencies had been so formed as to give KANU 19 seats and KADU 15.

The European press and radio have always been willing to give full publicity to new, dissident groups, although their policies seldom reflect a national outlook; they are sectional or tribal groups whose only effect—if not their purpose—is to delay the coming of freedom. Parties are formed because they are free to form, not because there is need for them. In our country a new trade union may not be formed if there is already one which serves the interests of workers in that field. No similar test of need is laid down for political parties. Anyone who feels like starting a political party can do so. The more sensational and unnecessary its program, the more publicity it will receive in the European press.

The worst of it is that in dependent countries imperialism has managed to keep the level of illiteracy and ignorance high so that every person who takes it into his head to become a leader can find some followers in his own district or tribe or religious denomination. No wonder that the parties in dependent, or erstwhile dependent, countries are not divided on ideological lines. There is generally one party which presses—and whose leaders suffer for—the nationalist cause. Other parties exist because the law allows them to, and because their alien sympathizers give them limelight, encouragement and sometimes money.

II

It is quite clear that the party system can exist without democracy. The only question is whether the converse is also true. To put it more strongly—and I hope agreeably to those brought up in the traditions of the West—we must ascertain whether democracy can function fully and fruitfully without a party system.

Here, a further distinction is necessary. There are states which allow the fullest freedom for the formation and working of political parties but where the multi-party system (which is what we really mean by the expression "party system") fails to flourish. In Tanganyika it has, in the past, been possible for anyone to start a political party. At least two parties have in fact existed there. Nevertheless, one of the parties (the Tanganyika African National Union led by Mr. Julius Nyerere) was able to win 70 seats out of a total 71 in a straight, completely free, general election. To all intents and purposes, therefore, Tanganyika has had a single-party system. Does it cease on that account to be a democracy?

To take another illustration, India has a multiplicity of political parties and there is freedom to form more if the people so desire. The country has had three general elections during the 15 years or so of her freedom, and each of them was vigorously contested. One of the parties (the Indian National Congress led by Mr. Jawaharlal Nehru) has won all three elections and still occupies a more or less unchallengeable position. Is India not to be called a democracy because of this?

The only conclusion one can draw from the political experience of newly freed countries in Asia and Africa is that the party system is not a necessary part of democracy, which is truly concerned with the views, wishes and interests of the individuals making up the nation. Democracy is not fundamentally or necessarily concerned with the existence or well-being of parties, which may represent either sections or cross-sections of the population.

A good, relevant definition of democracy is suggested by the late Dr. C. E. M. Joad:

If we define democracy as a method of government under which every citizen has an opportunity of participating, through discussion, in an attempt to reach voluntary agreement as to what shall be done for the good of the whole, we shall conclude that in offering to its members opportunities to shape its policy and to realize in action the policy they have shaped, it offers them also opportunities for the development of their nature. . . . It enables the individual to realize himself in service to the State, while not forgetting that the true end of the State must be sought in the lives of individuals.[1]

Even those who believe that there is a connection between democracy and the party system must therefore agree that what is necessary is the freedom to form parties. It is not necessary that more than one should in fact exist and function effectively.

Let us take the argument one step further. The chief theoretical justification for the party system is that it increases the force and effectiveness of the people's views. It is an instrument, a means to an end, not the end itself. If the end can be achieved by an alternative means, there is no reason why that alternative should not be adopted. And as in democratic theory the people are sovereign, they can, of course, decide to achieve their ends by another means. A sovereign legislature parts with its sovereignty to the parliament of a new state (say in Africa) which was hitherto a dependency. In the same way, the sovereign people may decide to forego their right to form parties and decree that there shall in future be only one party in the country.

Now, it can be argued that no people will ever do that, but the theoretical possibility is there. And can anyone question the competence of the sovereign people to make such a decision? The only condition is that the decision should be voluntary, and arrived at after free and frank discussion. But, it will be objected, dictators in the early years of their rule always command a persuasive tongue; will they not misuse the weapon of a single party which has been placed in their hands? Have they not in fact misused it in the past?

Perhaps the single-party system will be misused. But has anyone the right or power to stop the sovereign people from decreeing such a system? At the most, we can insist on two things. First, the original decision should be completely voluntary and without any coercion. Secondly, the people should be able, if they so desire, to restore the multi-party system by a further amendment of the constitution. Nevertheless, it should be said that if the people have the right to take a revocable decision to establish a single-party system, they also have the right to say that that decision shall be irrevocable. It is this unfettered right of the people which is difficult to exclude or outlaw.

Now, the people can either express themselves in the words of a

[1] "Guide to the Philosophy of Morals and Politics," London: Gollancz, 1938, p. 807.

constitutional amendment or by their conduct. Suppose Mr. Nyerere's party in Tanganyika repeats its electoral performance once, twice, thrice. Can anyone then doubt what are the wishes of the people? My view, therefore, is that the question whether a country is to have a single party or several parties is to be answered not in terms of any preconceived ideas of "democracy" but in the concrete terms of the wishes of the people.

III

It is unfortunate that the intentions and declarations of African leaders are so often misunderstood. Immediately the people of a country feel a need to strengthen their central government and take steps in that direction, there is a hue and cry in the West that a dictatorship is being created. The fears expressed may in some cases turn out to be justified, but the readiness with which they are expressed shows that the critics start with preconceived notions.

Only a short while ago, Mr. Julius Nyerere of Tanganyika made a public announcement on the subject of party organization in his country. Most newspapers noticed in his long, carefully prepared speech nothing but a determination to put an end to the party system. His essential arguments were carefully excluded from newspaper reports. I should like to quote only a few passages from the speech, omitting the general arguments against the multi-party system which can be found in any good political textbook:

In Tanganyika . . . we adopted the Westminster type of representative democracy. . . . But it soon became clear to us that, however ready we leaders might have been to accept the theory that an official Opposition was essential to democratic government, our own people thought otherwise . . . in spite of our having only one party, we were very democratic. But we were more democratic within the Party. . . . In Parliament it is no longer permissible for each Member to express his own personal opinion. . . . There is a party line to be followed . . . where there is no Opposition party, there is no reason why the debate in Parliament should not be as free as the debate in the National Executive. . . . It seems at least open to doubt, therefore, that a system which forces political parties to limit the freedom of their members is a democratic system, and that one which can permit a party to leave its members their freedom is undemocratic. . . .

The existence of a Two-Party system in the older democracies is best explained by reference to the history of those countries. . . . the genesis of the Two-Party system was a class society. . . .

Our own parties had a very different origin. They were not formed to

challenge any ruling group of our own people, they were formed to challenge the *foreigners* who ruled over us. They were . . . nationalist movements.

. . . where there is *one* party—provided it is identified with the nation as
a whole—the foundations of democracy can be firmer, and the people can
have more opportunity to exercise a real choice, than where you have two
or more parties. . . . we can conduct our elections in a way which is
genuinely free and democratic. . . .

. . . a National Movement is open to all. . . . Those forming the Government will, of course, be replaced from time to time; that is what elections are for. The leadership of our Movement is constantly changing. . . .
since such a National Movement leaves no room for the growth of discon-
tented elements excluded from its membership, it has nothing to fear from
criticism and the free expression of ideas. . . . Any member of the Movement . . . would be free to stand as a candidate if he so wishes . . . the
voters would be able to make their choice freely from among these candidates.

To elaborate briefly on the ideas expressed by Mr. Nyerere, there
are circumstances in Africa which favor emergence of single parties,
or systems in which there are many parties but with one in a dominat-
ing position. Those circumstances can now be listed.

First, the new states of Africa have hardly got out of the woods. In
the days of struggle against a foreign nation or against a racial minority placed in power by a foreign nation, the minds of the people
are preoccupied with their political troubles. They experience these
troubles not as individuals but as a racial group, all of whom suffer the
same disabilities and indignities. There are no exceptions made in
favor of anyone. Therefore, when the victims of discrimination combine to form a single party, it tends to be based on race. Small "moderate" groups may be formed here and there, but they are of no consequence. The essential point is that all opposition to foreign rule or a
mono-racial rule comes from what is to all intents and purposes a
single political party. As the tempo of struggle against racial policies
rises, this political party becomes better organized and more widely
based. In time, it becomes the mouthpiece of an oppressed nation, a
possible successor to the alien government.

Secondly, this party or movement comes to have a leader who, by
reason of his sincere and effective advocacy of the national cause and
by reason of his sacrifices in that cause, is regarded by the masses as
the leader, the hero, the father of the nation. He is a symbol of national unity. He is identified in the mind of the people and the outside
world with the party, with the nation. This serves to solidify the foun-

dations of the political organization and the general movement for unity.

Thirdly, this movement for unity continues after independence. The original party which fought for, and brought about, freedom continues in being—maybe as the government of the country. The same leader with the same group of collaborators is now the leader of both the people and the government. This in itself works against the emergence of a multi-party system. Again, the problems facing the new government are serious and urgent. It was easy in the pre-independence days to blame the foreign or the racial minority government for the poverty, the ignorance and the poor health of the people. Now, these causes of backwardness have to be removed—a process which requires planning, money and popular enthusiasm. This is the time when the government feels it must somehow persuade the people to give it all the support possible. The opposition parties, which were always small and weak, try to justify themselves by increasing their opposition to government measures—opposition largely for its own sake. This irritates the government which is engaged in the work of nation-building. At this stage, two courses are possible: either the government acts as a steamroller, ignoring the existence of the opposition, or it takes steps to put an end to opposition for its own sake— completely and permanently.

There is another force which militates against the establishment of a multi-party democracy of the Western type. The majority party in a dependent country—that is, the party which represents the nationalist movement—comes into conflict with the ruling race almost from the start. To establish a counterweight the rulers choose dissident individuals and groups and build them up. When the nationalist majority, naturally, demands a one-man-one-vote democracy on the Westminster model, the favorite minorities oppose it and ask for safeguards against majority rule. The rulers side with the minorities and a democratic system crippled by a crop of entrenched clauses is ultimately introduced. The majority party has to agree to this crippling in order to get rid of the foreign rule.

Our own experience in Kenya serves as an illustration. The African community was united in its demand for freedom and had the support of many of the Asians and some of the Europeans. At the Constitutional Conference in London in 1960, the African Elected Members presented a unanimous demand, speaking as one single party led by one leader. This Conference accepted two aims of constitutional development in Kenya: "first, to build a nation based on parliamentary institutions on the Westminster model and enjoying responsible self-government under certain traditional conditions; and secondly, a general acceptance by all of the right of each community to remain in Kenya and play a part in public life."

In pursuance of the second of these aims, the majority party (that is, KANU) proposed a comprehensive Bill of Rights guaranteeing full and equal political, economic and social rights to members of all races. As regards the first aim, the memorandum presented by KANU to the 1962 Constitutional Conference stated: "We understand this to mean majority rule, with the majority party, for the time being, running the Government, and the acceptance of an opposition party or parties who—on their part—accept parliamentary rules and methods as the means of advancing their policies and in pursuance of their political activities."

Can anyone in the face of these clear statements maintain that the majority party wanted to establish either a dictatorship or a one-party system? Nevertheless, we did not get the necessary backing from the British Government and many British papers were hostile to us.

IV

I think it will be useful if I now summarize my conclusions in a few brief paragraphs:

1. Democracy is government of the *people*, by the *people*, for the *people*. The supporters of the party system argue as though the word "people" in this definition read "party."

2. A government which gives all citizens the right to vote, the right to contest elections and the right to express themselves freely inside and outside parliament is not undemocratic.

3. The current aims of, and the history behind, the parties in the older countries of the West are different from the aims and history of the parties (or national movements) in the countries of Africa.

4. The responsibility for the emergence in African countries of a single political party or of one strong and several weak parties must be laid at the door of imperialist nations which created the conditions militating against the establishment of democracy based on two or more political parties.

5. The imperialist nations of the West and the Western press continue their traditional attitude of encouraging and actively instigating

disgruntled, dissident elements which oppose the establishment of a parliamentary system of government (implying one-man-one-vote and majority rule). The Western statesmen and their representatives in Africa never tire of asserting that majority rule suits the countries of the West but that in Africa the minority tribes and races stand in need of special protection against majorities.

6. The countries of Africa emerging from political subjection are entitled to modify, to suit their own needs, the institutions of democracy as developed in the West. No one has the right to cavil at this so long as all citizens—irrespective of their racial, tribal or religious affiliations—are treated alike.

Index

ARMS AND POLITICS IN LATIN AMERICA (Revised Edition), by Edwin Lieuwen.

THE FUTURE OF UNDERDEVELOPED COUNTRIES: Political Implications of Economic Development (Revised Edition), by Eugene Staley.

SPAIN AND DEFENSE OF THE WEST: Ally and Liability, by Arthur P. Whitaker.

SOCIAL CHANGE IN LATIN AMERICA TODAY: Its Implications for United States Policy, by Richard N. Adams, John P. Gillin, Allan R. Holmberg, Oscar Lewis, Richard W. Patch, and Charles W. Wagley.

FOREIGN POLICY: THE NEXT PHASE: The 1960s (Revised Edition), by Thomas K. Finletter.

DEFENSE OF THE MIDDLE EAST: Problems of American Policy (Revised Edition), by John C. Campbell.

COMMUNIST CHINA AND ASIA: Challenge to American Policy, by A. Doak Barnett.

FRANCE, TROUBLED ALLY: De Gaulle's Heritage and Prospects, by Edgar S. Furniss, Jr.

THE SCHUMAN PLAN: A Study in Economic Cooperation, 1950–1959, by William Diebold, Jr.

SOVIET ECONOMIC AID: The New Aid and Trade Policy in Underdeveloped Countries, by Joseph S. Berliner.

RAW MATERIALS: A Study of American Policy, by Percy W. Bidwell.

NATO AND THE FUTURE OF EUROPE, by Ben T. Moore.

AFRICAN ECONOMIC DEVELOPMENT, by William Hance.

INDIA AND AMERICA: A Study of Their Relations, by Phillips Talbot and S. L. Poplai.

JAPAN BETWEEN EAST AND WEST, by Hugh Borton, Jerome B. Cohen, William J. Jorden, Donald Keene, Paul F. Langer and C. Martin Wilbur.

NUCLEAR WEAPONS AND FOREIGN POLICY, by Henry A. Kissinger.

MOSCOW-PEKING AXIS: Strengths and Strains, by Howard L. Boorman, Alexander Eckstein, Philip E. Mosely and Benjamin Schwartz.

RUSSIA AND AMERICA: Dangers and Prospects, by Henry L. Roberts.

FOREIGN AFFAIRS BIBLIOGRAPHY, 1942–1952, by Henry L. Roberts.